Collection Editor: Jennifer Grünwald
Assistant Editor: Caitlin O'Connell
Associate Managing Editor: Kateri Woody
Editor, Special Projects: Mark D. Beazley
VP Production & Special Projects: Jeff Youngquist
SVP Print, Sales & Marketing: David Gabriel

Editor in Chief: Axel Alonso
Chief Creative Officer: Joe Quesada
President: Dan Buckley
Executive Producer: Alan Fine

SPIDER-WOMAN: SHIFTING GEARS VOL. 3 — SCARE TACTICS. Contains material originally published in magazine form as SPIDER-WOMAN #13-17. First printing 2017. ISBN# 978-1-302-90330-5. Published by MARVEL WORLDWIDE, INC., a subsidiary of MARVEL ENTERTAINMENT, LLC. OFFICE OF PUBLICATION: 135 West 50th Street, New York, NY 10020. **Printed in the U.S.A.** DAN BUCKLEY, President, Marvel Entertainment; JOE QUESADA, Chief Creative Officer; TOM BREVOORT, SVP of Publishing; DAVID BOGART, SVP of Business Affairs & Operations, Publishing & Partnership; C.B. CEBULSKI, VP of Brand Management & Development, Asia; DAVID GABRIEL, SVP of Sales & Marketing, Publishing; JEFF YOUNGQUIST, VP of Production & Special Projects; DAN CARR, Executive Director of Publishing Technology; ALEX MORALES, Director of Publishing Operations; SUSAN CRESPI, Production Manager; STAN LEE, Chairman Emeritus. For information regarding advertising in Marvel Comics or on Marvel.com, please contact Vit DeBellis, Integrated Sales Manager, at vdebellis@marvel.com. For Marvel subscription inquiries, please call 888-511-5480. **Manufactured between 4/7/2017 and 5/9/2017 by QUAD/GRAPHICS WASECA, WASECA, MN, USA.**

10 9 8 7 6 5 4 3 2 1

PREVIOUSLY

Jessica Drew rarely gets a break. Being a single mom, a private investigator and a super hero doesn't leave much time for...well, anything.

Fortunately, *Daily Bugle* reporter Ben Urich and reformed criminal Roger Gocking (A.K.A. the Porcupine) are the best babysitters a girl could ask for. And after taking his old pal, the Sandman, down all by himself, Roger has not only proven that he's one of the good guys now, but also that he can handle himself in a fight.

But in the world of web-slinging, wall-crawling and spider-sleuthing, trouble is never far...

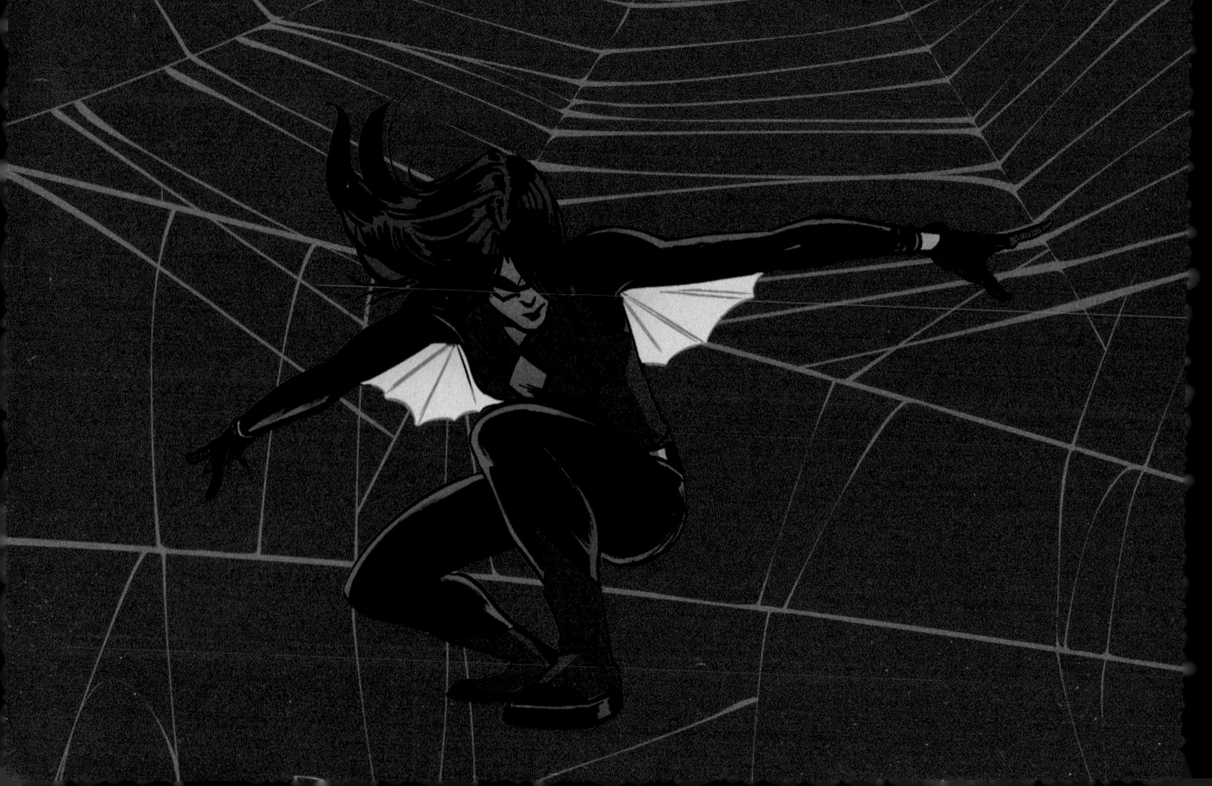

SPIDER·WOMAN
SHIFTING GEARS

SCARE TACTICS

WRITER
DENNIS HOPELESS

ARTIST
VERONICA FISH

INKING ASSIST, #16-17
ANDY FISH

COLORIST
RACHELLE ROSENBERG

LETTERER
VC'S TRAVIS LANHAM

COVER ART
JAVIER RODRIGUEZ

ASSISTANT EDITOR
ALLISON STOCK

EDITOR
DEVIN LEWIS

SENIOR EDITOR
NICK LOWE

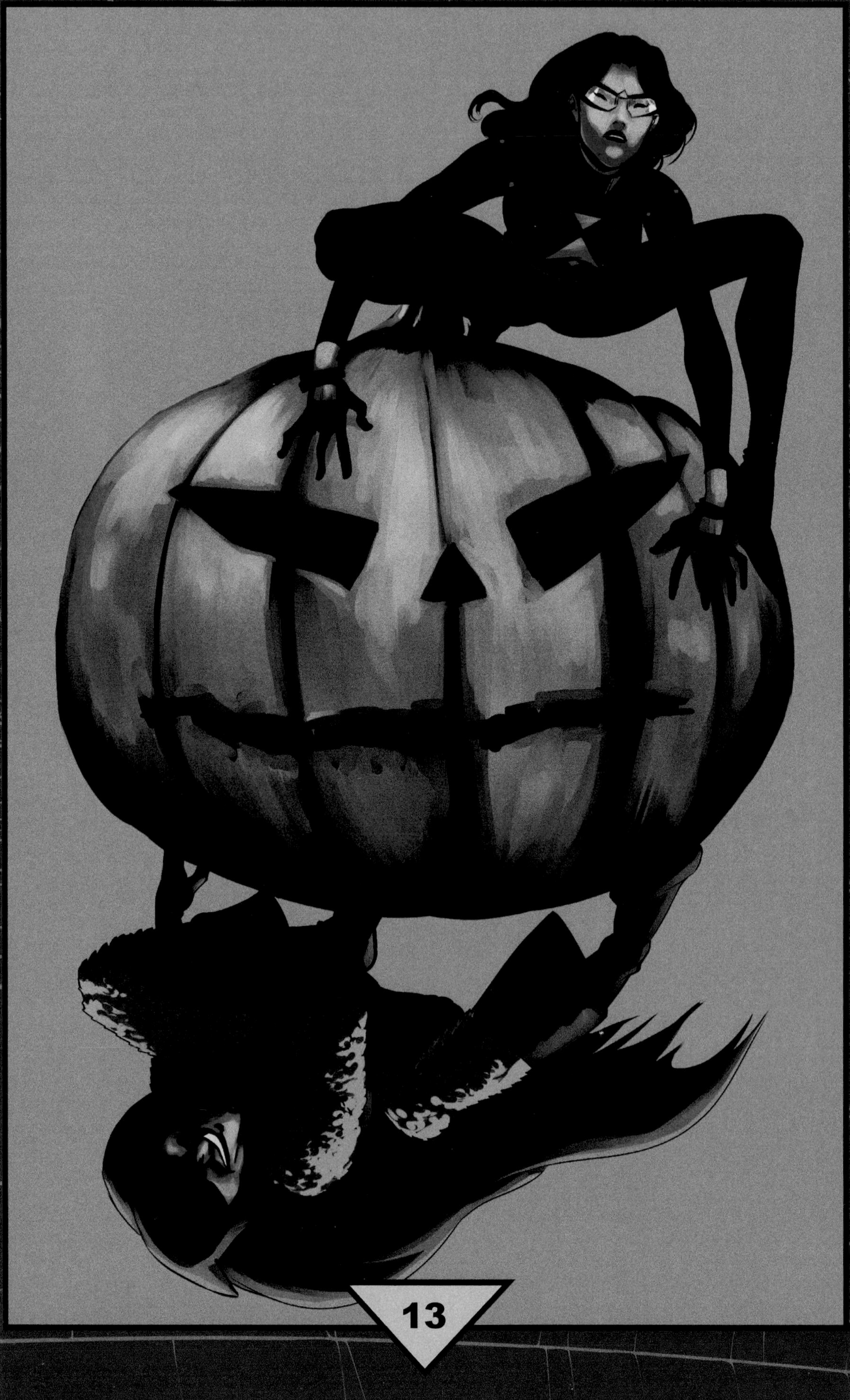
13

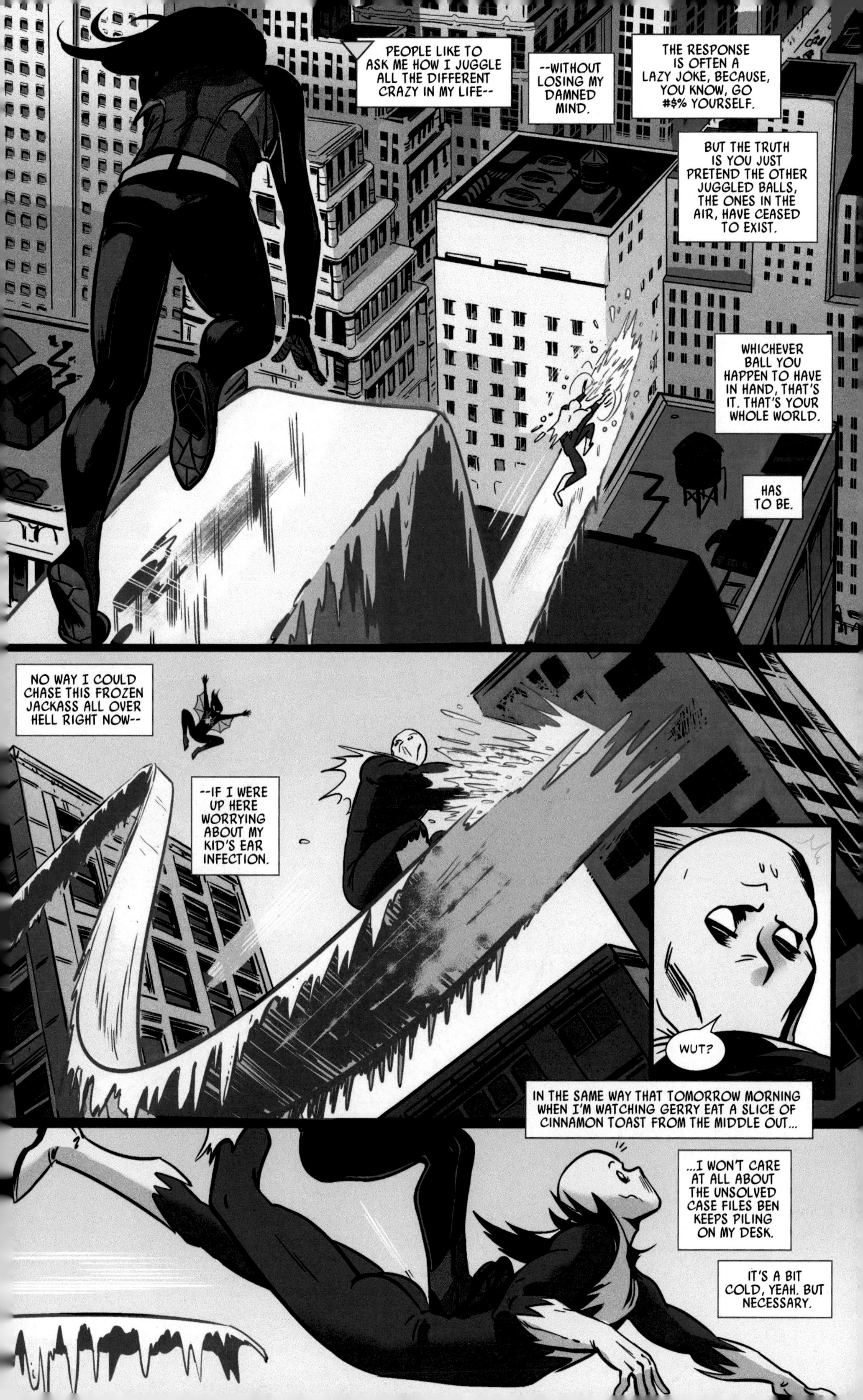
PEOPLE LIKE TO ASK ME HOW I JUGGLE ALL THE DIFFERENT CRAZY IN MY LIFE--
--WITHOUT LOSING MY DAMNED MIND.
THE RESPONSE IS OFTEN A LAZY JOKE, BECAUSE, YOU KNOW, GO #$% YOURSELF.
BUT THE TRUTH IS YOU JUST PRETEND THE OTHER JUGGLED BALLS, THE ONES IN THE AIR, HAVE CEASED TO EXIST.
WHICHEVER BALL YOU HAPPEN TO HAVE IN HAND, THAT'S IT. THAT'S YOUR WHOLE WORLD.
HAS TO BE.
NO WAY I COULD CHASE THIS FROZEN JACKASS ALL OVER HELL RIGHT NOW--
--IF I WERE UP HERE WORRYING ABOUT MY KID'S EAR INFECTION.
WUT?
IN THE SAME WAY THAT TOMORROW MORNING WHEN I'M WATCHING GERRY EAT A SLICE OF CINNAMON TOAST FROM THE MIDDLE OUT...
...I WON'T CARE AT ALL ABOUT THE UNSOLVED CASE FILES BEN KEEPS PILING ON MY DESK.
IT'S A BIT COLD, YEAH. BUT NECESSARY.

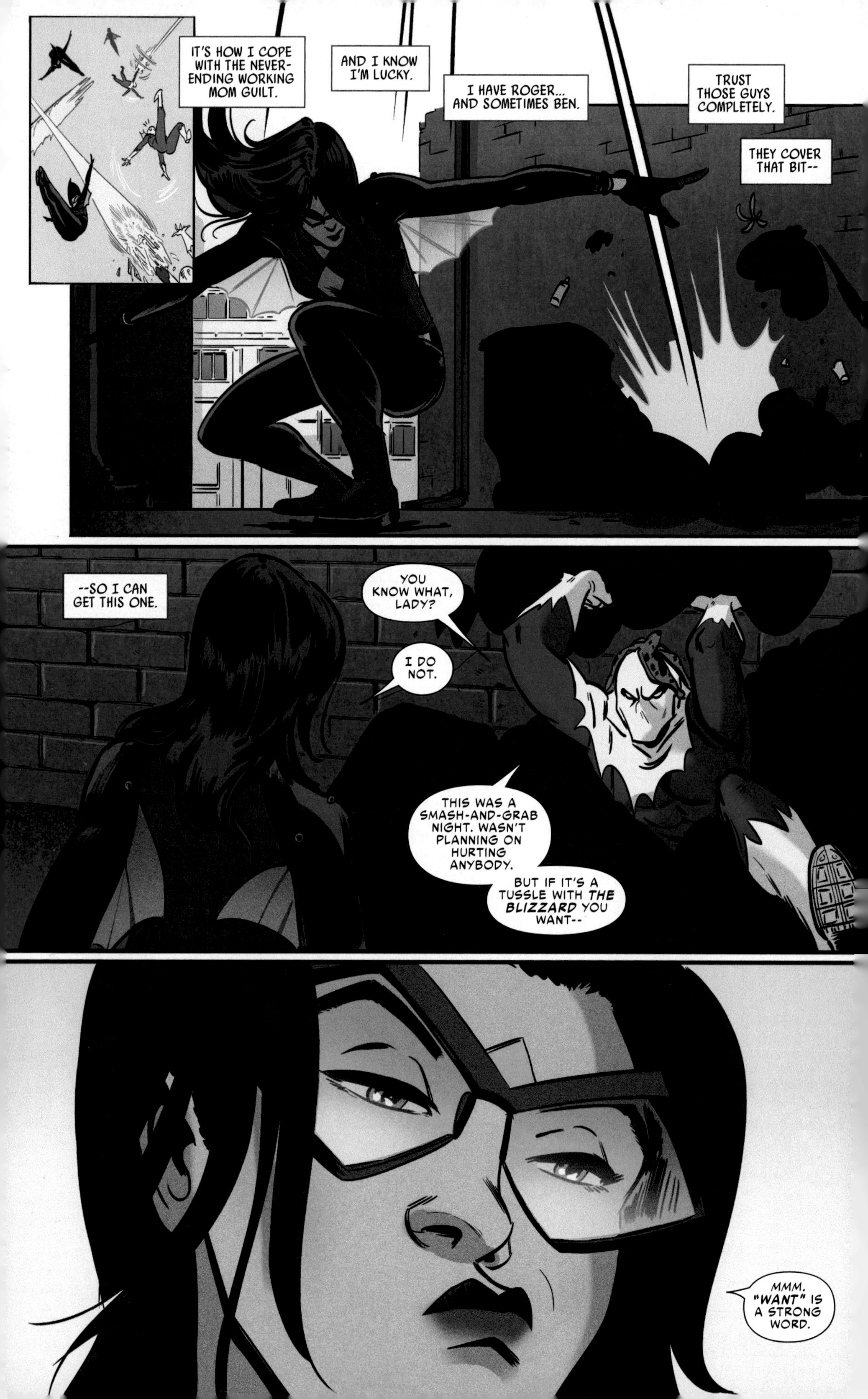
IT'S HOW I COPE WITH THE NEVER-ENDING WORKING MOM GUILT.
AND I KNOW I'M LUCKY.
I HAVE ROGER... AND SOMETIMES BEN.
TRUST THOSE GUYS COMPLETELY.
THEY COVER THAT BIT--
--SO I CAN GET THIS ONE.
YOU KNOW WHAT, LADY?
I DO NOT.
THIS WAS A SMASH-AND-GRAB NIGHT. WASN'T PLANNING ON HURTING ANYBODY.
BUT IF IT'S A TUSSLE WITH *THE BLIZZARD* YOU WANT--
MMM. *"WANT"* IS A STRONG WORD.

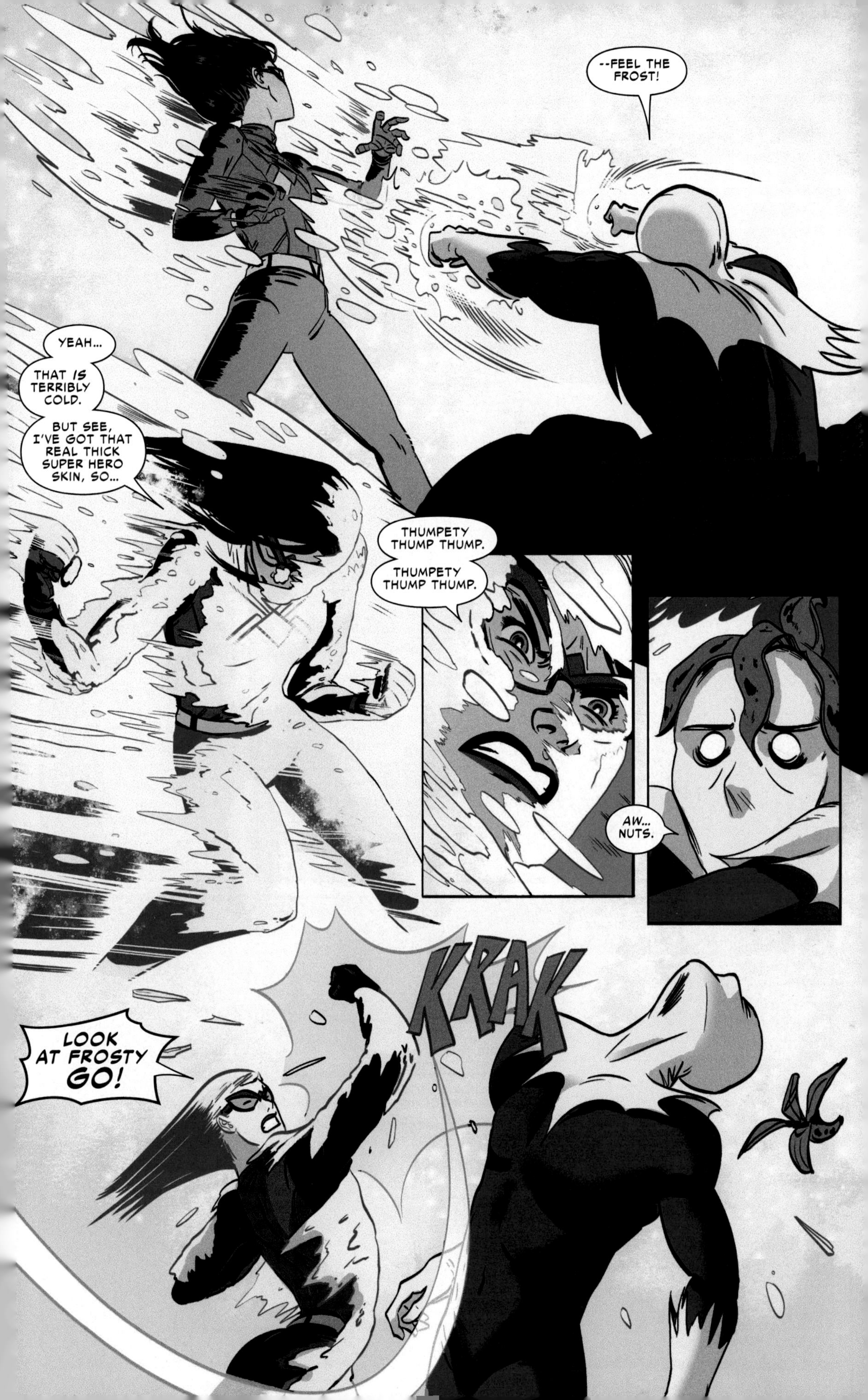
--FEEL THE FROST!
YEAH...
THAT IS TERRIBLY COLD.
BUT SEE, I'VE GOT THAT REAL THICK SUPER HERO SKIN, SO...
THUMPETY THUMP THUMP.
THUMPETY THUMP THUMP.
AW... NUTS.
KRAK
LOOK AT FROSTY GO!

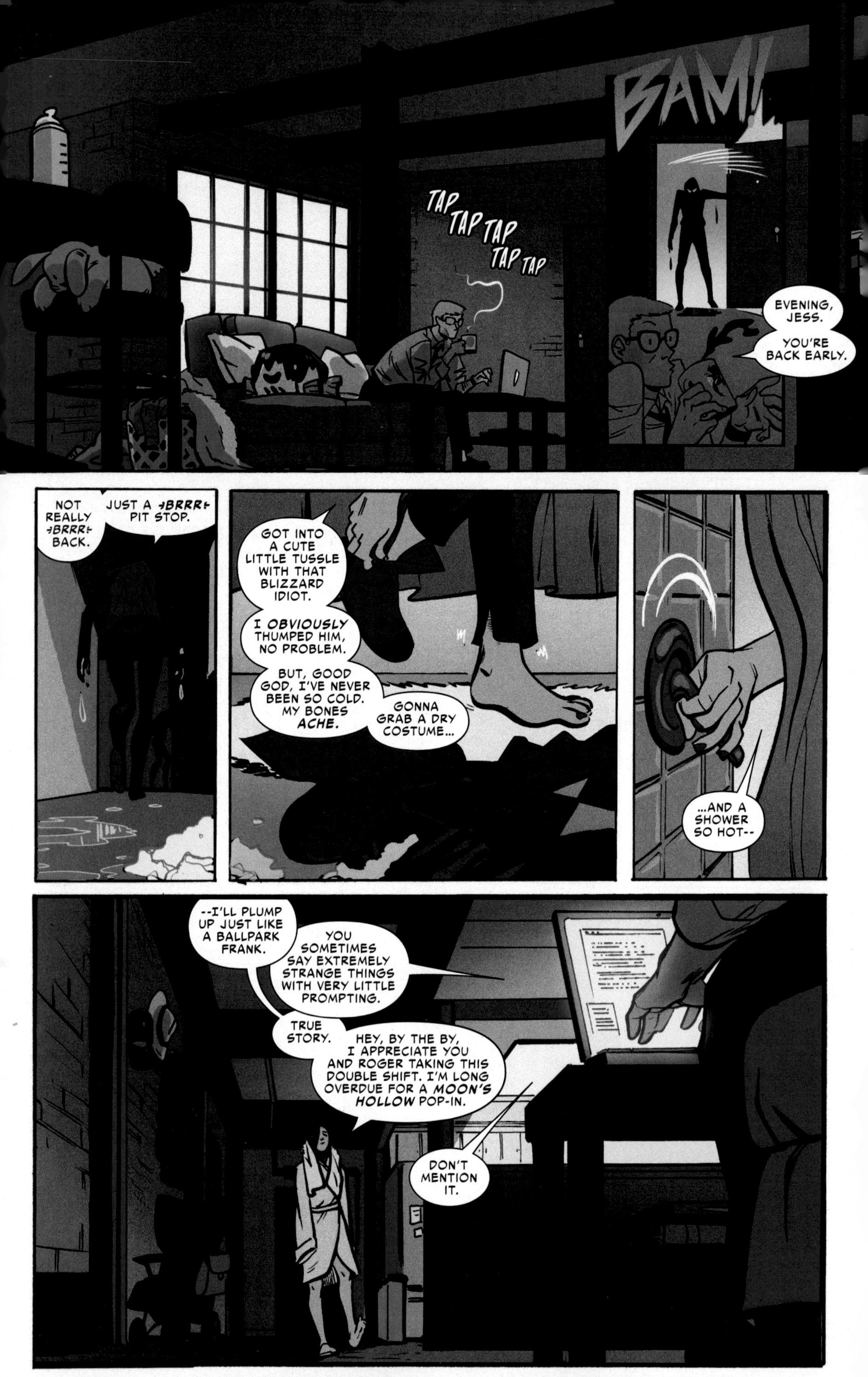
BAM!
TAP TAP TAP TAP TAP
EVENING, JESS.
YOU'RE BACK EARLY.
NOT REALLY -BRRR- BACK.
JUST A -BRRR- PIT STOP.
GOT INTO A CUTE LITTLE TUSSLE WITH THAT BLIZZARD IDIOT.
I OBVIOUSLY THUMPED HIM, NO PROBLEM.
BUT, GOOD GOD, I'VE NEVER BEEN SO COLD. MY BONES ACHE.
GONNA GRAB A DRY COSTUME...
...AND A SHOWER SO HOT--
--I'LL PLUMP UP JUST LIKE A BALLPARK FRANK.
YOU SOMETIMES SAY EXTREMELY STRANGE THINGS WITH VERY LITTLE PROMPTING.
TRUE STORY.
HEY, BY THE BY, I APPRECIATE YOU AND ROGER TAKING THIS DOUBLE SHIFT. I'M LONG OVERDUE FOR A MOON'S HOLLOW POP-IN.
DON'T MENTION IT.

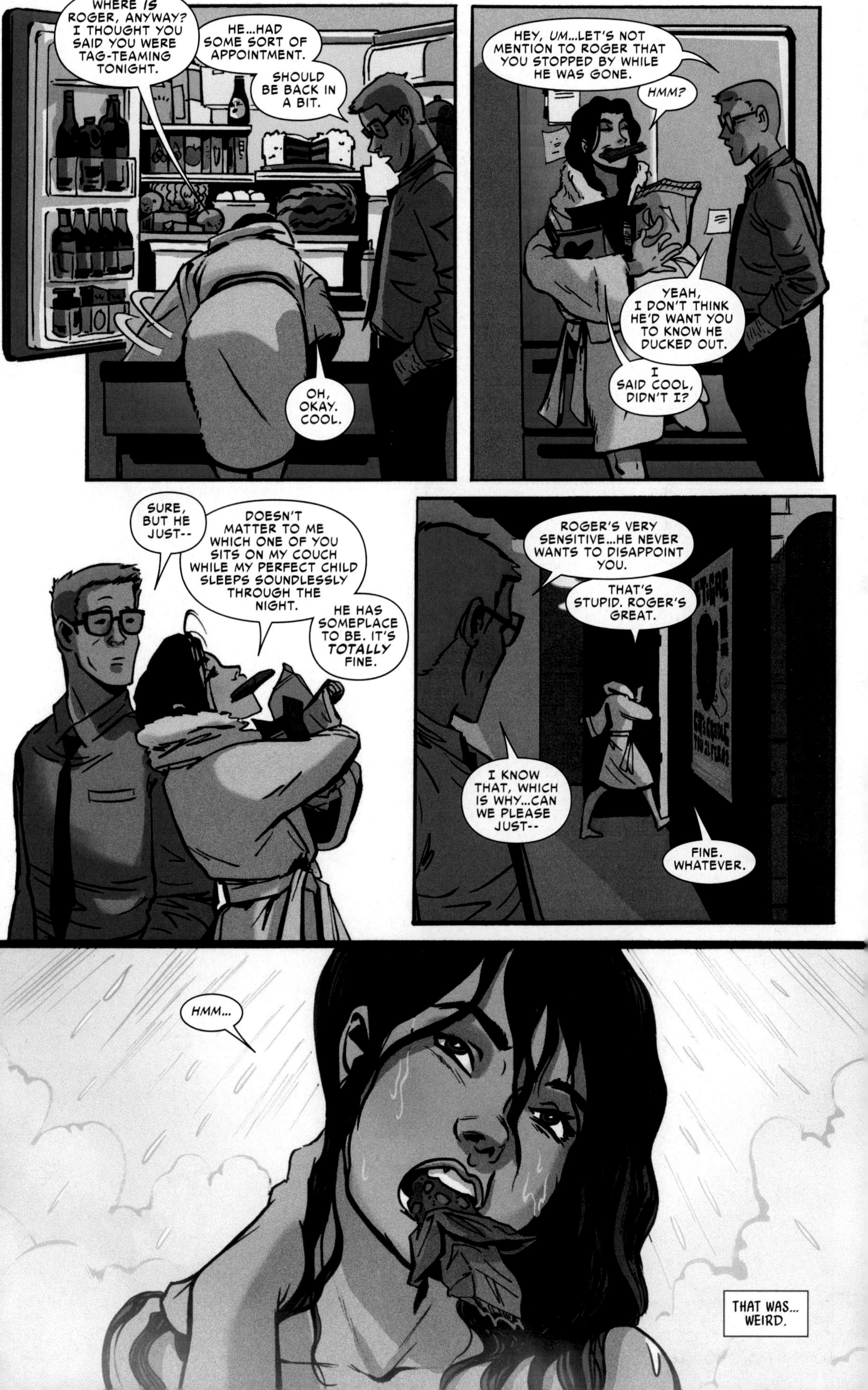

WHERE *IS* ROGER, ANYWAY? I THOUGHT YOU SAID YOU WERE TAG-TEAMING TONIGHT.
HE...HAD SOME SORT OF APPOINTMENT.
SHOULD BE BACK IN A BIT.
OH, OKAY. COOL.
HEY, *UM*...LET'S NOT MENTION TO ROGER THAT YOU STOPPED BY WHILE HE WAS GONE.
HMM?
YEAH, I DON'T THINK HE'D WANT YOU TO KNOW HE DUCKED OUT.
I SAID COOL, DIDN'T I?
SURE, BUT HE JUST--
DOESN'T MATTER TO ME WHICH ONE OF YOU SITS ON MY COUCH WHILE MY PERFECT CHILD SLEEPS SOUNDLESSLY THROUGH THE NIGHT.
HE HAS SOMEPLACE TO BE. IT'S *TOTALLY* FINE.
ROGER'S VERY SENSITIVE...HE NEVER WANTS TO DISAPPOINT YOU.
THAT'S STUPID. ROGER'S GREAT.
I KNOW THAT, WHICH IS WHY...CAN WE PLEASE JUST--
FINE. WHATEVER.
HMM...
THAT WAS... WEIRD.

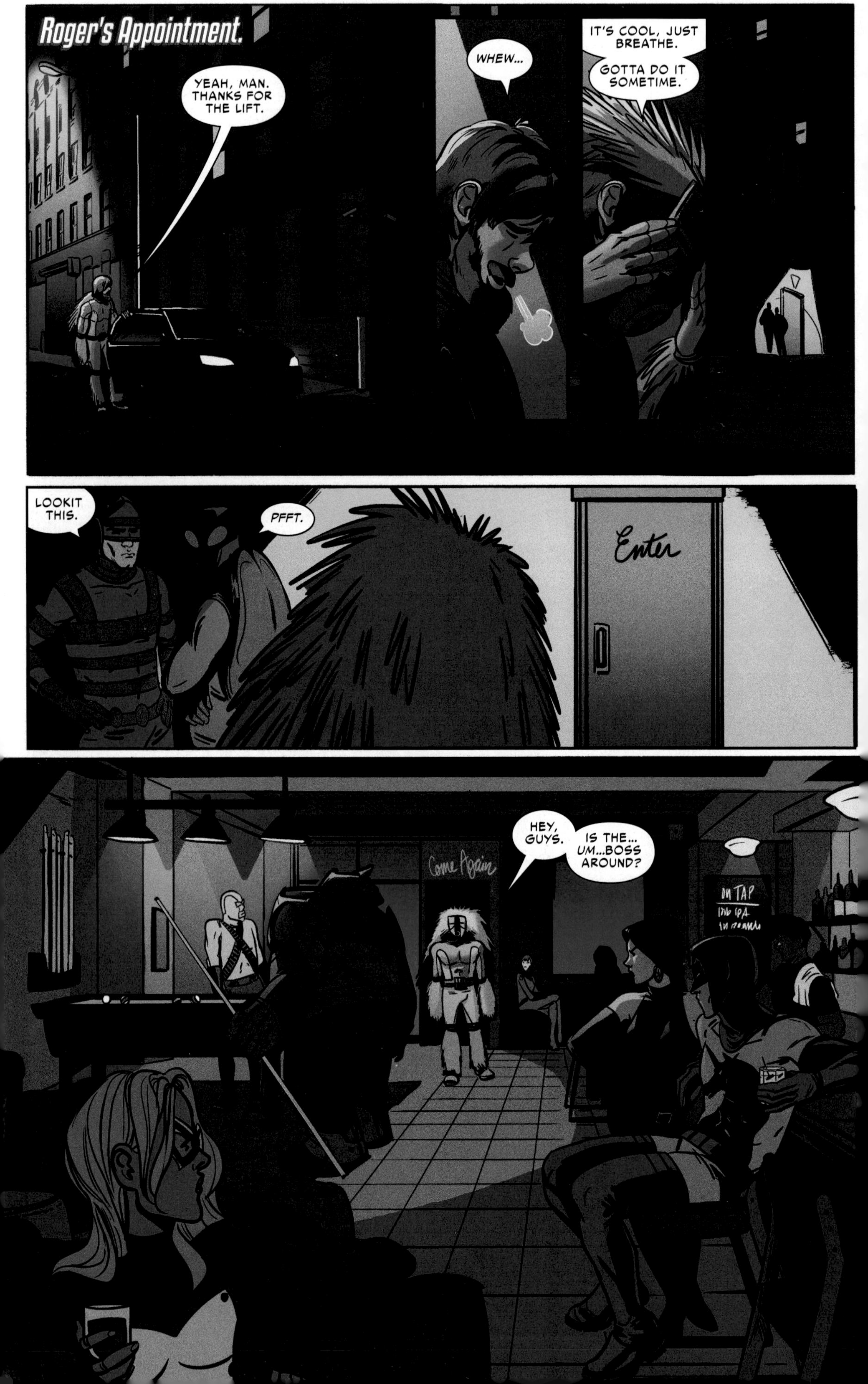
Roger's Appointment.
YEAH, MAN. THANKS FOR THE LIFT.
WHEW...
IT'S COOL, JUST BREATHE.
GOTTA DO IT SOMETIME.
LOOKIT THIS.
PFFT.
Enter
Come Again
HEY, GUYS.
IS THE... UM...BOSS AROUND?
ON TAP

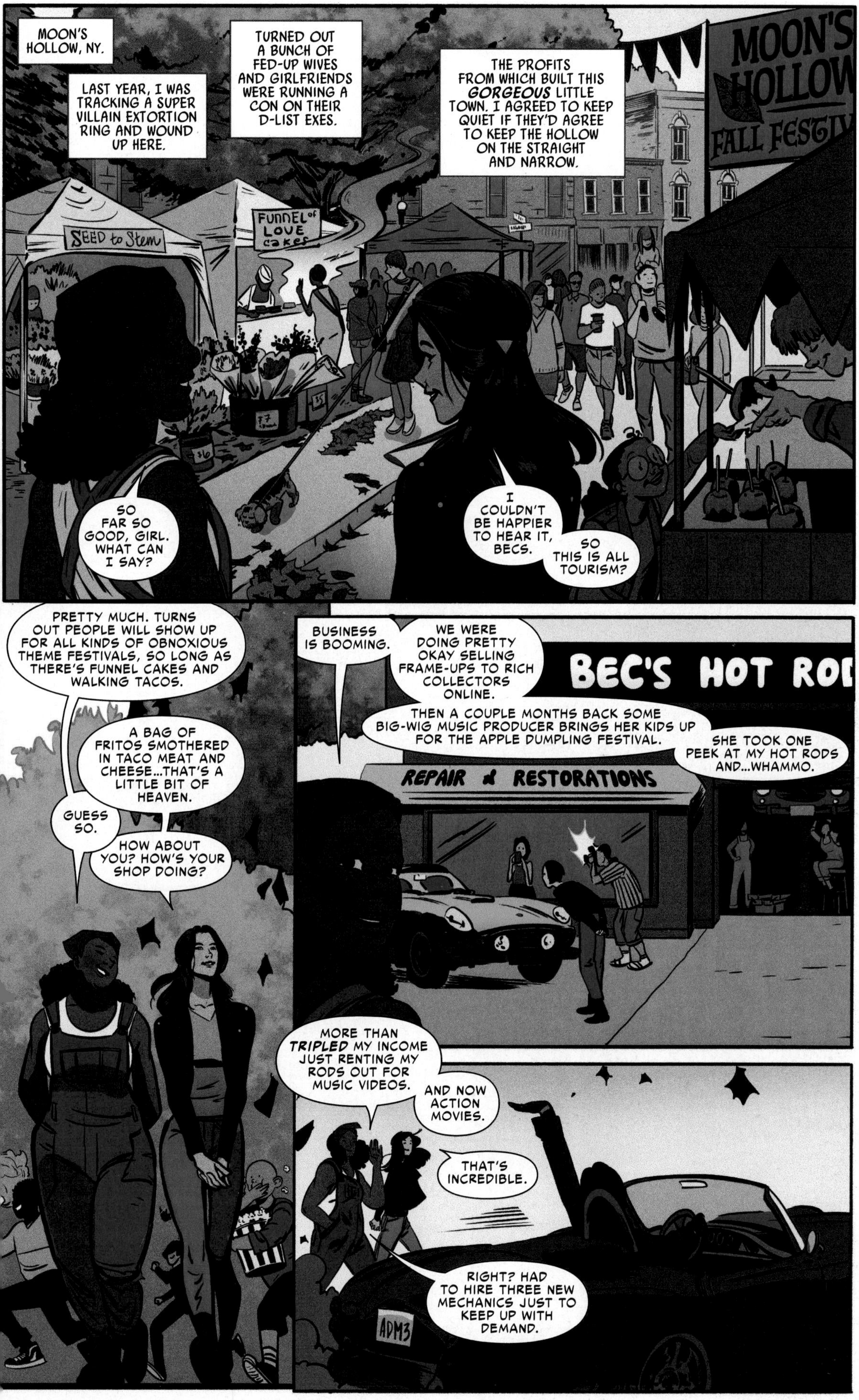
MOON'S HOLLOW, NY.
LAST YEAR, I WAS TRACKING A SUPER VILLAIN EXTORTION RING AND WOUND UP HERE.
TURNED OUT A BUNCH OF FED-UP WIVES AND GIRLFRIENDS WERE RUNNING A CON ON THEIR D-LIST EXES.
THE PROFITS FROM WHICH BUILT THIS *GORGEOUS* LITTLE TOWN. I AGREED TO KEEP QUIET IF THEY'D AGREE TO KEEP THE HOLLOW ON THE STRAIGHT AND NARROW.
MOON'S HOLLOW FALL FESTIV
SEED to Stem
FUNNEL of LOVE cakes
SO FAR SO GOOD, GIRL. WHAT CAN I SAY?
I COULDN'T BE HAPPIER TO HEAR IT, BECS.
SO THIS IS ALL TOURISM?
PRETTY MUCH. TURNS OUT PEOPLE WILL SHOW UP FOR ALL KINDS OF OBNOXIOUS THEME FESTIVALS, SO LONG AS THERE'S FUNNEL CAKES AND WALKING TACOS.
A BAG OF FRITOS SMOTHERED IN TACO MEAT AND CHEESE...THAT'S A LITTLE BIT OF HEAVEN.
GUESS SO.
HOW ABOUT YOU? HOW'S YOUR SHOP DOING?
BUSINESS IS BOOMING.
WE WERE DOING PRETTY OKAY SELLING FRAME-UPS TO RICH COLLECTORS ONLINE.
BEC'S HOT ROD
THEN A COUPLE MONTHS BACK SOME BIG-WIG MUSIC PRODUCER BRINGS HER KIDS UP FOR THE APPLE DUMPLING FESTIVAL.
SHE TOOK ONE PEEK AT MY HOT RODS AND...WHAMMO.
REPAIR & RESTORATIONS
MORE THAN *TRIPLED* MY INCOME JUST RENTING MY RODS OUT FOR MUSIC VIDEOS.
AND NOW ACTION MOVIES.
THAT'S INCREDIBLE.
RIGHT? HAD TO HIRE THREE NEW MECHANICS JUST TO KEEP UP WITH DEMAND.
ADM3

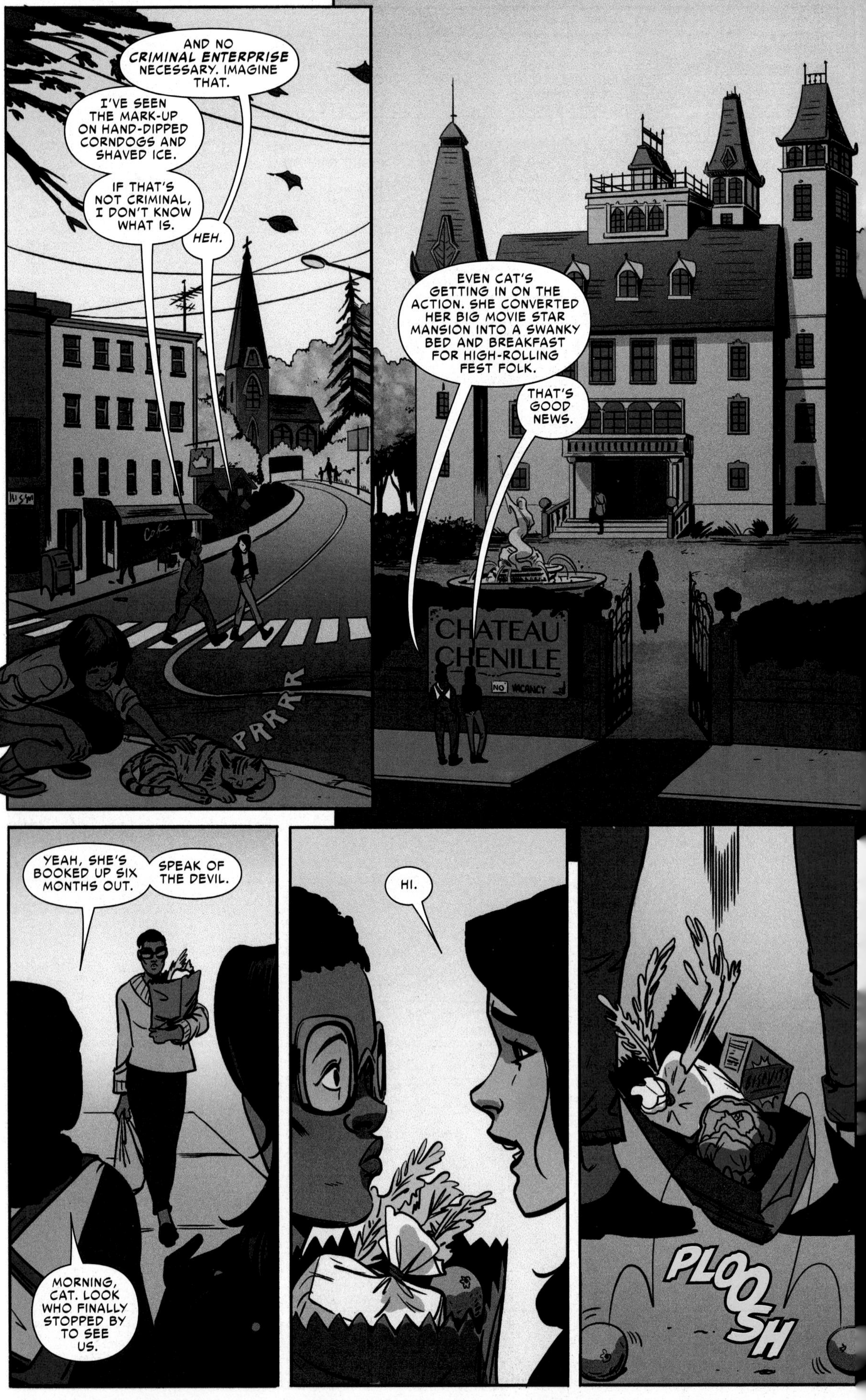

AND NO *CRIMINAL ENTERPRISE* NECESSARY. IMAGINE THAT.
I'VE SEEN THE MARK-UP ON HAND-DIPPED CORNDOGS AND SHAVED ICE.
IF THAT'S NOT CRIMINAL, I DON'T KNOW WHAT IS.
HEH.
PRRRR
EVEN CAT'S GETTING IN ON THE ACTION. SHE CONVERTED HER BIG MOVIE STAR MANSION INTO A SWANKY BED AND BREAKFAST FOR HIGH-ROLLING FEST FOLK.
THAT'S GOOD NEWS.
CHATEAU CHENILLE
NO VACANCY
YEAH, SHE'S BOOKED UP SIX MONTHS OUT.
SPEAK OF THE DEVIL.
MORNING, CAT. LOOK WHO FINALLY STOPPED BY TO SEE US.
HI.
PLOOSH

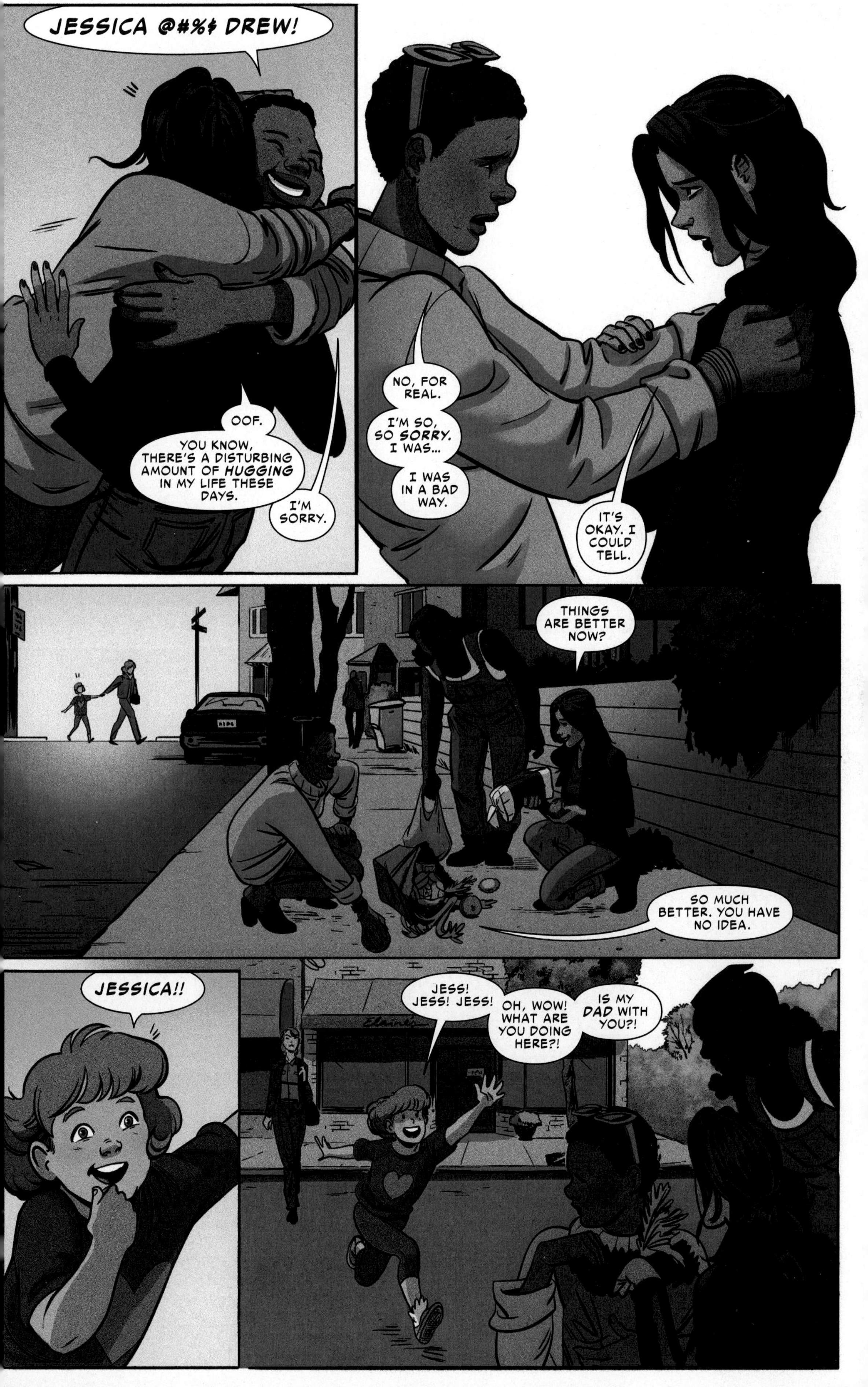
JESSICA @#%$ DREW!
OOF.
YOU KNOW, THERE'S A DISTURBING AMOUNT OF HUGGING IN MY LIFE THESE DAYS.
I'M SORRY.
NO, FOR REAL.
I'M SO, SO SORRY. I WAS...
I WAS IN A BAD WAY.
IT'S OKAY. I COULD TELL.
THINGS ARE BETTER NOW?
SO MUCH BETTER. YOU HAVE NO IDEA.
JESSICA!!
JESS! JESS! JESS!
OH, WOW! WHAT ARE YOU DOING HERE?!
IS MY DAD WITH YOU?!

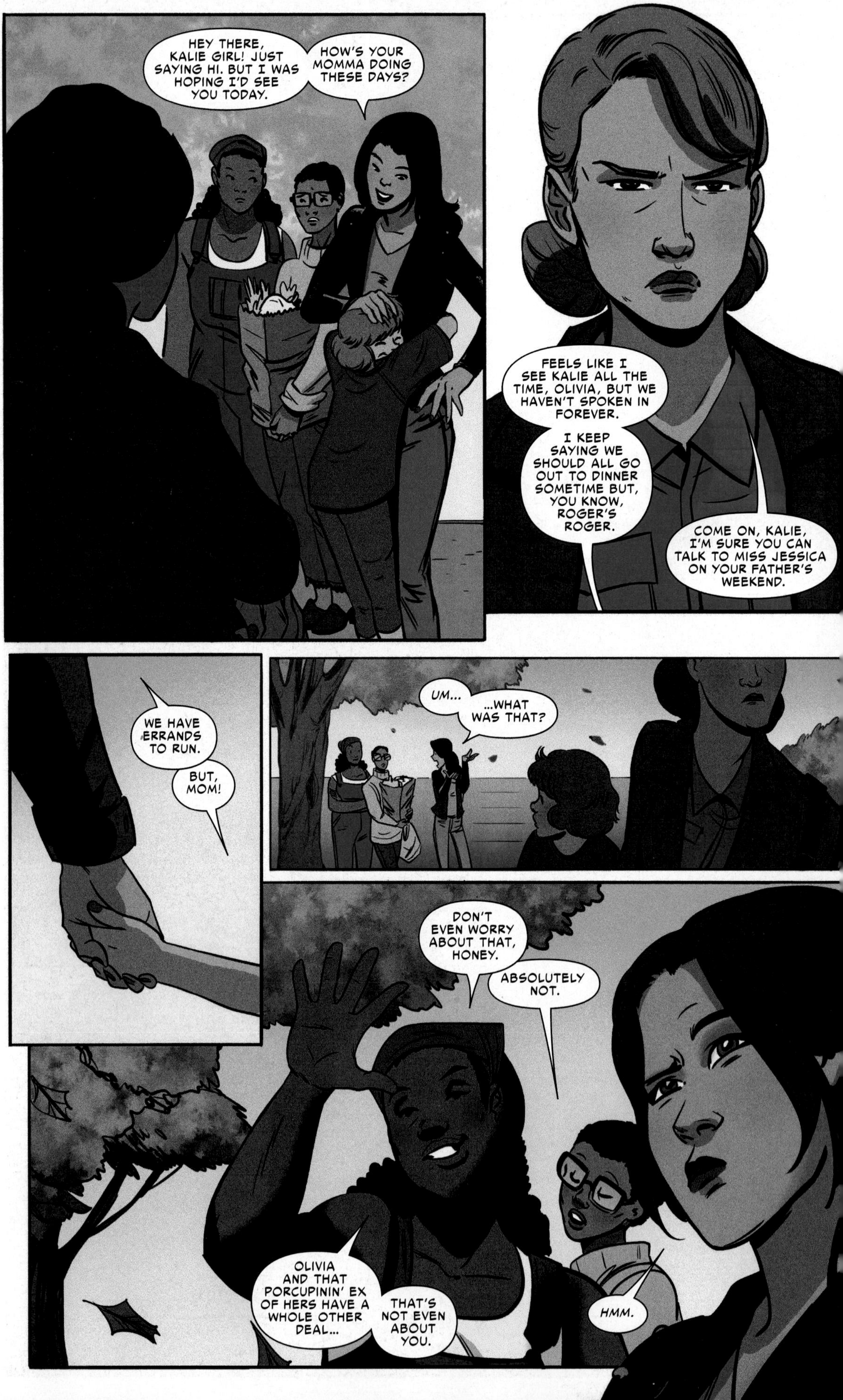
HEY THERE, KALIE GIRL! JUST SAYING HI. BUT I WAS HOPING I'D SEE YOU TODAY.
HOW'S YOUR MOMMA DOING THESE DAYS?
FEELS LIKE I SEE KALIE ALL THE TIME, OLIVIA, BUT WE HAVEN'T SPOKEN IN FOREVER.
I KEEP SAYING WE SHOULD ALL GO OUT TO DINNER SOMETIME BUT, YOU KNOW, ROGER'S ROGER.
COME ON, KALIE, I'M SURE YOU CAN TALK TO MISS JESSICA ON YOUR FATHER'S WEEKEND.
WE HAVE ERRANDS TO RUN.
BUT, MOM!
UM...
...WHAT WAS THAT?
DON'T EVEN WORRY ABOUT THAT, HONEY.
ABSOLUTELY NOT.
OLIVIA AND THAT PORCUPININ' EX OF HERS HAVE A WHOLE OTHER DEAL...
THAT'S NOT EVEN ABOUT YOU.
HMM.

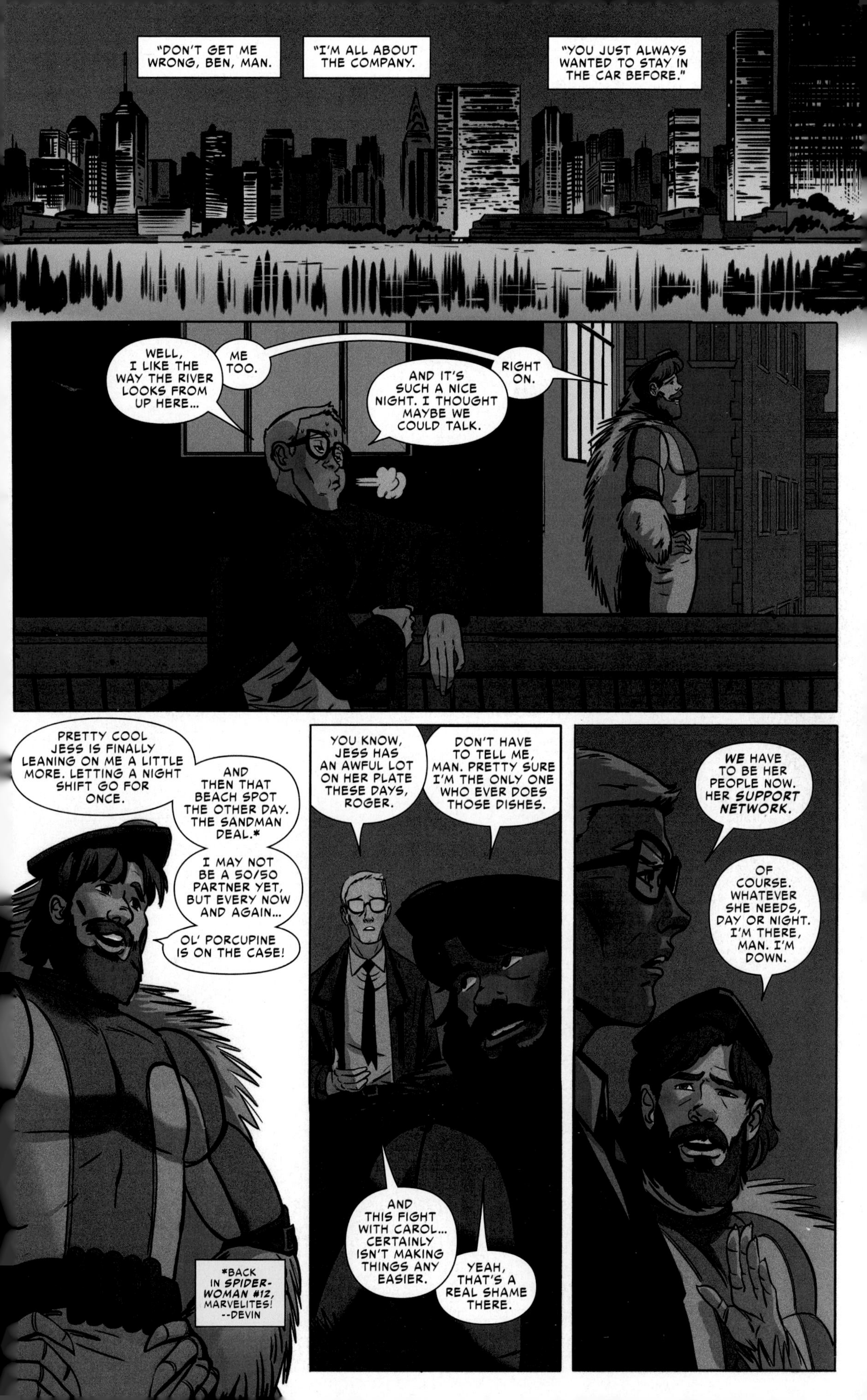
"DON'T GET ME WRONG, BEN, MAN.
"I'M ALL ABOUT THE COMPANY.
"YOU JUST ALWAYS WANTED TO STAY IN THE CAR BEFORE."
WELL, I LIKE THE WAY THE RIVER LOOKS FROM UP HERE...
ME TOO.
RIGHT ON.
AND IT'S SUCH A NICE NIGHT. I THOUGHT MAYBE WE COULD TALK.
PRETTY COOL JESS IS FINALLY LEANING ON ME A LITTLE MORE. LETTING A NIGHT SHIFT GO FOR ONCE.
AND THEN THAT BEACH SPOT THE OTHER DAY. THE SANDMAN DEAL.*
I MAY NOT BE A 50/50 PARTNER YET, BUT EVERY NOW AND AGAIN...
OL' PORCUPINE IS ON THE CASE!
*BACK IN SPIDER-WOMAN #12, MARVELITES! --DEVIN
YOU KNOW, JESS HAS AN AWFUL LOT ON HER PLATE THESE DAYS, ROGER.
DON'T HAVE TO TELL ME, MAN. PRETTY SURE I'M THE ONLY ONE WHO EVER DOES THOSE DISHES.
AND THIS FIGHT WITH CAROL... CERTAINLY ISN'T MAKING THINGS ANY EASIER.
YEAH, THAT'S A REAL SHAME THERE.
WE HAVE TO BE HER PEOPLE NOW. HER SUPPORT NETWORK.
OF COURSE. WHATEVER SHE NEEDS, DAY OR NIGHT. I'M THERE, MAN. I'M DOWN.

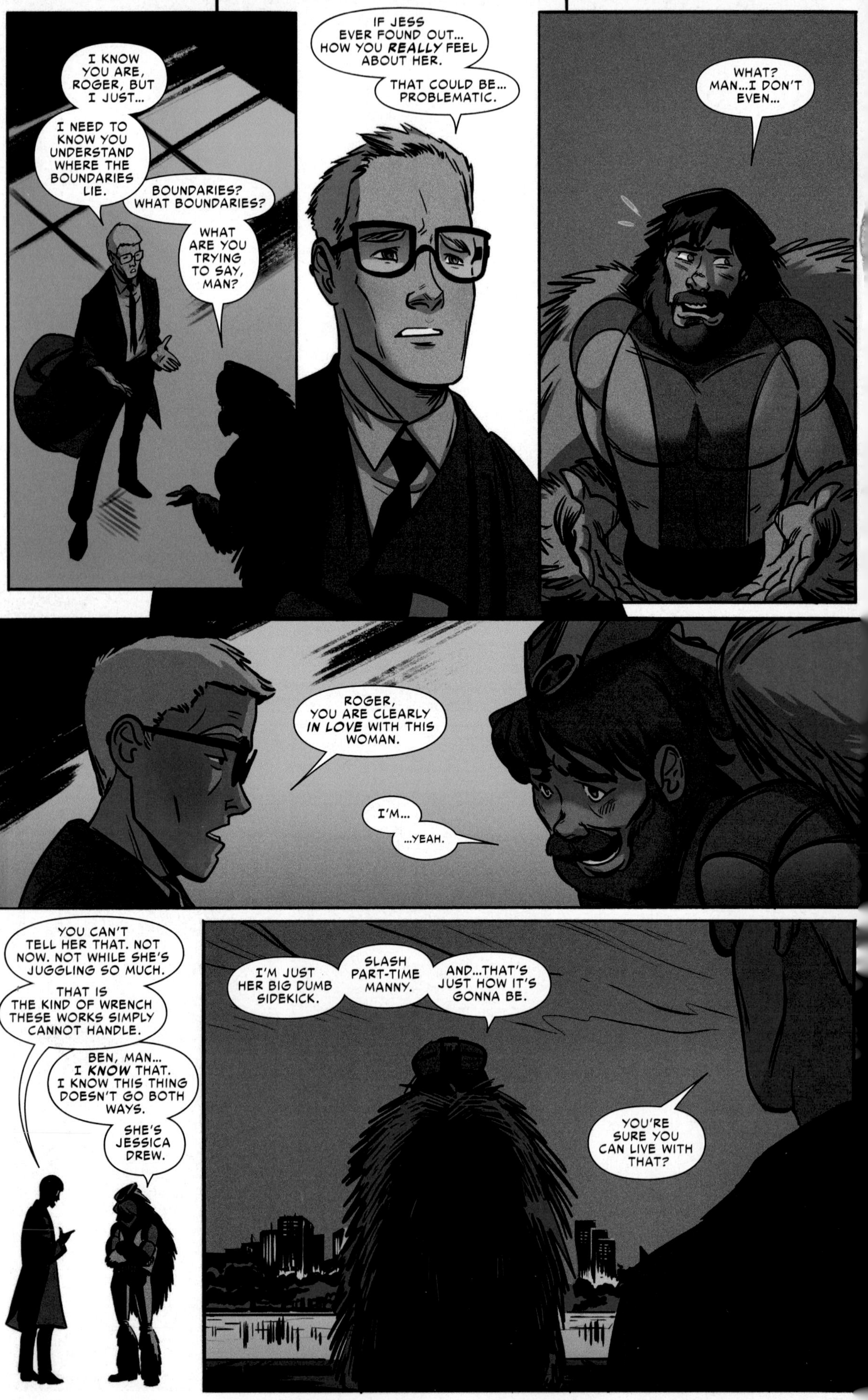

I KNOW YOU ARE, ROGER, BUT I JUST...
I NEED TO KNOW YOU UNDERSTAND WHERE THE BOUNDARIES LIE.
BOUNDARIES? WHAT BOUNDARIES?
WHAT ARE YOU TRYING TO SAY, MAN?
IF JESS EVER FOUND OUT... HOW YOU REALLY FEEL ABOUT HER.
THAT COULD BE... PROBLEMATIC.
WHAT? MAN...I DON'T EVEN...
ROGER, YOU ARE CLEARLY IN LOVE WITH THIS WOMAN.
I'M...
...YEAH.
YOU CAN'T TELL HER THAT. NOT NOW. NOT WHILE SHE'S JUGGLING SO MUCH.
THAT IS THE KIND OF WRENCH THESE WORKS SIMPLY CANNOT HANDLE.
BEN, MAN... I KNOW THAT. I KNOW THIS THING DOESN'T GO BOTH WAYS.
SHE'S JESSICA DREW.
I'M JUST HER BIG DUMB SIDEKICK.
SLASH PART-TIME MANNY.
AND...THAT'S JUST HOW IT'S GONNA BE.
YOU'RE SURE YOU CAN LIVE WITH THAT?

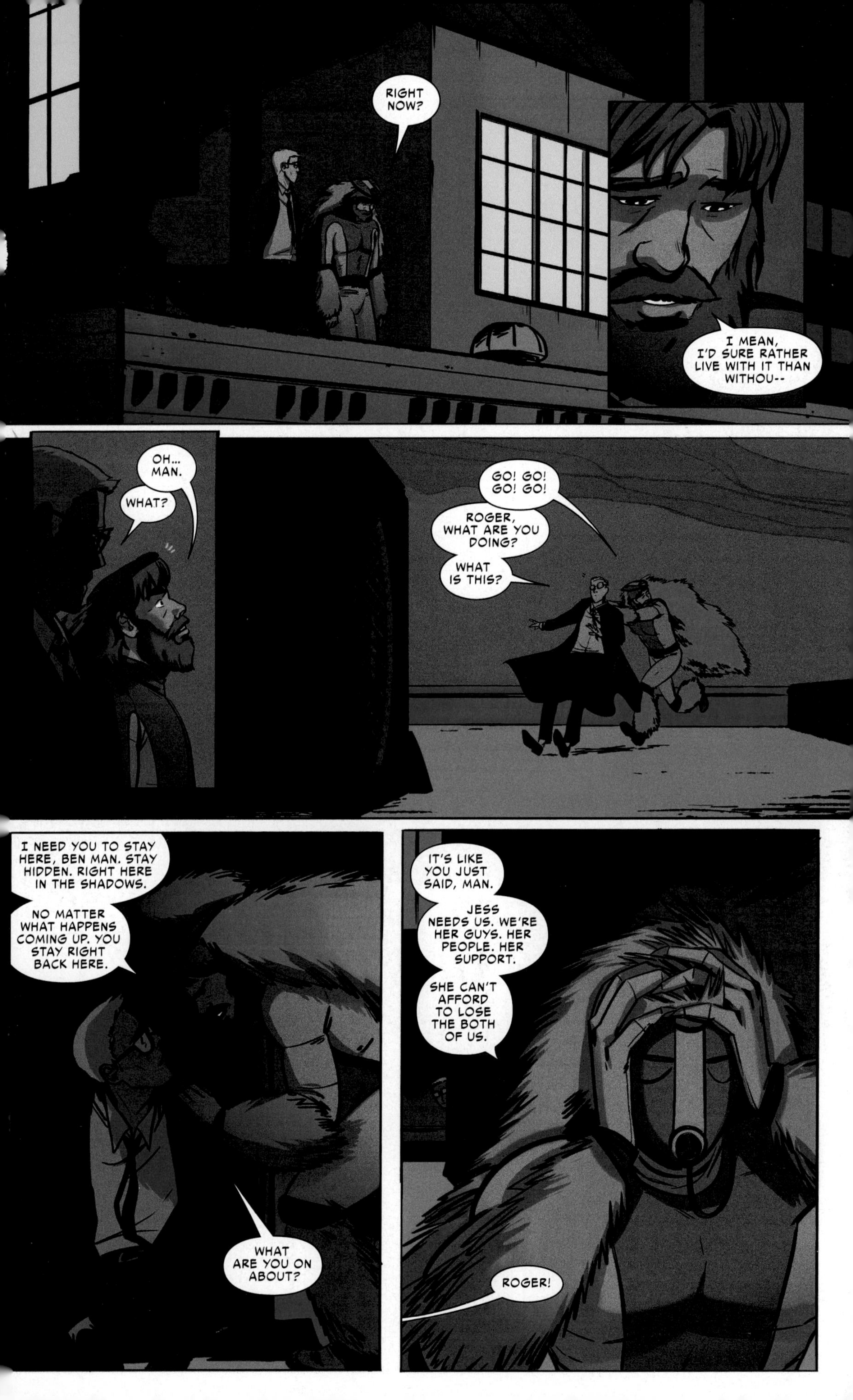
RIGHT NOW?
I MEAN, I'D SURE RATHER LIVE WITH IT THAN WITHOU--
OH... MAN.
WHAT?
GO! GO! GO! GO!
ROGER, WHAT ARE YOU DOING?
WHAT IS THIS?
I NEED YOU TO STAY HERE, BEN MAN. STAY HIDDEN. RIGHT HERE IN THE SHADOWS.
NO MATTER WHAT HAPPENS COMING UP. YOU STAY RIGHT BACK HERE.
WHAT ARE YOU ON ABOUT?
IT'S LIKE YOU JUST SAID, MAN.
JESS NEEDS US. WE'RE HER GUYS. HER PEOPLE. HER SUPPORT.
SHE CAN'T AFFORD TO LOSE THE BOTH OF US.
ROGER!

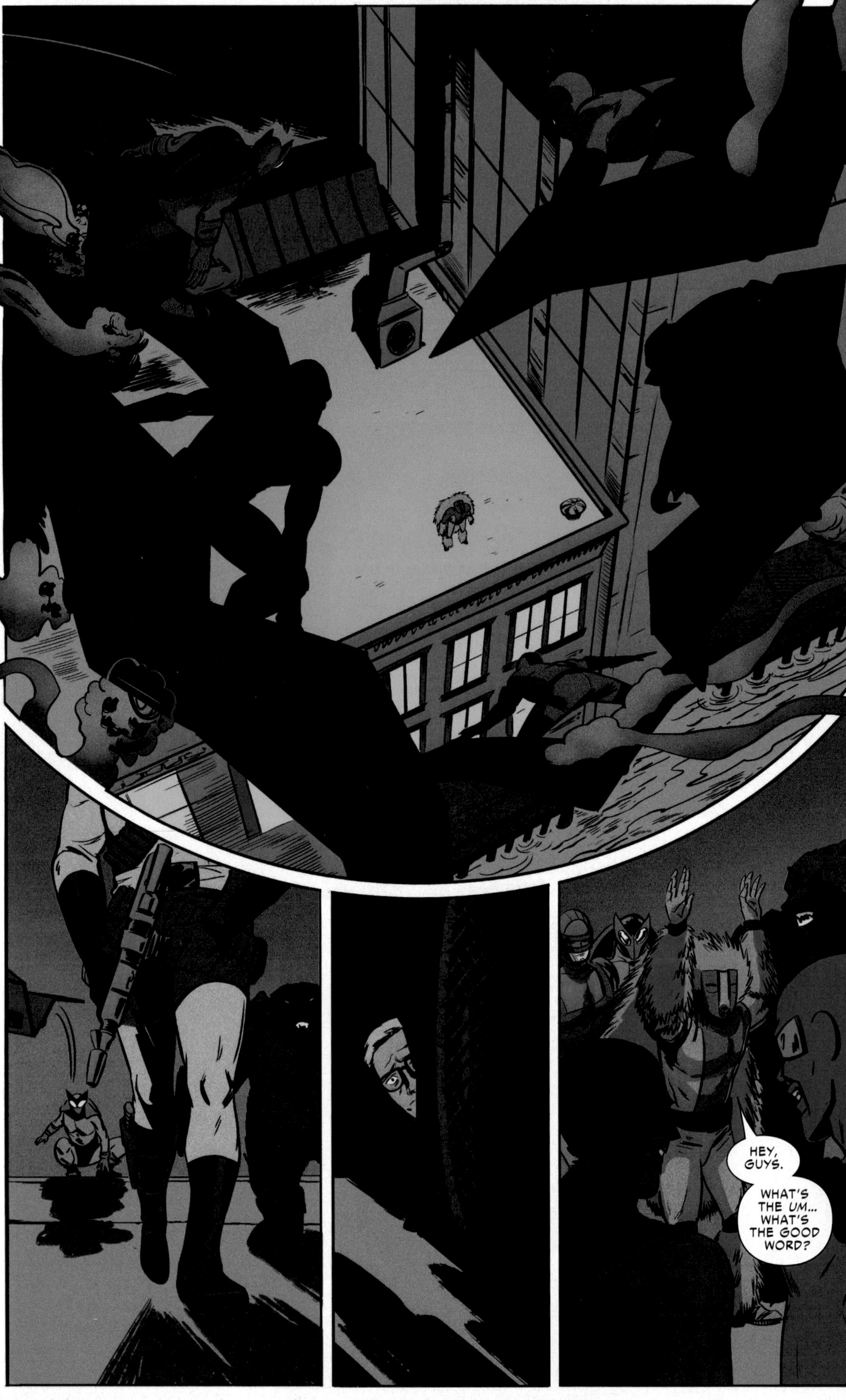
HEY, GUYS.
WHAT'S THE *UM*... WHAT'S THE GOOD WORD?

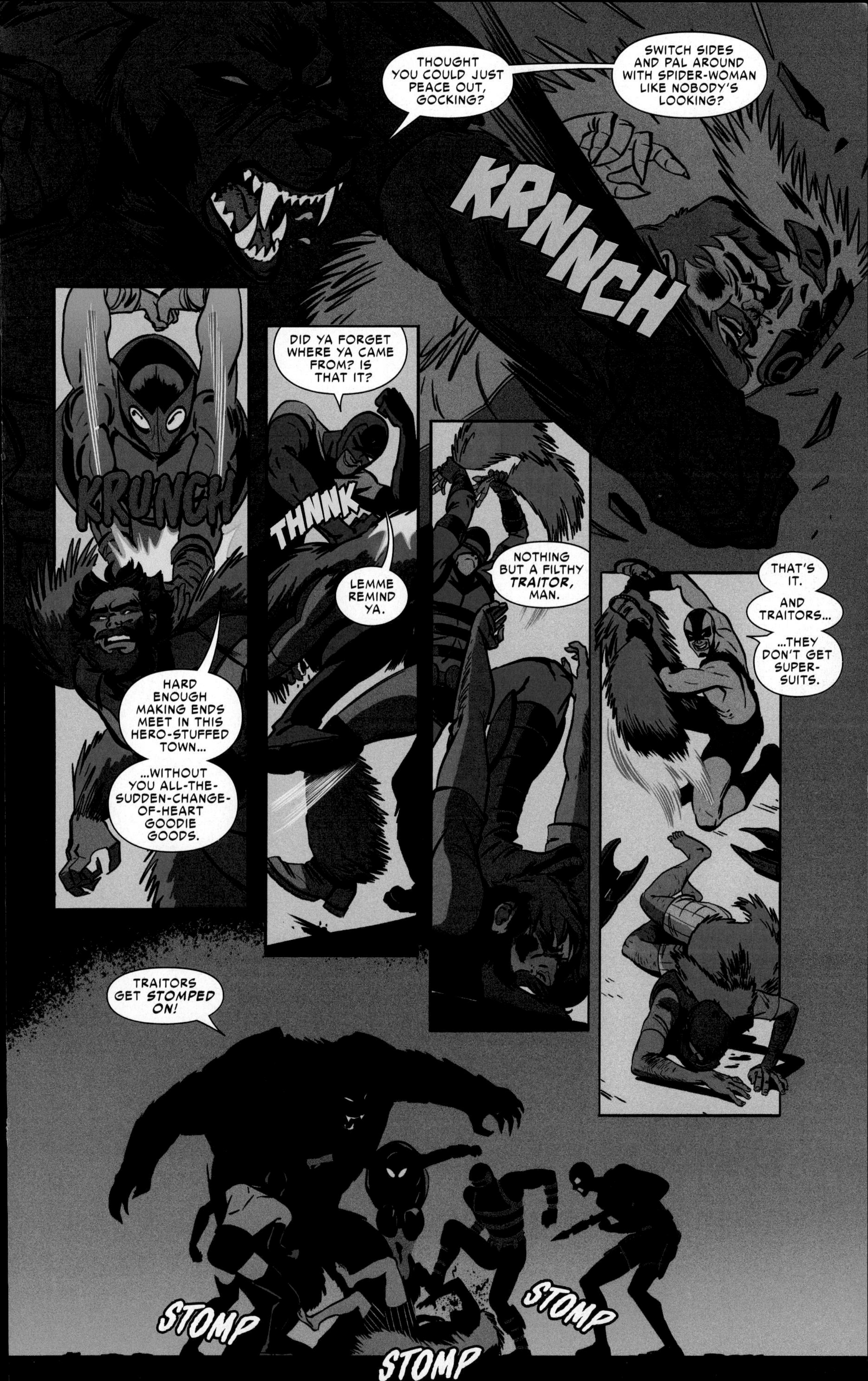
THOUGHT YOU COULD JUST PEACE OUT, GOCKING?
SWITCH SIDES AND PAL AROUND WITH SPIDER-WOMAN LIKE NOBODY'S LOOKING?
KRNNCH
KRUNCH
HARD ENOUGH MAKING ENDS MEET IN THIS HERO-STUFFED TOWN...
...WITHOUT YOU ALL-THE-SUDDEN-CHANGE-OF-HEART GOODIE GOODS.
DID YA FORGET WHERE YA CAME FROM? IS THAT IT?
THNNK
LEMME REMIND YA.
NOTHING BUT A FILTHY TRAITOR, MAN.
THAT'S IT.
AND TRAITORS...
...THEY DON'T GET SUPER-SUITS.
TRAITORS GET STOMPED ON!
STOMP
STOMP
STOMP

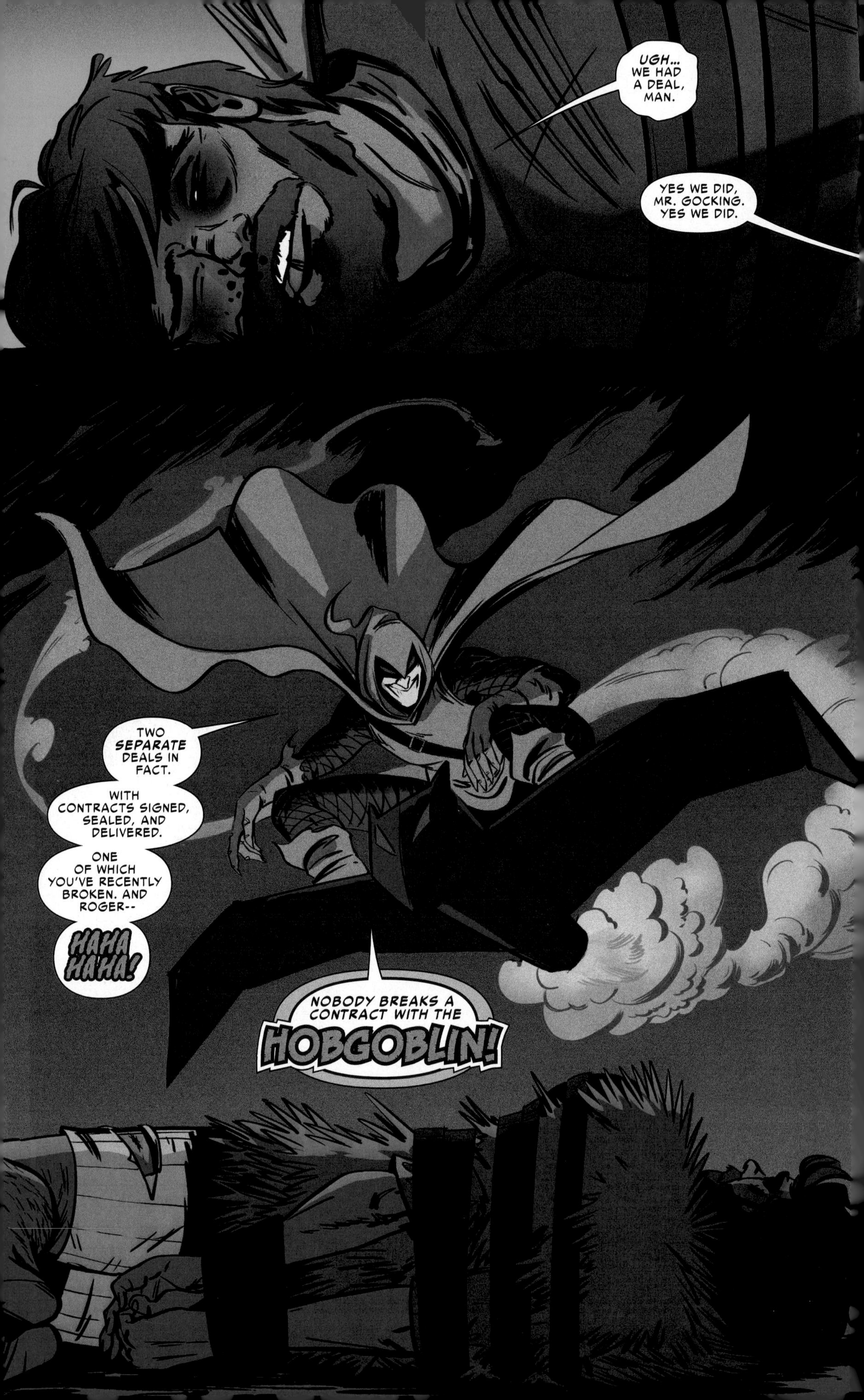
UGH... WE HAD A DEAL, MAN.
YES WE DID, MR. GOCKING. YES WE DID.
TWO *SEPARATE* DEALS IN FACT.
WITH CONTRACTS SIGNED, SEALED, AND DELIVERED.
ONE OF WHICH YOU'VE RECENTLY BROKEN. AND ROGER--
HAHA HAHA!
NOBODY BREAKS A CONTRACT WITH THE HOBGOBLIN!

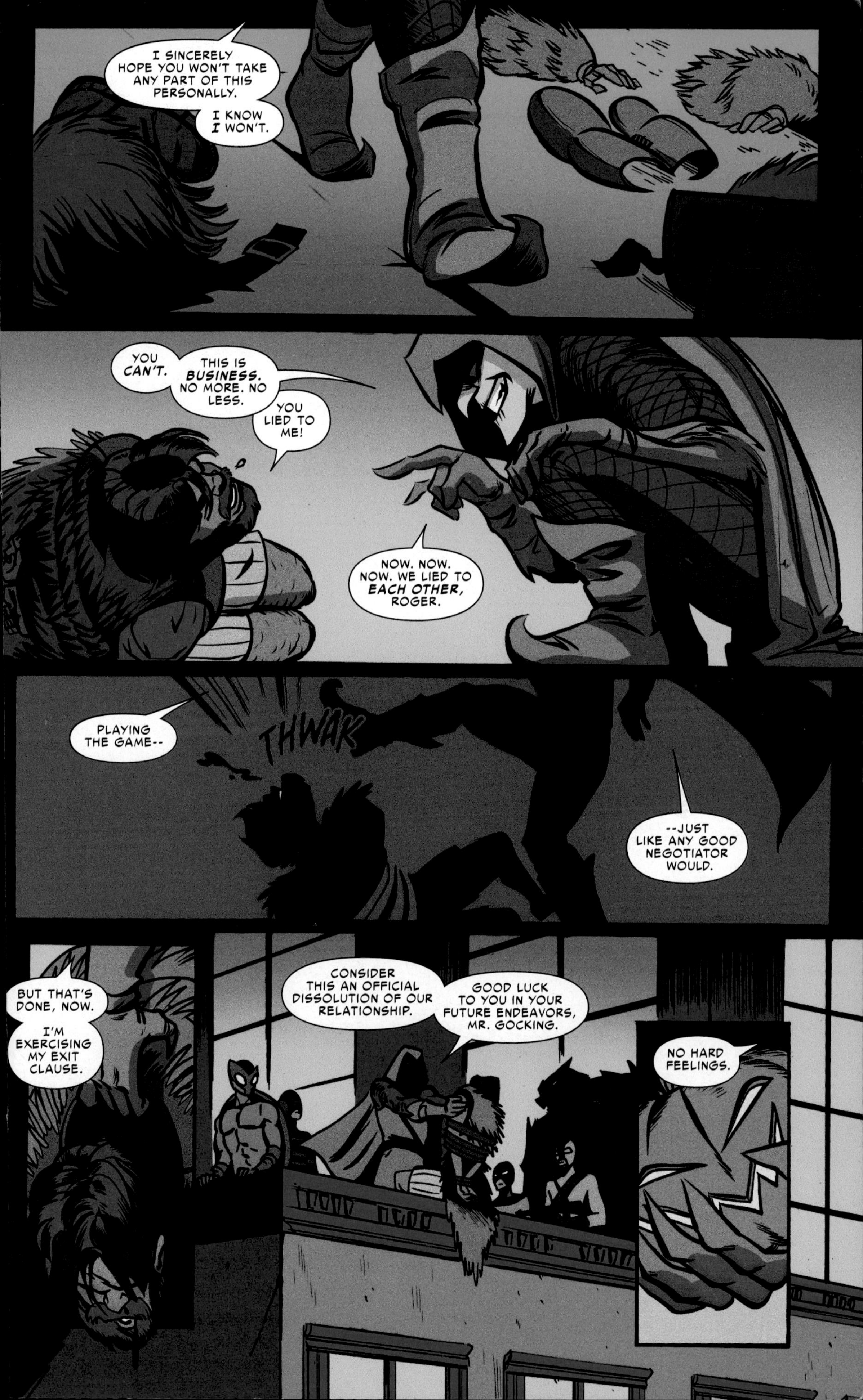
I SINCERELY HOPE YOU WON'T TAKE ANY PART OF THIS PERSONALLY.
I KNOW *I* WON'T.
YOU *CAN'T.*
THIS IS *BUSINESS.* NO MORE. NO LESS.
YOU LIED TO ME!
NOW. NOW. NOW. WE LIED TO *EACH OTHER,* ROGER.
PLAYING THE GAME--
THWAK
--JUST LIKE ANY GOOD NEGOTIATOR WOULD.
BUT THAT'S DONE, NOW.
I'M EXERCISING MY EXIT CLAUSE.
CONSIDER THIS AN OFFICIAL DISSOLUTION OF OUR RELATIONSHIP.
GOOD LUCK TO YOU IN YOUR FUTURE ENDEAVORS, MR. GOCKING.
NO HARD FEELINGS.

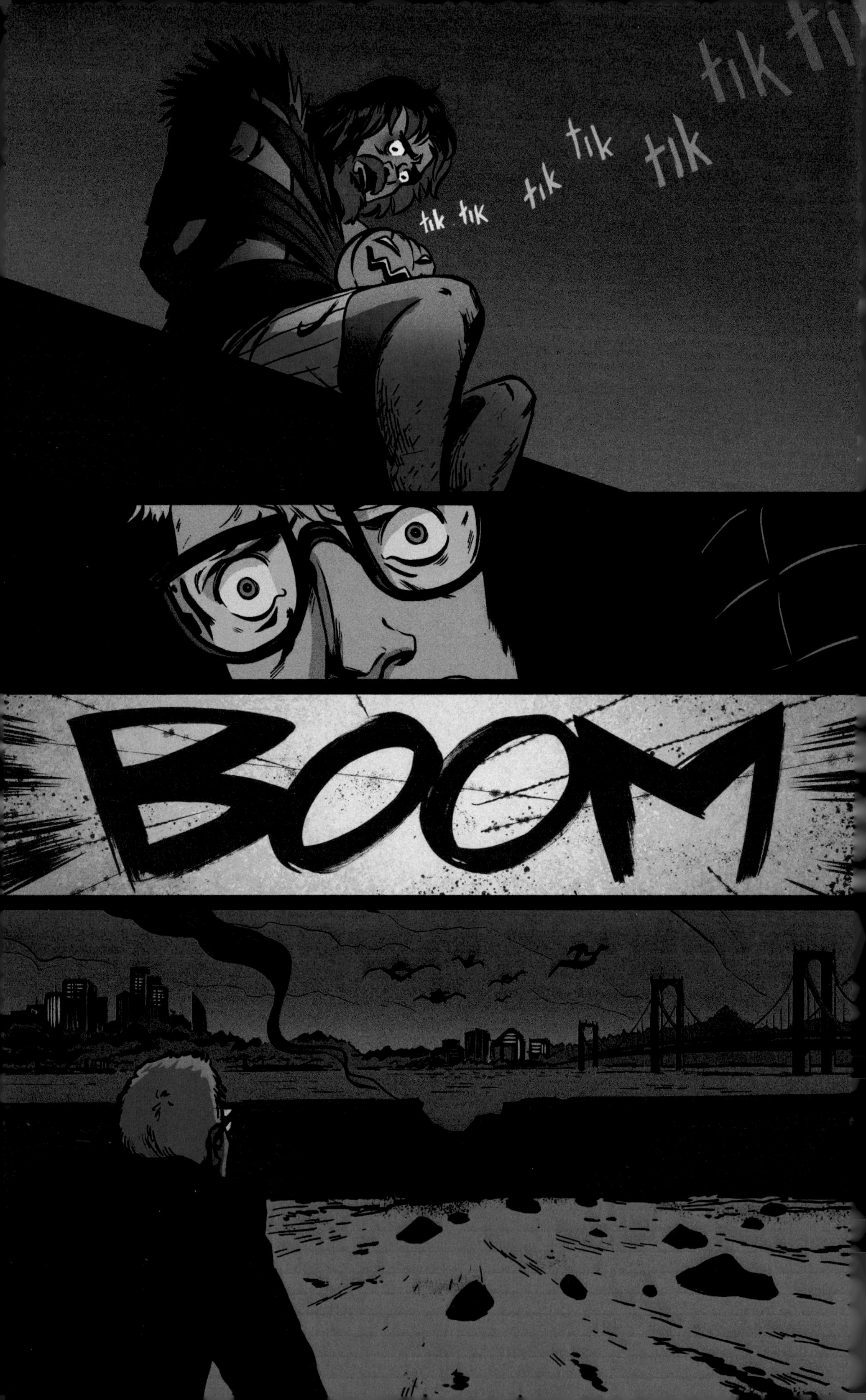
tik tik
tik
tik
tik
tik
tik ti
BOOM

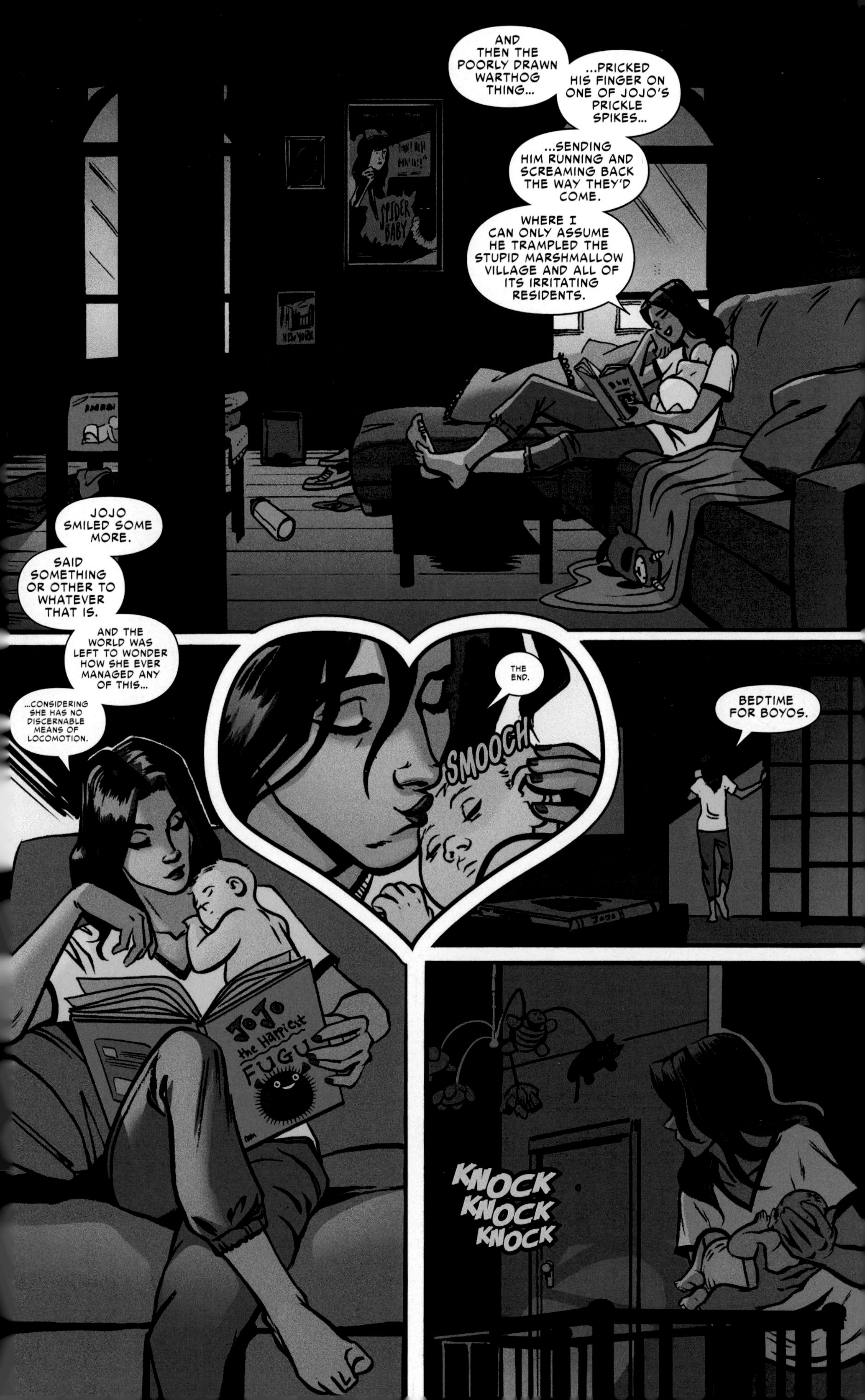
AND THEN THE POORLY DRAWN WARTHOG THING...
...PRICKED HIS FINGER ON ONE OF JOJO'S PRICKLE SPIKES...
...SENDING HIM RUNNING AND SCREAMING BACK THE WAY THEY'D COME.
WHERE I CAN ONLY ASSUME HE TRAMPLED THE STUPID MARSHMALLOW VILLAGE AND ALL OF ITS IRRITATING RESIDENTS.
SPIDER BABY
NEW YORK
JOJO SMILED SOME MORE.
SAID SOMETHING OR OTHER TO WHATEVER THAT IS.
AND THE WORLD WAS LEFT TO WONDER HOW SHE EVER MANAGED ANY OF THIS...
...CONSIDERING SHE HAS NO DISCERNABLE MEANS OF LOCOMOTION.
JoJo the Happiest FUGU
THE END.
SMOOCH
BEDTIME FOR BOYOS.
KNOCK KNOCK KNOCK

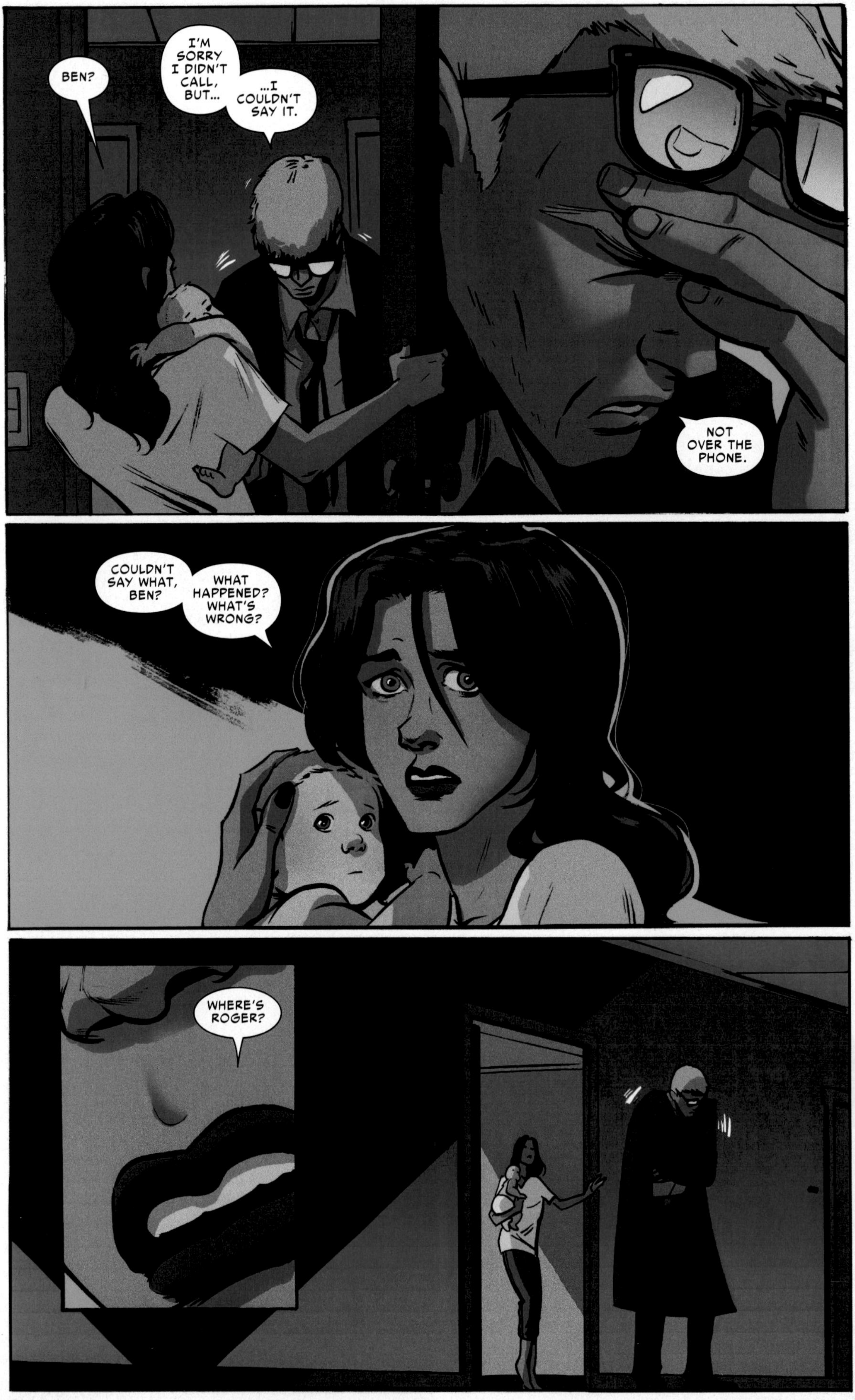
BEN?
I'M SORRY I DIDN'T CALL, BUT...
...I COULDN'T SAY IT.
NOT OVER THE PHONE.
COULDN'T SAY WHAT, BEN?
WHAT HAPPENED? WHAT'S WRONG?
WHERE'S ROGER?

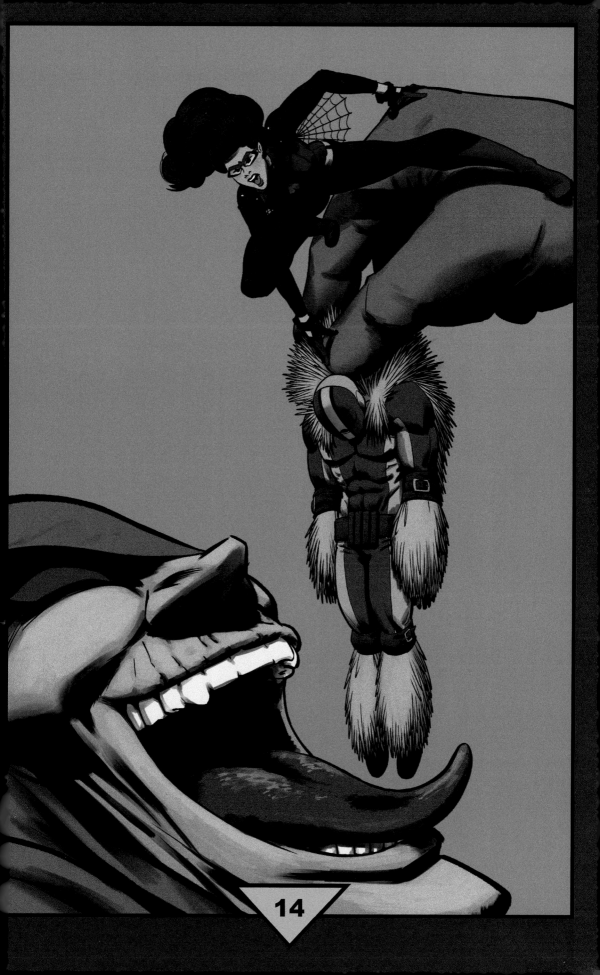

14

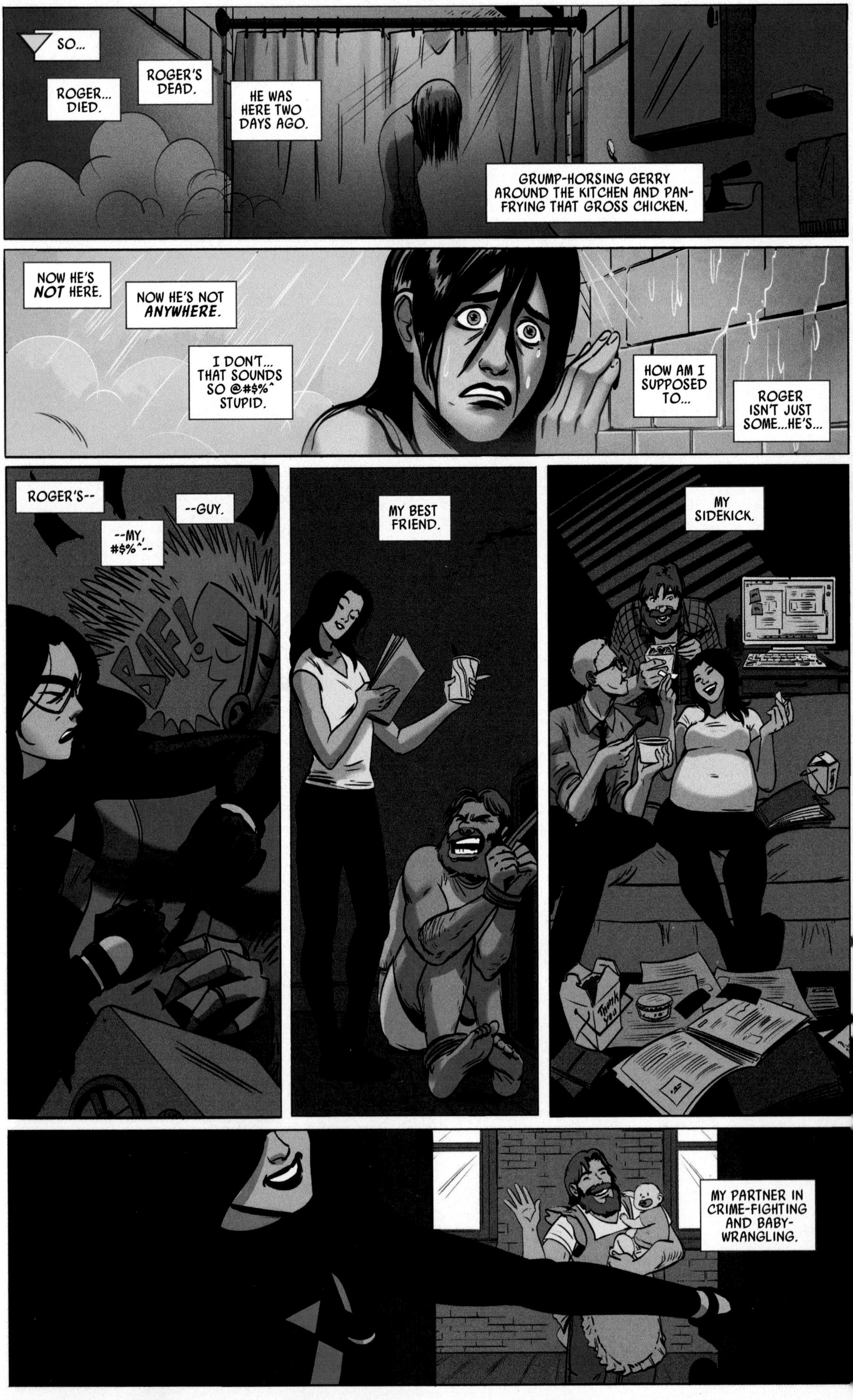
SO...
ROGER... DIED.
ROGER'S DEAD.
HE WAS HERE TWO DAYS AGO.
GRUMP-HORSING GERRY AROUND THE KITCHEN AND PAN-FRYING THAT GROSS CHICKEN.
NOW HE'S *NOT* HERE.
NOW HE'S NOT *ANYWHERE.*
I DON'T... THAT SOUNDS SO @#$%^ STUPID.
HOW AM I SUPPOSED TO...
ROGER ISN'T JUST SOME...HE'S...
ROGER'S--
--MY, #$%^--
--GUY.
BAF!
MY BEST FRIEND.
MY SIDEKICK.
MY PARTNER IN CRIME-FIGHTING AND BABY-WRANGLING.

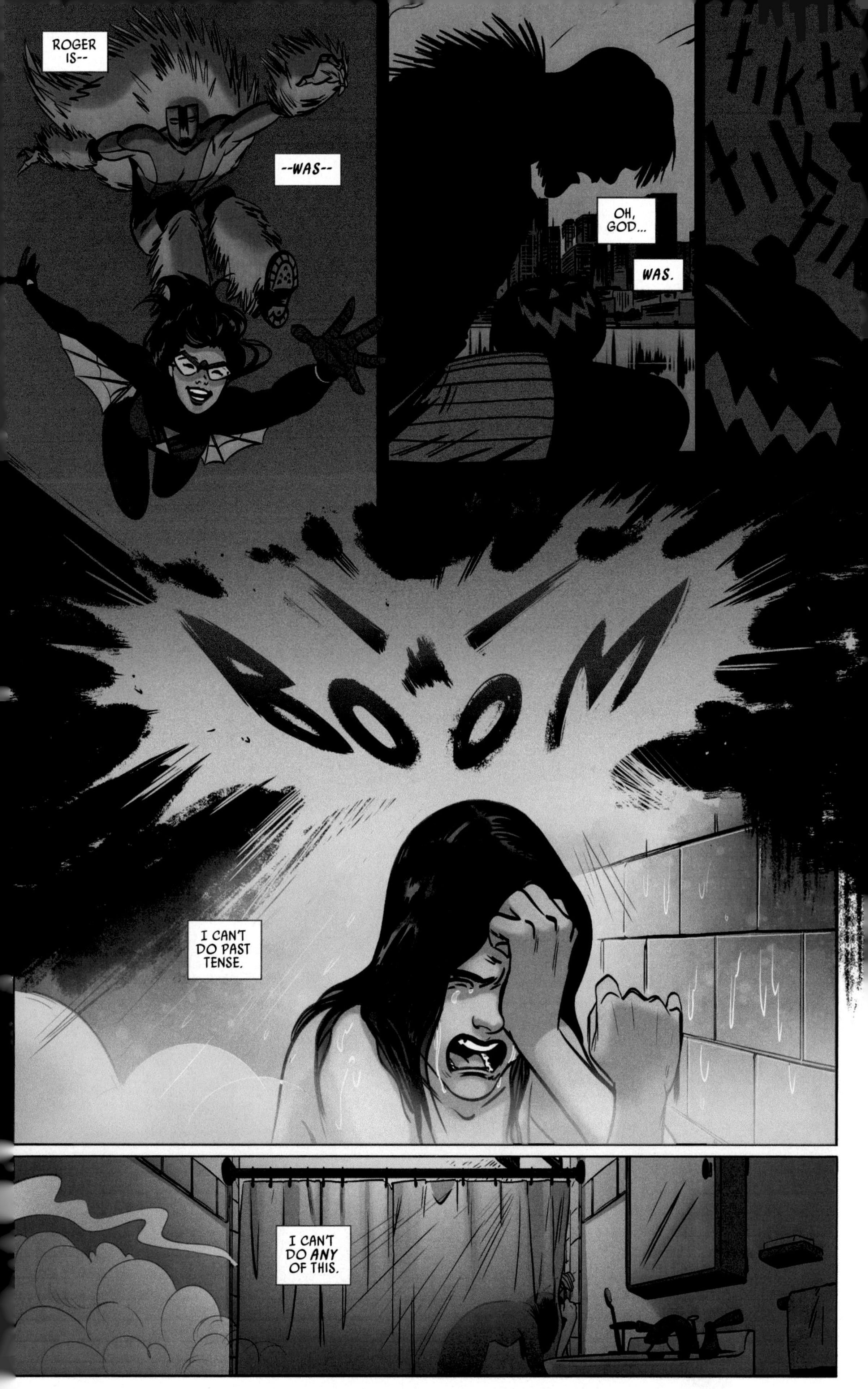

ROGER IS--
--WAS--
OH, GOD...
WAS.
BOOM
I CAN'T DO PAST TENSE.
I CAN'T DO ANY OF THIS.

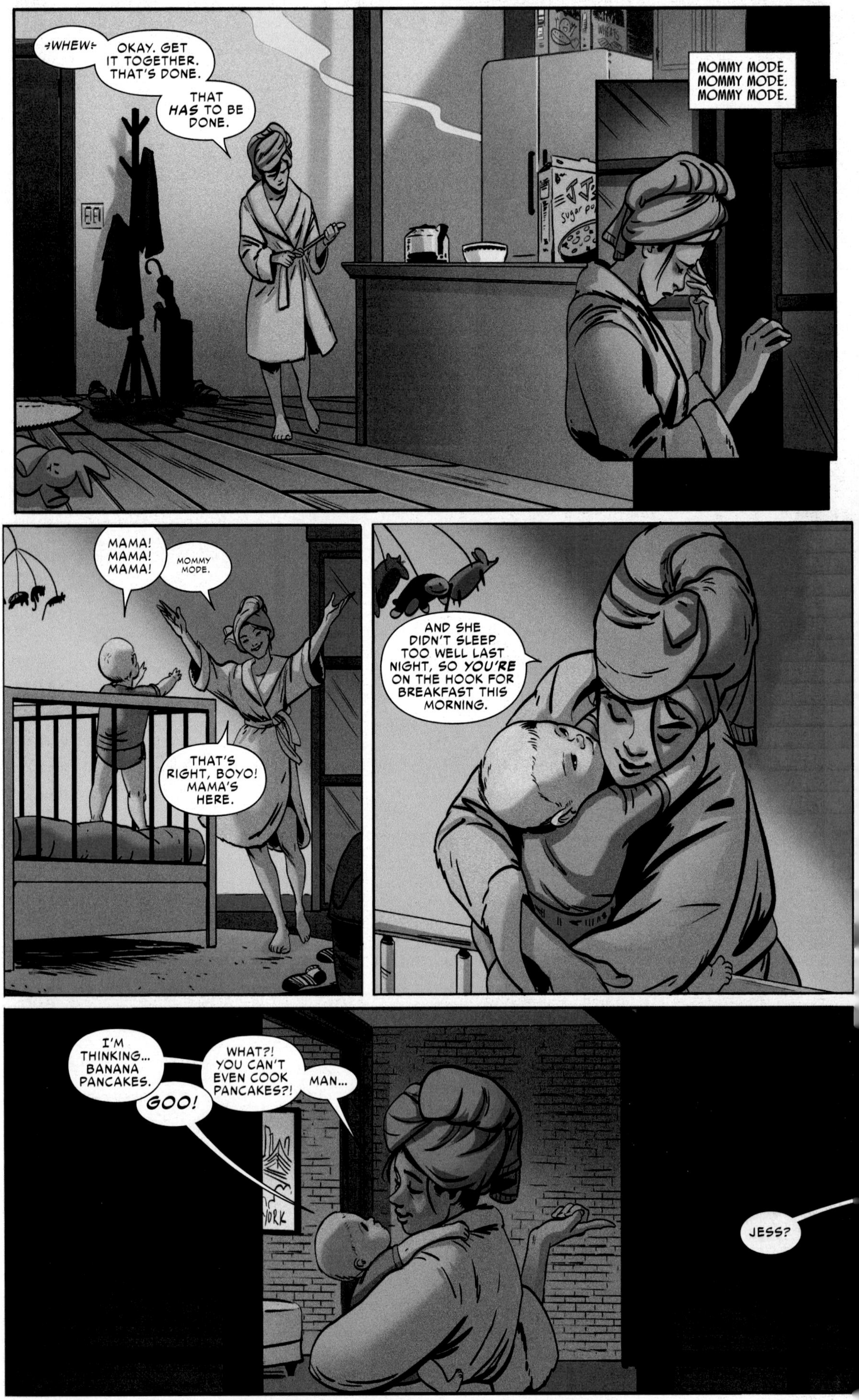

-WHEW-
OKAY. GET IT TOGETHER. THAT'S DONE.
THAT HAS TO BE DONE.
MOMMY MODE. MOMMY MODE. MOMMY MODE.
MAMA! MAMA! MAMA!
MOMMY MODE.
THAT'S RIGHT, BOYO! MAMA'S HERE.
AND SHE DIDN'T SLEEP TOO WELL LAST NIGHT, SO YOU'RE ON THE HOOK FOR BREAKFAST THIS MORNING.
I'M THINKING... BANANA PANCAKES.
GOO!
WHAT?! YOU CAN'T EVEN COOK PANCAKES?!
MAN...
JESS?

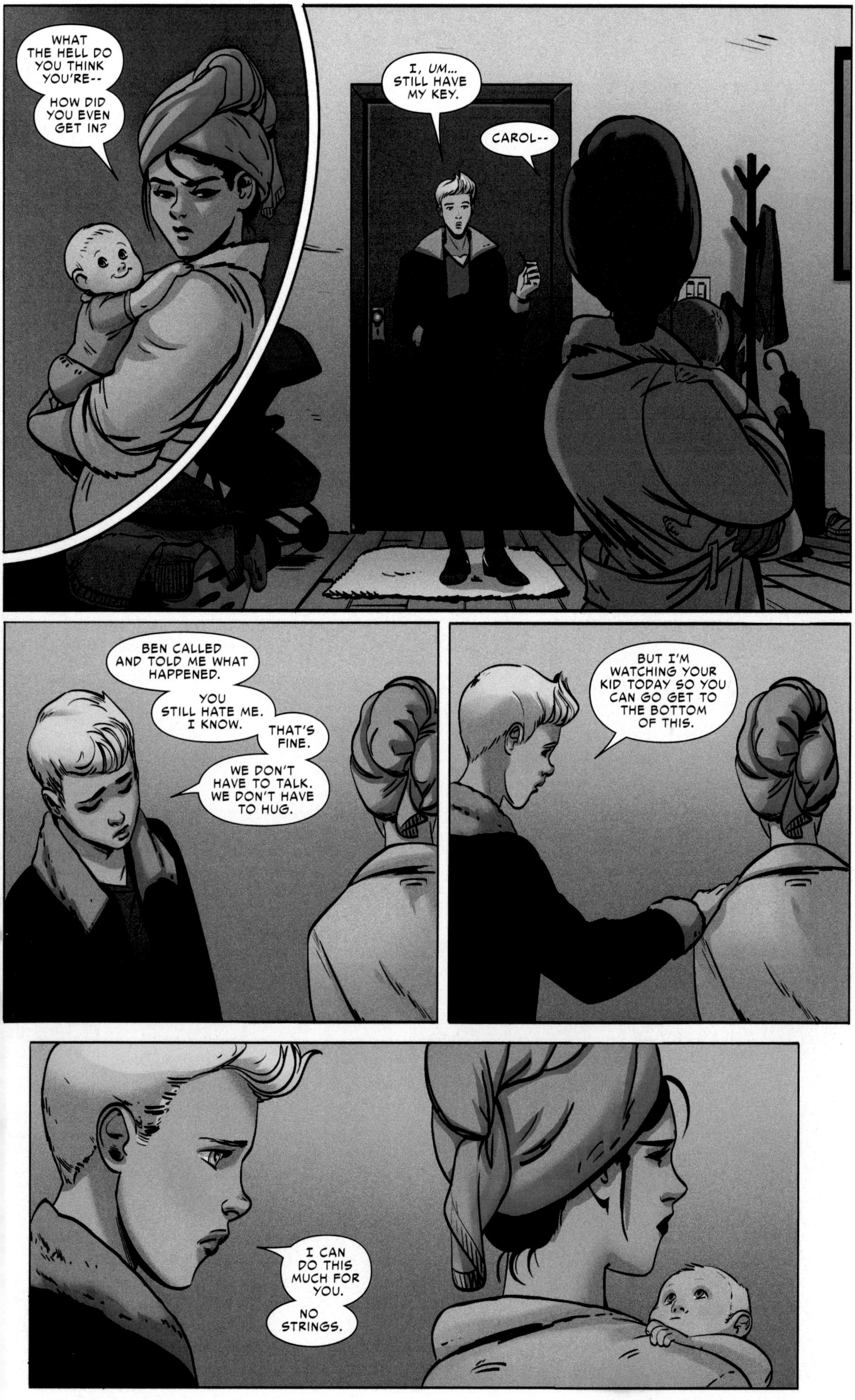
WHAT THE HELL DO YOU THINK YOU'RE--
HOW DID YOU EVEN GET IN?
I, UM... STILL HAVE MY KEY.
CAROL--
BEN CALLED AND TOLD ME WHAT HAPPENED.
YOU STILL HATE ME. I KNOW.
THAT'S FINE.
WE DON'T HAVE TO TALK. WE DON'T HAVE TO HUG.
BUT I'M WATCHING YOUR KID TODAY SO YOU CAN GO GET TO THE BOTTOM OF THIS.
I CAN DO THIS MUCH FOR YOU.
NO STRINGS.

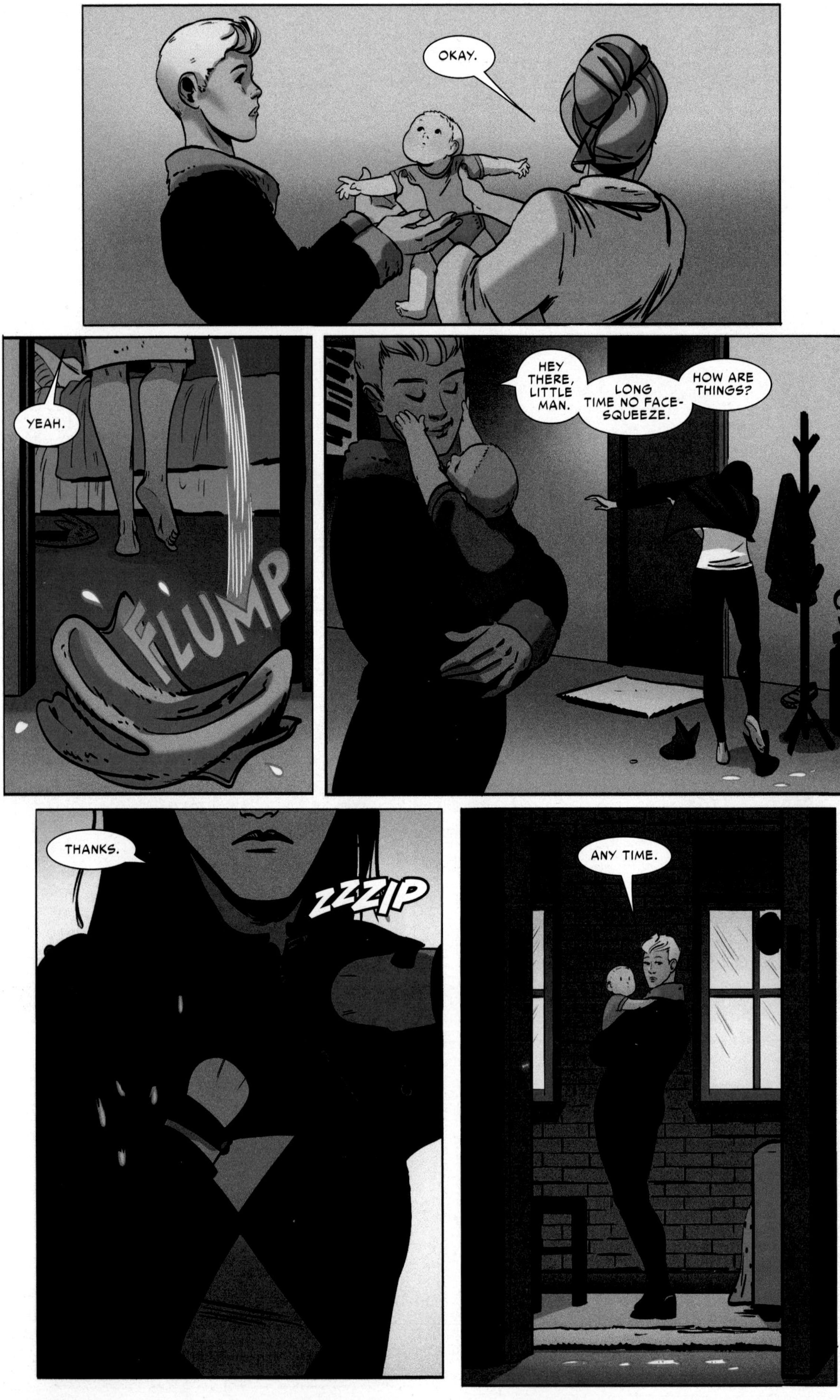
OKAY.
YEAH.
FLUMP
HEY THERE, LITTLE MAN.
LONG TIME NO FACE-SQUEEZE.
HOW ARE THINGS?
THANKS.
ZZZIP
ANY TIME.

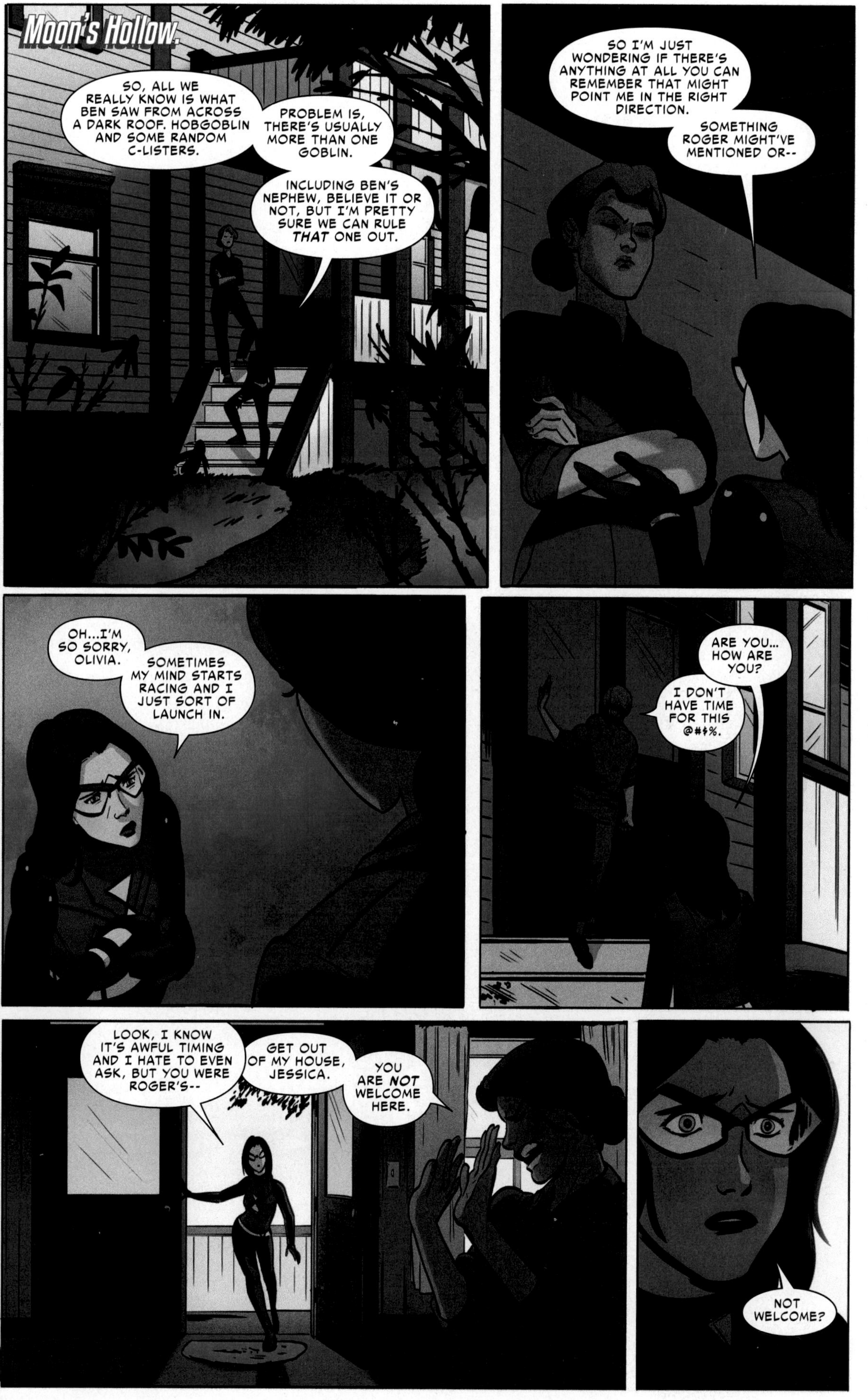
Moon's Hollow.
SO, ALL WE REALLY KNOW IS WHAT BEN SAW FROM ACROSS A DARK ROOF. HOBGOBLIN AND SOME RANDOM C-LISTERS.
PROBLEM IS, THERE'S USUALLY MORE THAN ONE GOBLIN.
INCLUDING BEN'S NEPHEW, BELIEVE IT OR NOT, BUT I'M PRETTY SURE WE CAN RULE *THAT* ONE OUT.
SO I'M JUST WONDERING IF THERE'S ANYTHING AT ALL YOU CAN REMEMBER THAT MIGHT POINT ME IN THE RIGHT DIRECTION.
SOMETHING ROGER MIGHT'VE MENTIONED OR--
OH...I'M SO SORRY, OLIVIA.
SOMETIMES MY MIND STARTS RACING AND I JUST SORT OF LAUNCH IN.
ARE YOU... HOW ARE YOU?
I DON'T HAVE TIME FOR THIS @#$%.
LOOK, I KNOW IT'S AWFUL TIMING AND I HATE TO EVEN ASK, BUT YOU WERE ROGER'S--
GET OUT OF MY HOUSE, JESSICA.
YOU ARE *NOT* WELCOME HERE.
NOT WELCOME?

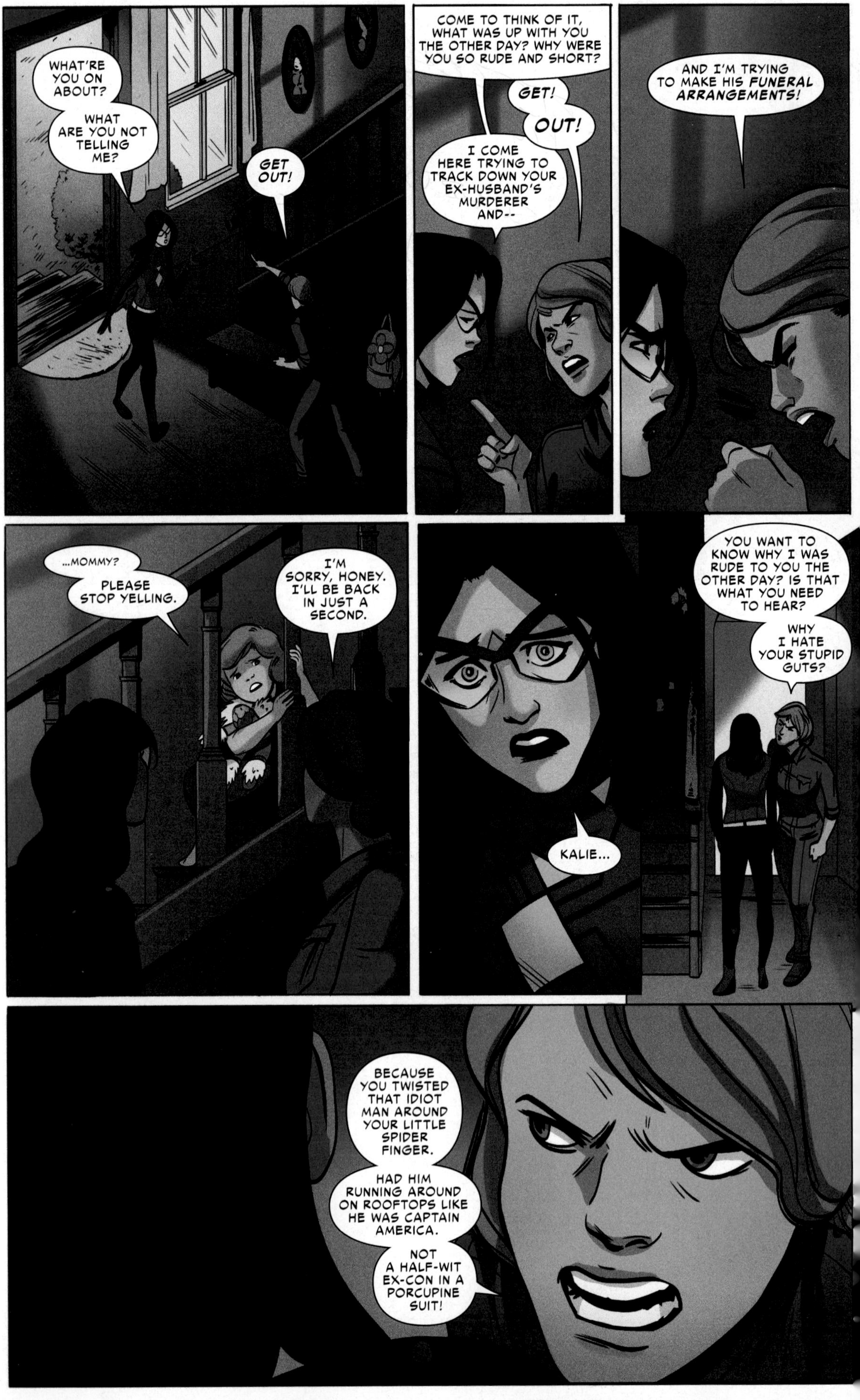
WHAT'RE YOU ON ABOUT?
WHAT ARE YOU NOT TELLING ME?
GET OUT!
COME TO THINK OF IT, WHAT WAS UP WITH YOU THE OTHER DAY? WHY WERE YOU SO RUDE AND SHORT?
GET!
OUT!
I COME HERE TRYING TO TRACK DOWN YOUR EX-HUSBAND'S MURDERER AND--
AND I'M TRYING TO MAKE HIS *FUNERAL ARRANGEMENTS!*
...MOMMY?
PLEASE STOP YELLING.
I'M SORRY, HONEY. I'LL BE BACK IN JUST A SECOND.
KALIE...
YOU WANT TO KNOW WHY I WAS RUDE TO YOU THE OTHER DAY? IS THAT WHAT YOU NEED TO HEAR?
WHY I HATE YOUR STUPID GUTS?
BECAUSE YOU TWISTED THAT IDIOT MAN AROUND YOUR LITTLE SPIDER FINGER.
HAD HIM RUNNING AROUND ON ROOFTOPS LIKE HE WAS CAPTAIN AMERICA.
NOT A HALF-WIT EX-CON IN A PORCUPINE SUIT!

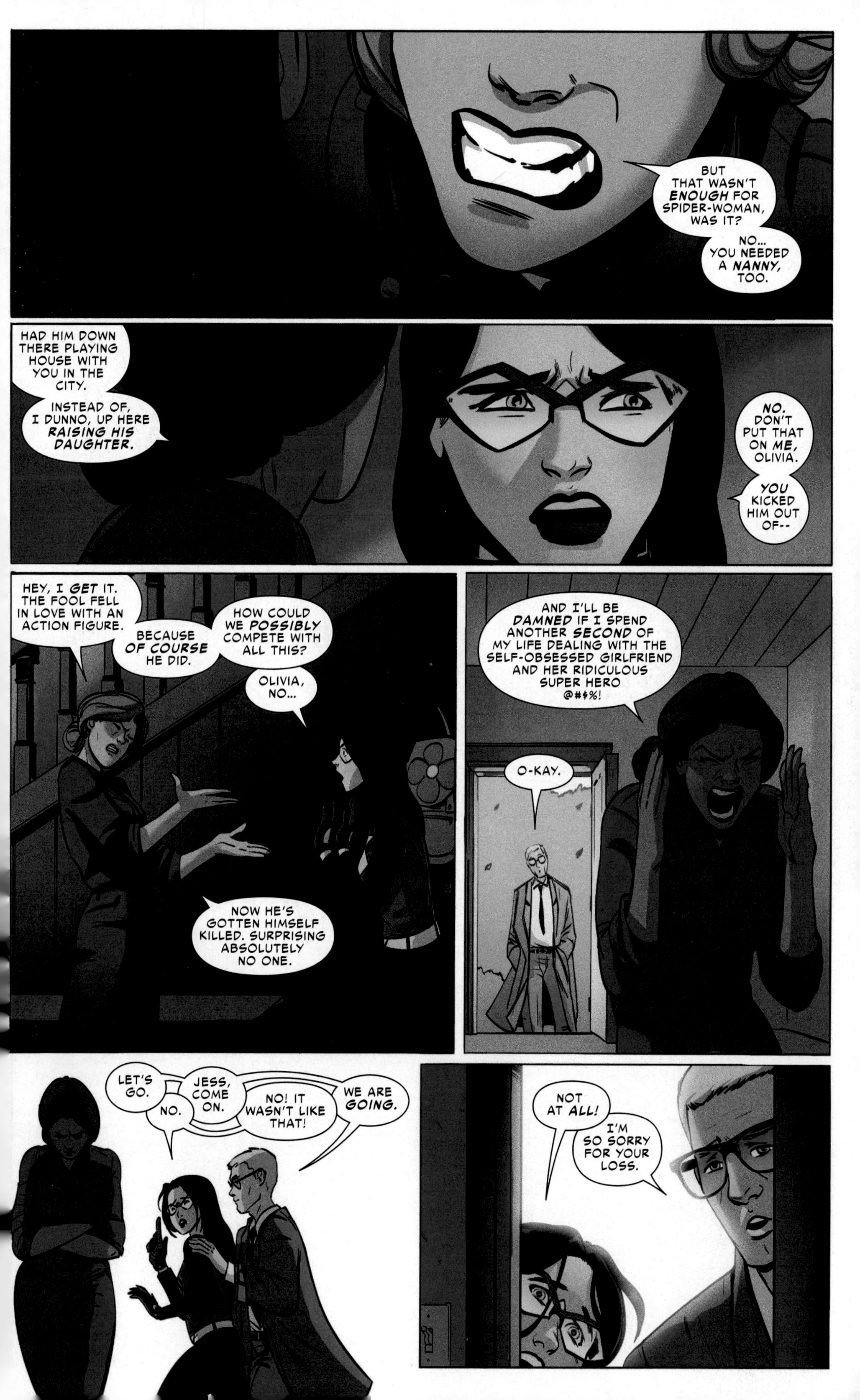

BUT THAT WASN'T ENOUGH FOR SPIDER-WOMAN, WAS IT?
NO... YOU NEEDED A NANNY, TOO.
HAD HIM DOWN THERE PLAYING HOUSE WITH YOU IN THE CITY.
INSTEAD OF, I DUNNO, UP HERE RAISING HIS DAUGHTER.
NO. DON'T PUT THAT ON ME, OLIVIA.
YOU KICKED HIM OUT OF--
HEY, I GET IT. THE FOOL FELL IN LOVE WITH AN ACTION FIGURE.
BECAUSE OF COURSE HE DID.
HOW COULD WE POSSIBLY COMPETE WITH ALL THIS?
OLIVIA, NO...
NOW HE'S GOTTEN HIMSELF KILLED. SURPRISING ABSOLUTELY NO ONE.
AND I'LL BE DAMNED IF I SPEND ANOTHER SECOND OF MY LIFE DEALING WITH THE SELF-OBSESSED GIRLFRIEND AND HER RIDICULOUS SUPER HERO @#$%!
O-KAY.
LET'S GO.
NO.
JESS, COME ON.
NO! IT WASN'T LIKE THAT!
WE ARE GOING.
NOT AT ALL!
I'M SO SORRY FOR YOUR LOSS.

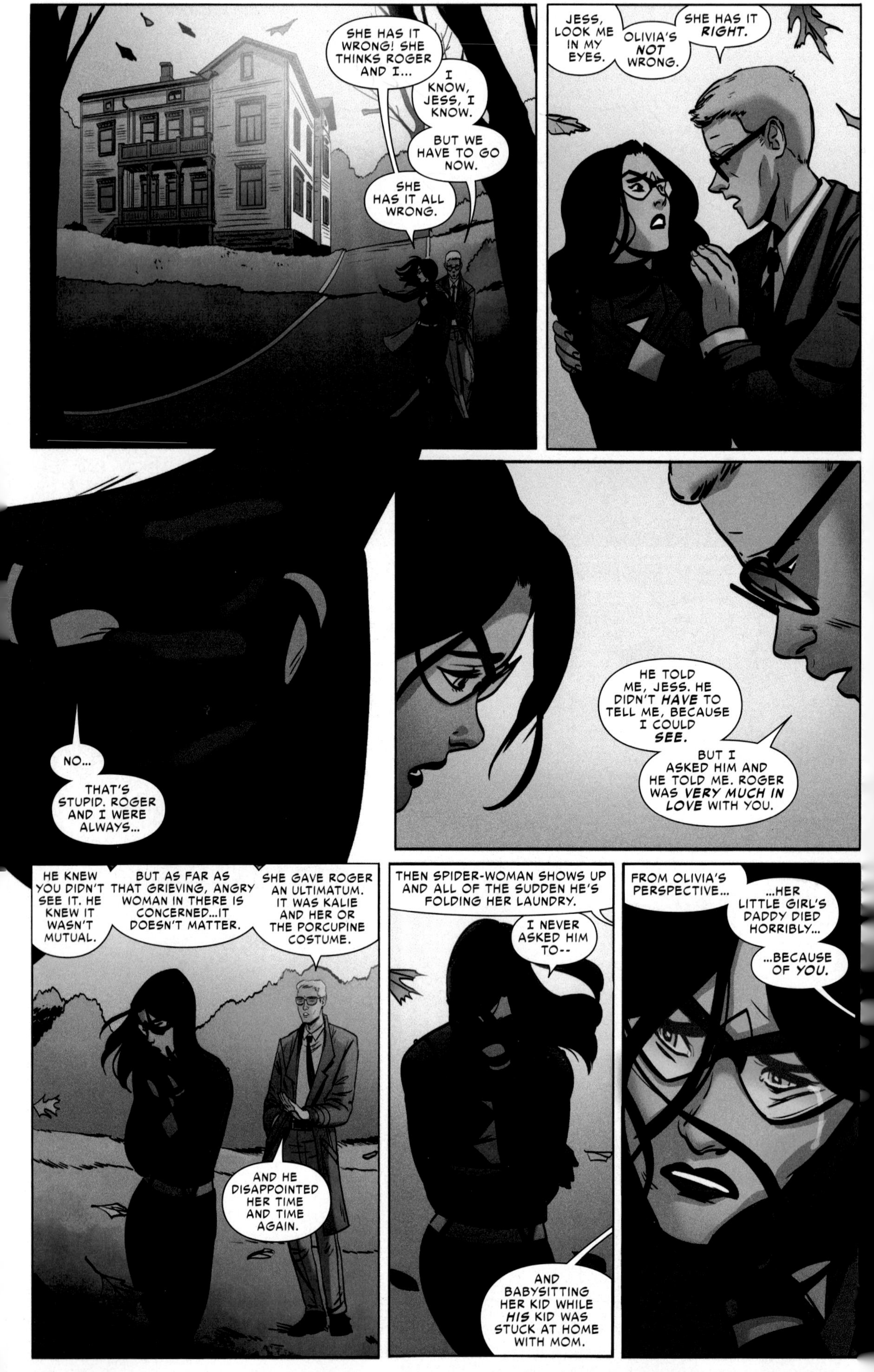
SHE HAS IT WRONG! SHE THINKS ROGER AND I...
I KNOW, JESS, I KNOW.
BUT WE HAVE TO GO NOW.
SHE HAS IT ALL WRONG.
JESS, LOOK ME IN MY EYES.
OLIVIA'S NOT WRONG.
SHE HAS IT RIGHT.
NO...
THAT'S STUPID. ROGER AND I WERE ALWAYS...
HE TOLD ME, JESS. HE DIDN'T HAVE TO TELL ME, BECAUSE I COULD SEE.
BUT I ASKED HIM AND HE TOLD ME. ROGER WAS VERY MUCH IN LOVE WITH YOU.
HE KNEW YOU DIDN'T SEE IT. HE KNEW IT WASN'T MUTUAL.
BUT AS FAR AS THAT GRIEVING, ANGRY WOMAN IN THERE IS CONCERNED...IT DOESN'T MATTER.
SHE GAVE ROGER AN ULTIMATUM. IT WAS KALIE AND HER OR THE PORCUPINE COSTUME.
AND HE DISAPPOINTED HER TIME AND TIME AGAIN.
THEN SPIDER-WOMAN SHOWS UP AND ALL OF THE SUDDEN HE'S FOLDING HER LAUNDRY.
I NEVER ASKED HIM TO--
AND BABYSITTING HER KID WHILE HIS KID WAS STUCK AT HOME WITH MOM.
FROM OLIVIA'S PERSPECTIVE...
...HER LITTLE GIRL'S DADDY DIED HORRIBLY...
...BECAUSE OF YOU.

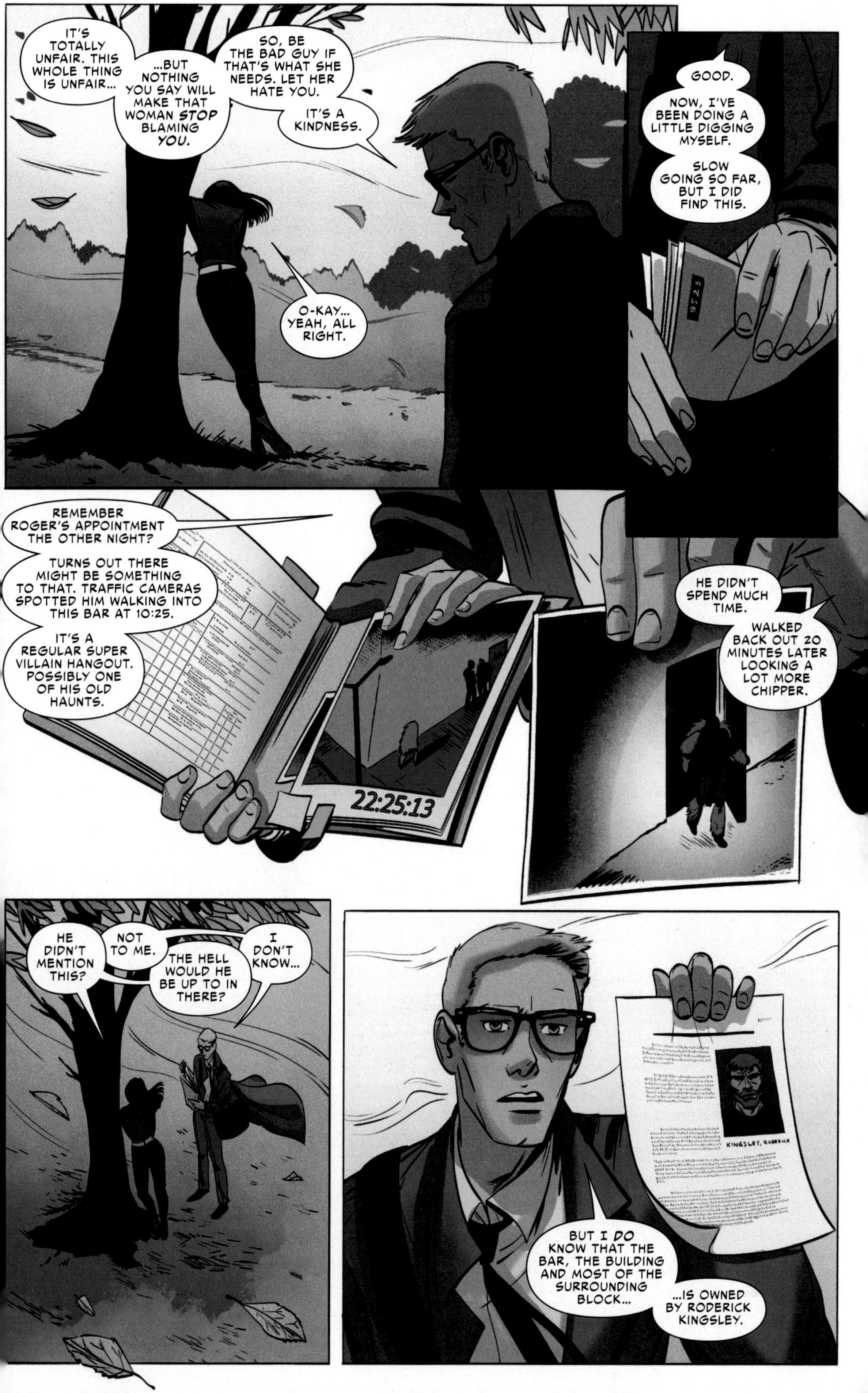
IT'S TOTALLY UNFAIR. THIS WHOLE THING IS UNFAIR...
...BUT NOTHING YOU SAY WILL MAKE THAT WOMAN STOP BLAMING YOU.
SO, BE THE BAD GUY IF THAT'S WHAT SHE NEEDS. LET HER HATE YOU.
IT'S A KINDNESS.
O-KAY... YEAH, ALL RIGHT.
GOOD.
NOW, I'VE BEEN DOING A LITTLE DIGGING MYSELF.
SLOW GOING SO FAR, BUT I DID FIND THIS.
REMEMBER ROGER'S APPOINTMENT THE OTHER NIGHT?
TURNS OUT THERE MIGHT BE SOMETHING TO THAT. TRAFFIC CAMERAS SPOTTED HIM WALKING INTO THIS BAR AT 10:25.
IT'S A REGULAR SUPER VILLAIN HANGOUT. POSSIBLY ONE OF HIS OLD HAUNTS.
22:25:13
HE DIDN'T SPEND MUCH TIME.
WALKED BACK OUT 20 MINUTES LATER LOOKING A LOT MORE CHIPPER.
HE DIDN'T MENTION THIS?
NOT TO ME.
I DON'T KNOW...
THE HELL WOULD HE BE UP TO IN THERE?
KINGSLEY, RODERICK
BUT I DO KNOW THAT THE BAR, THE BUILDING AND MOST OF THE SURROUNDING BLOCK...
...IS OWNED BY RODERICK KINGSLEY.

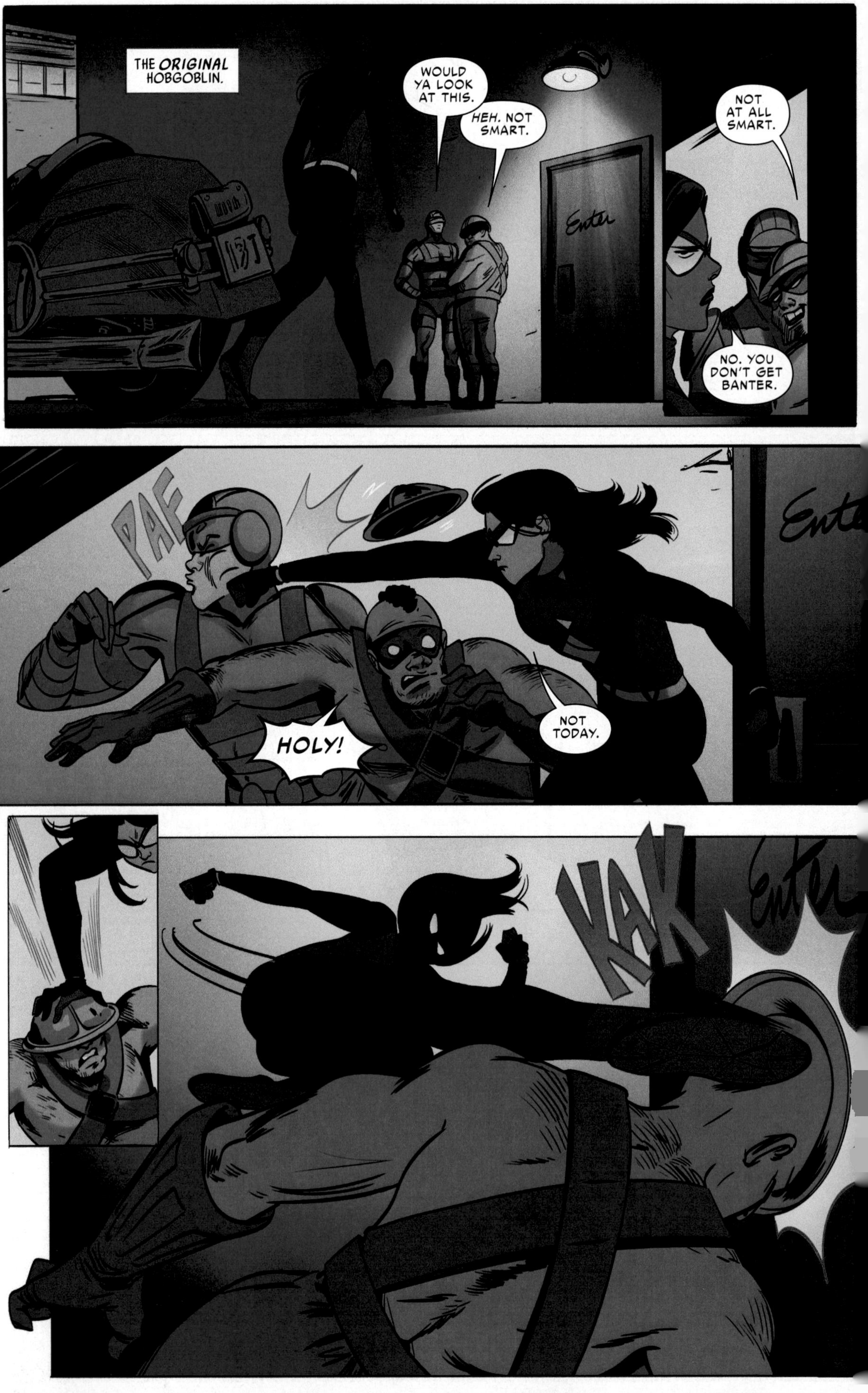
THE ORIGINAL HOBGOBLIN.
WOULD YA LOOK AT THIS.
HEH. NOT SMART.
NOT AT ALL SMART.
NO. YOU DON'T GET BANTER.
PAF
HOLY!
NOT TODAY.
Enter
KAK

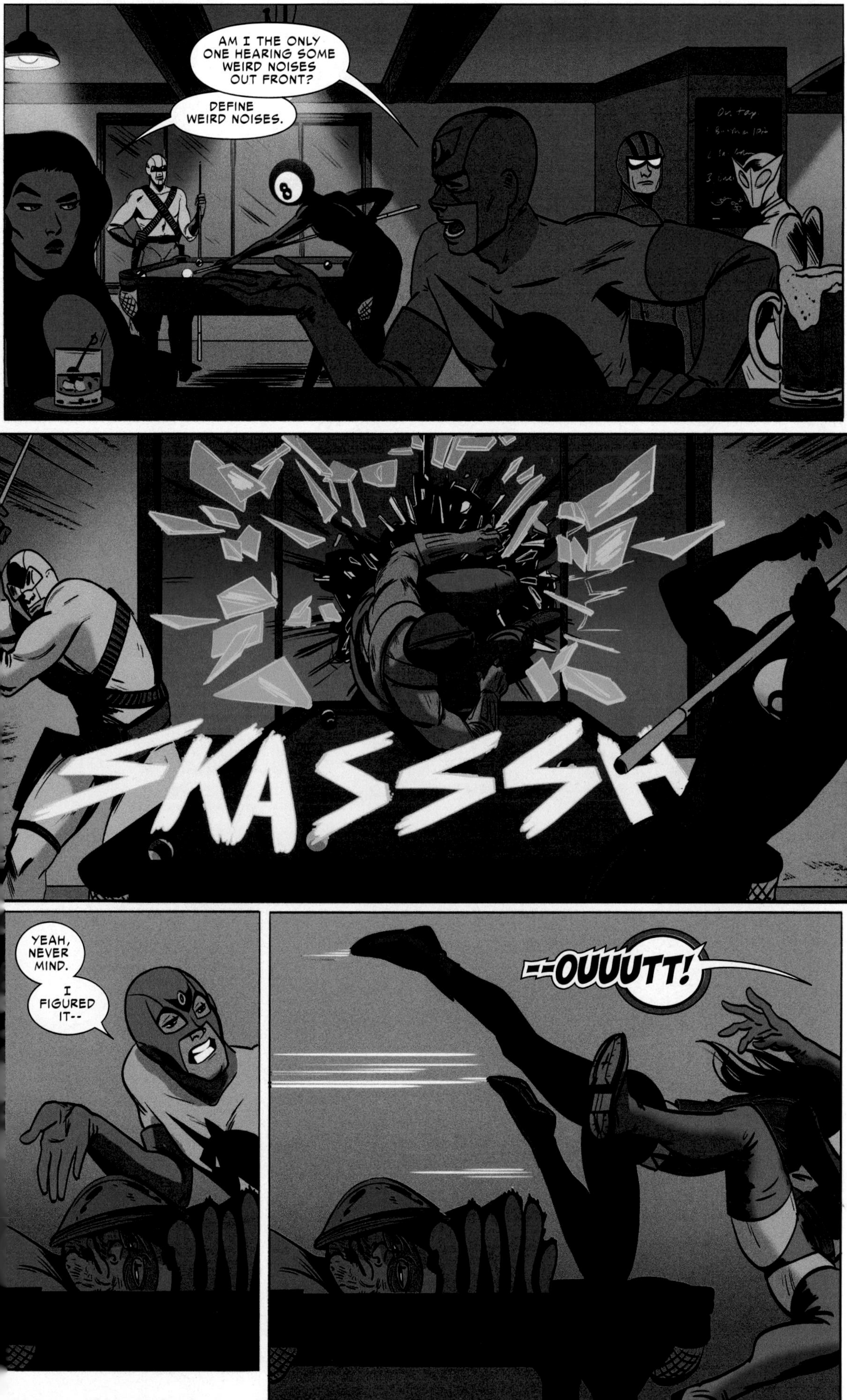
AM I THE ONLY ONE HEARING SOME WEIRD NOISES OUT FRONT?
DEFINE WEIRD NOISES.
SKASSSH
YEAH, NEVER MIND.
I FIGURED IT--
--OUUUTT!

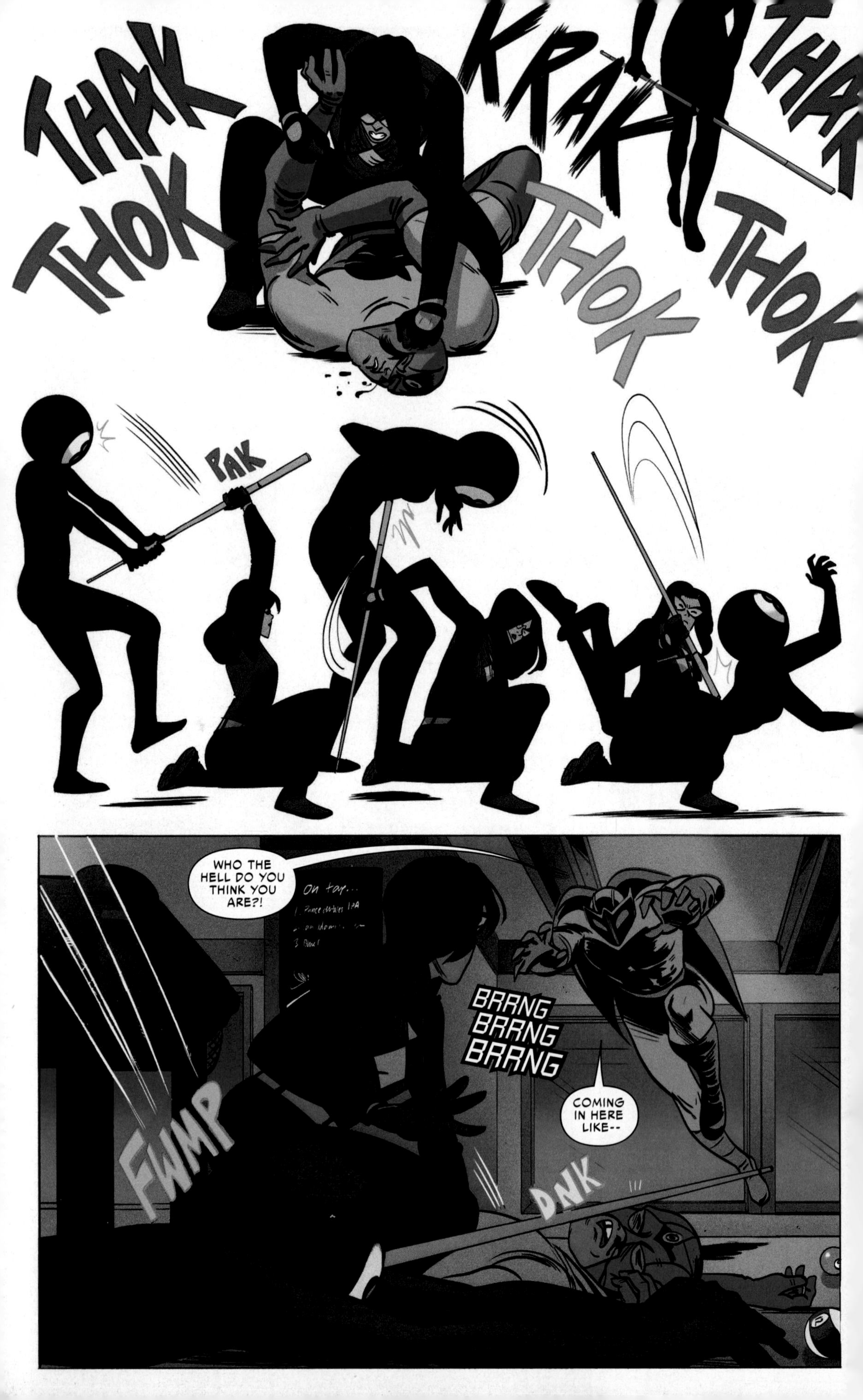
THAK
THOK
KRAK
THAK
THOK
THOK
PAK
WHO THE HELL DO YOU THINK YOU ARE?!
On tap...
BRRNG BRRNG BRRNG
COMING IN HERE LIKE--
FWMP
DNK

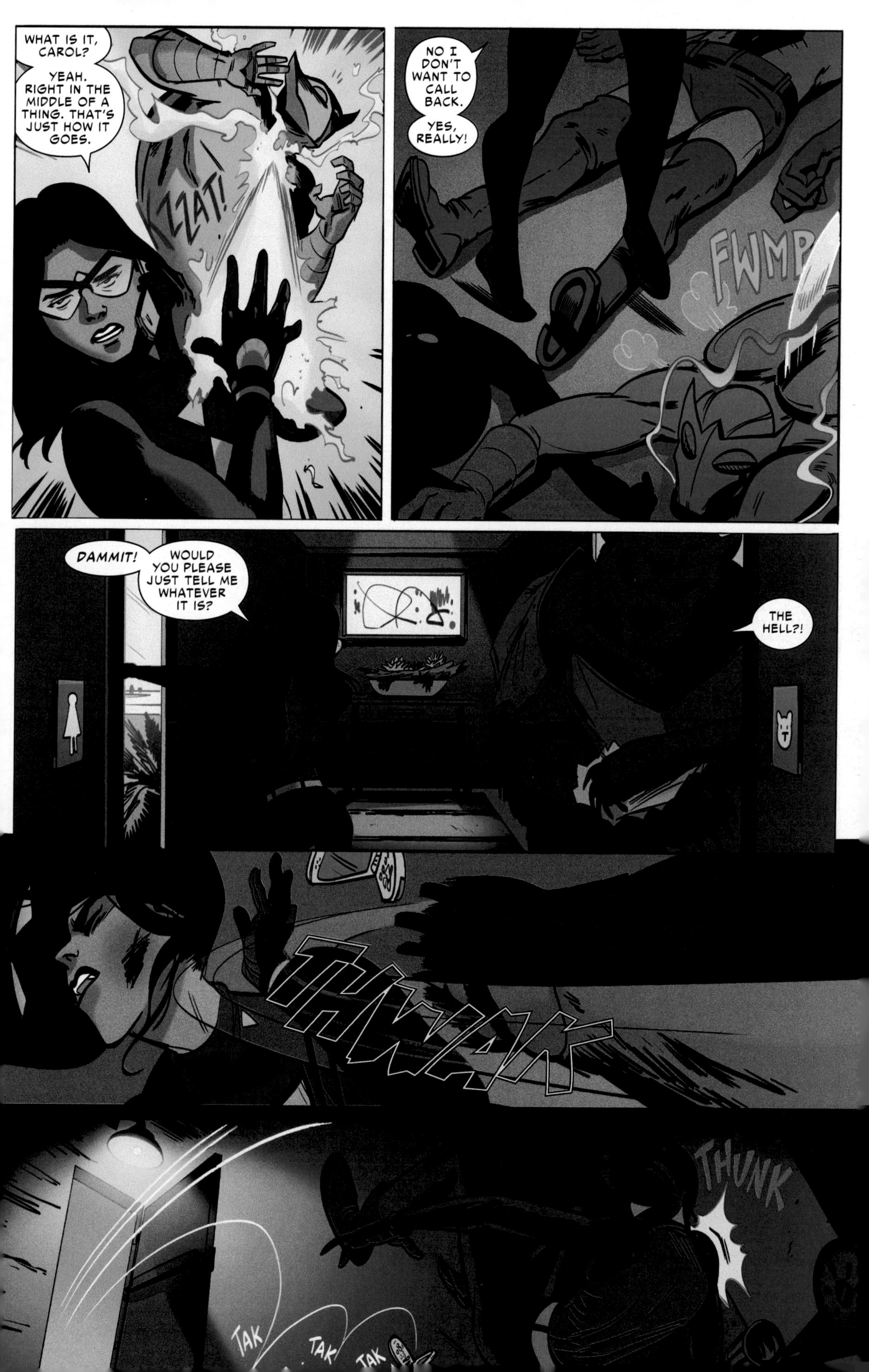
WHAT IS IT, CAROL?
YEAH. RIGHT IN THE MIDDLE OF A THING. THAT'S JUST HOW IT GOES.
ZZZAT!
NO I DON'T WANT TO CALL BACK.
YES, REALLY!
FWMP
DAMMIT!
WOULD YOU PLEASE JUST TELL ME WHATEVER IT IS?
THE HELL?!
THWAK
THUNK
TAK
TAK
TAK

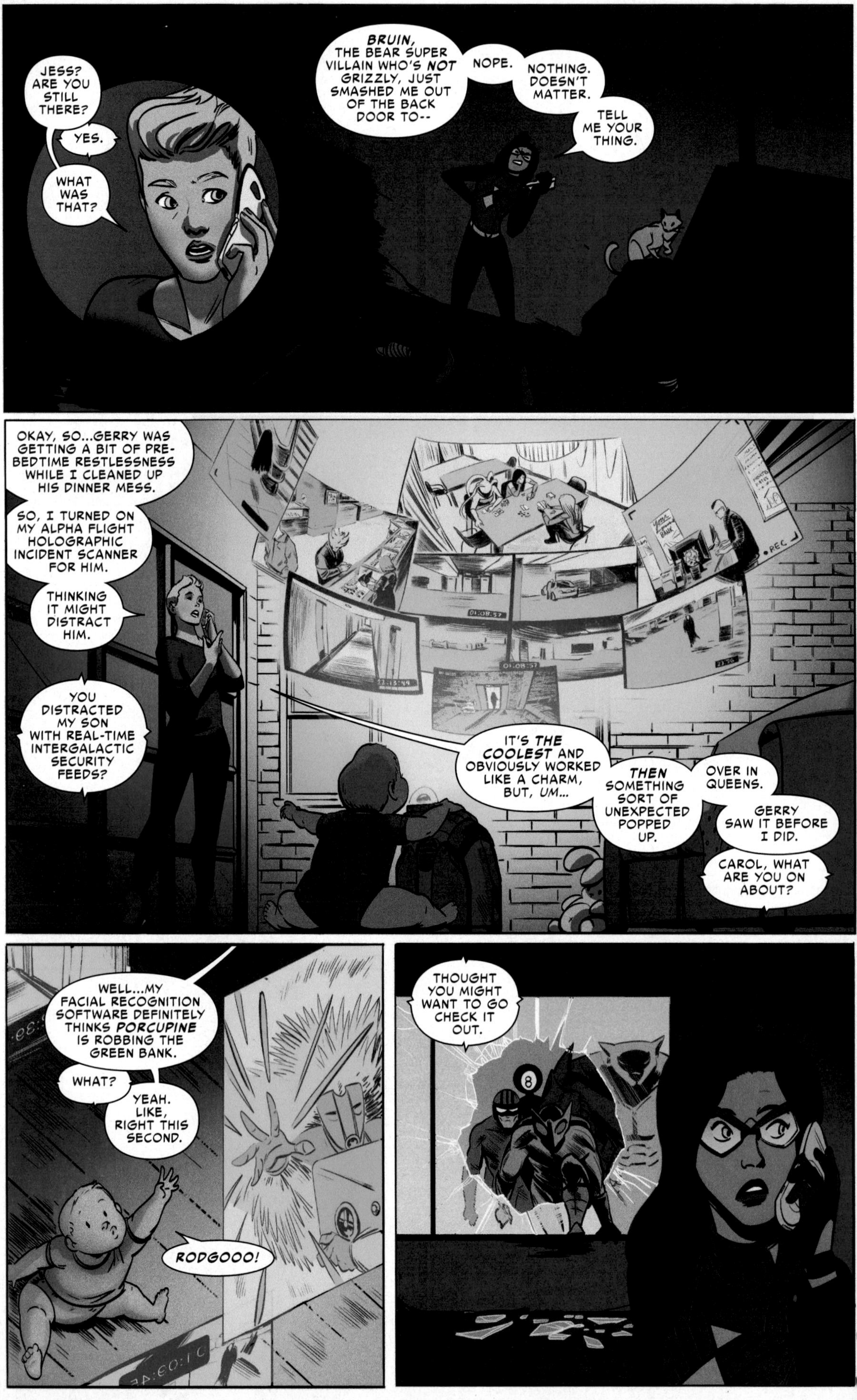
JESS? ARE YOU STILL THERE?
YES.
WHAT WAS THAT?
BRUIN, THE BEAR SUPER VILLAIN WHO'S NOT GRIZZLY, JUST SMASHED ME OUT OF THE BACK DOOR TO--
NOPE.
NOTHING. DOESN'T MATTER.
TELL ME YOUR THING.
OKAY, SO...GERRY WAS GETTING A BIT OF PRE-BEDTIME RESTLESSNESS WHILE I CLEANED UP HIS DINNER MESS.
SO, I TURNED ON MY ALPHA FLIGHT HOLOGRAPHIC INCIDENT SCANNER FOR HIM.
THINKING IT MIGHT DISTRACT HIM.
YOU DISTRACTED MY SON WITH REAL-TIME INTERGALACTIC SECURITY FEEDS?
IT'S THE COOLEST AND OBVIOUSLY WORKED LIKE A CHARM, BUT, UM...
THEN SOMETHING SORT OF UNEXPECTED POPPED UP.
OVER IN QUEENS.
GERRY SAW IT BEFORE I DID.
CAROL, WHAT ARE YOU ON ABOUT?
WELL...MY FACIAL RECOGNITION SOFTWARE DEFINITELY THINKS PORCUPINE IS ROBBING THE GREEN BANK.
WHAT?
YEAH. LIKE, RIGHT THIS SECOND.
RODGOOO!
THOUGHT YOU MIGHT WANT TO GO CHECK IT OUT.

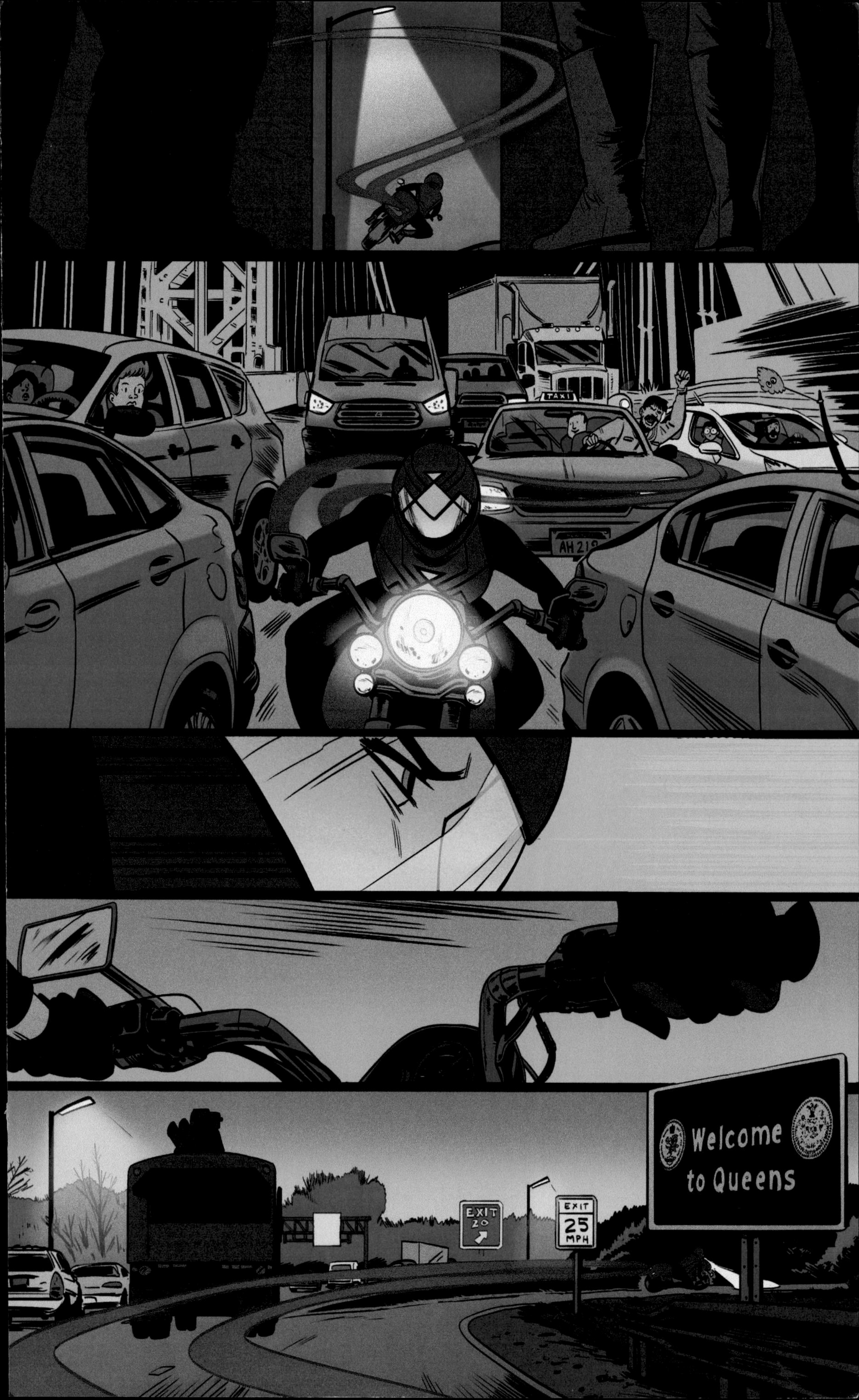
TAXI
Welcome to Queens
EXIT 20
EXIT
25
MPH

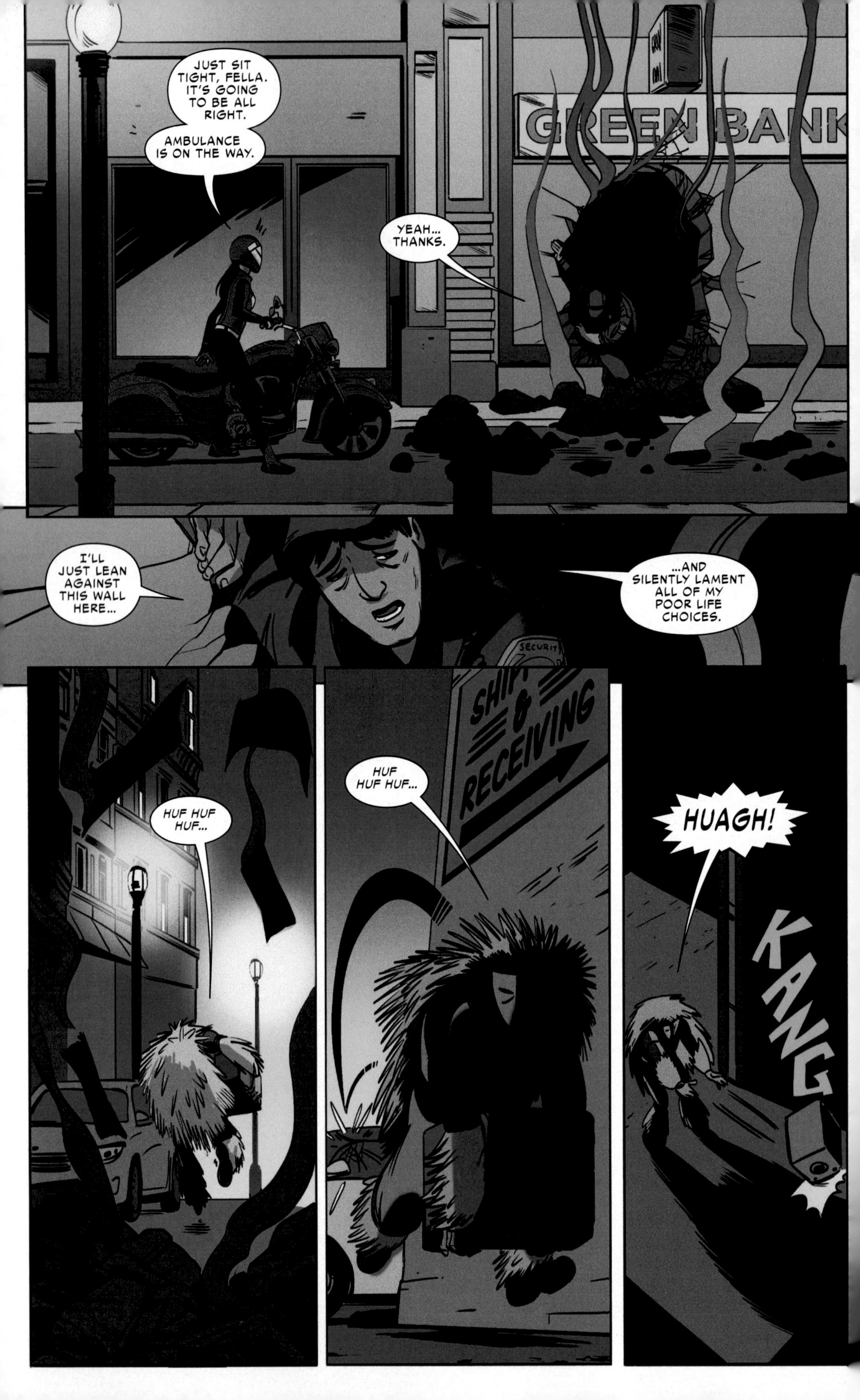
JUST SIT TIGHT, FELLA. IT'S GOING TO BE ALL RIGHT.
AMBULANCE IS ON THE WAY.
YEAH... THANKS.
GREEN BANK
I'LL JUST LEAN AGAINST THIS WALL HERE...
...AND SILENTLY LAMENT ALL OF MY POOR LIFE CHOICES.
SECURITY
HUF HUF HUF...
SHIP & RECEIVING
HUF HUF HUF...
HUAGH!
KANG

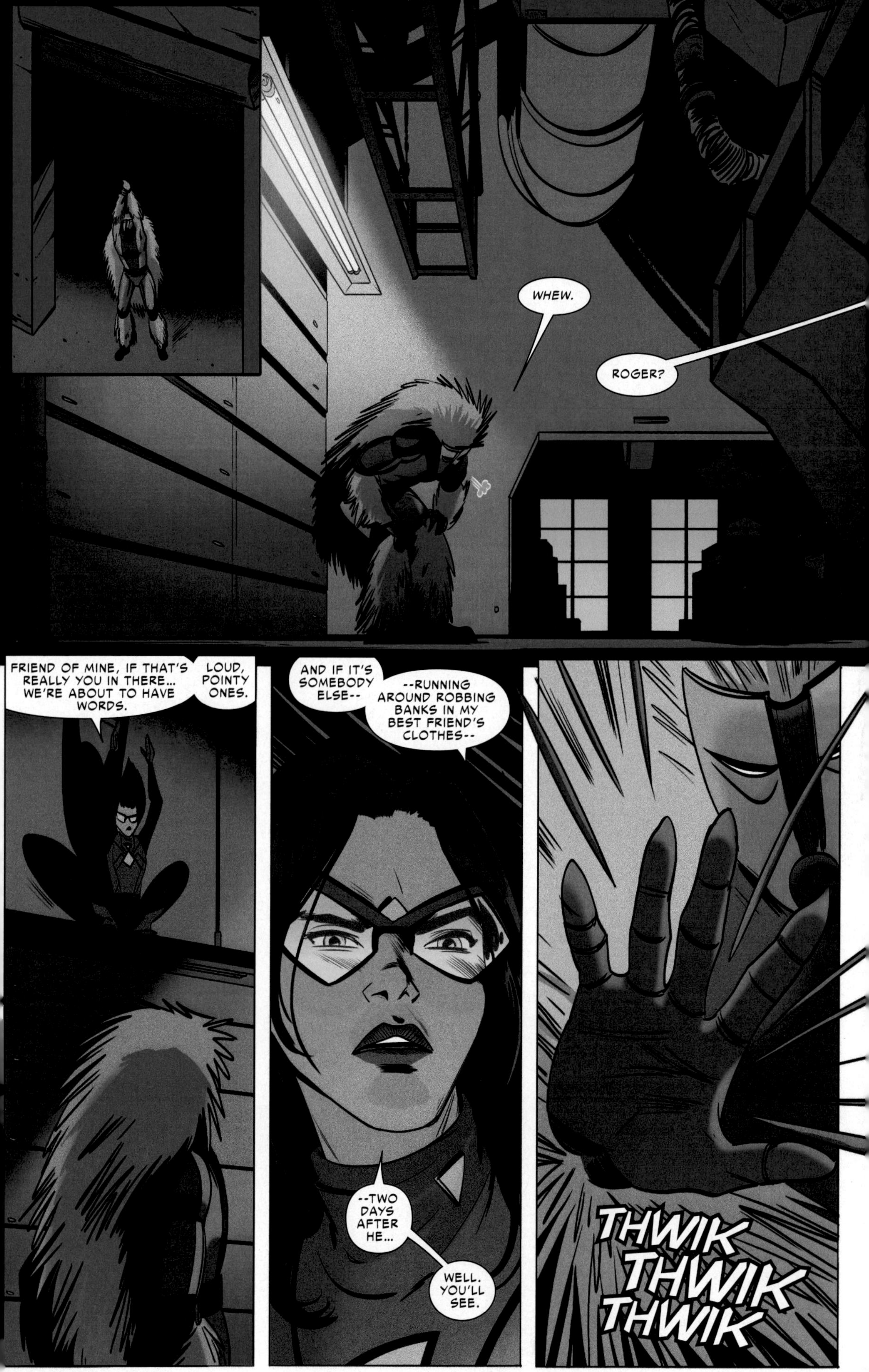
WHEW.
ROGER?
FRIEND OF MINE, IF THAT'S REALLY YOU IN THERE... WE'RE ABOUT TO HAVE WORDS.
LOUD, POINTY ONES.
AND IF IT'S SOMEBODY ELSE--
--RUNNING AROUND ROBBING BANKS IN MY BEST FRIEND'S CLOTHES--
--TWO DAYS AFTER HE...
WELL. YOU'LL SEE.
THWIK THWIK THWIK

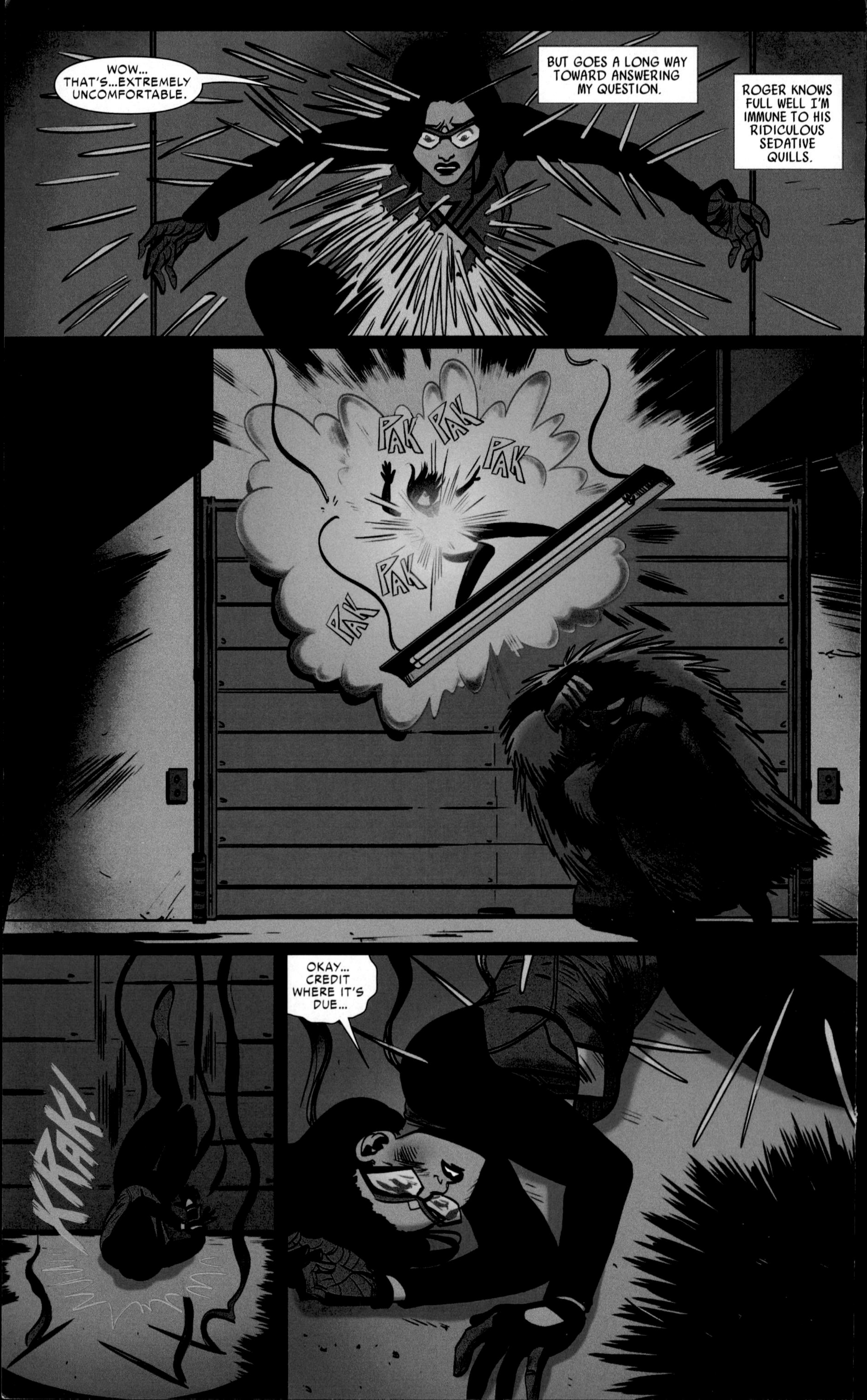
WOW... THAT'S...EXTREMELY UNCOMFORTABLE.
BUT GOES A LONG WAY TOWARD ANSWERING MY QUESTION.
ROGER KNOWS FULL WELL I'M IMMUNE TO HIS RIDICULOUS SEDATIVE QUILLS.
PAK PAK PAK
PAK PAK
KRAK!
OKAY... CREDIT WHERE IT'S DUE...

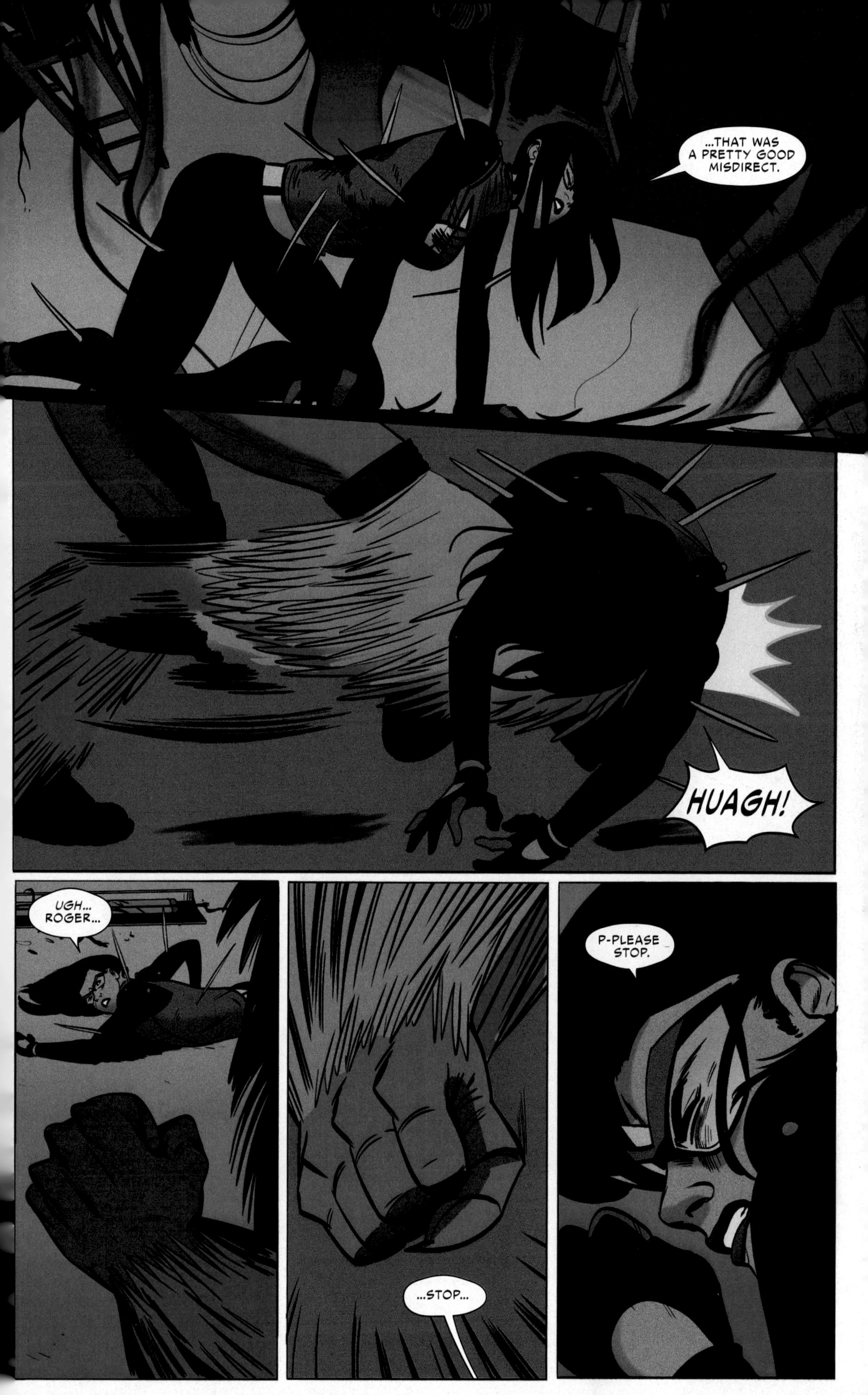
...THAT WAS A PRETTY GOOD MISDIRECT.
HUAGH!
UGH... ROGER...
...STOP...
P-PLEASE STOP.

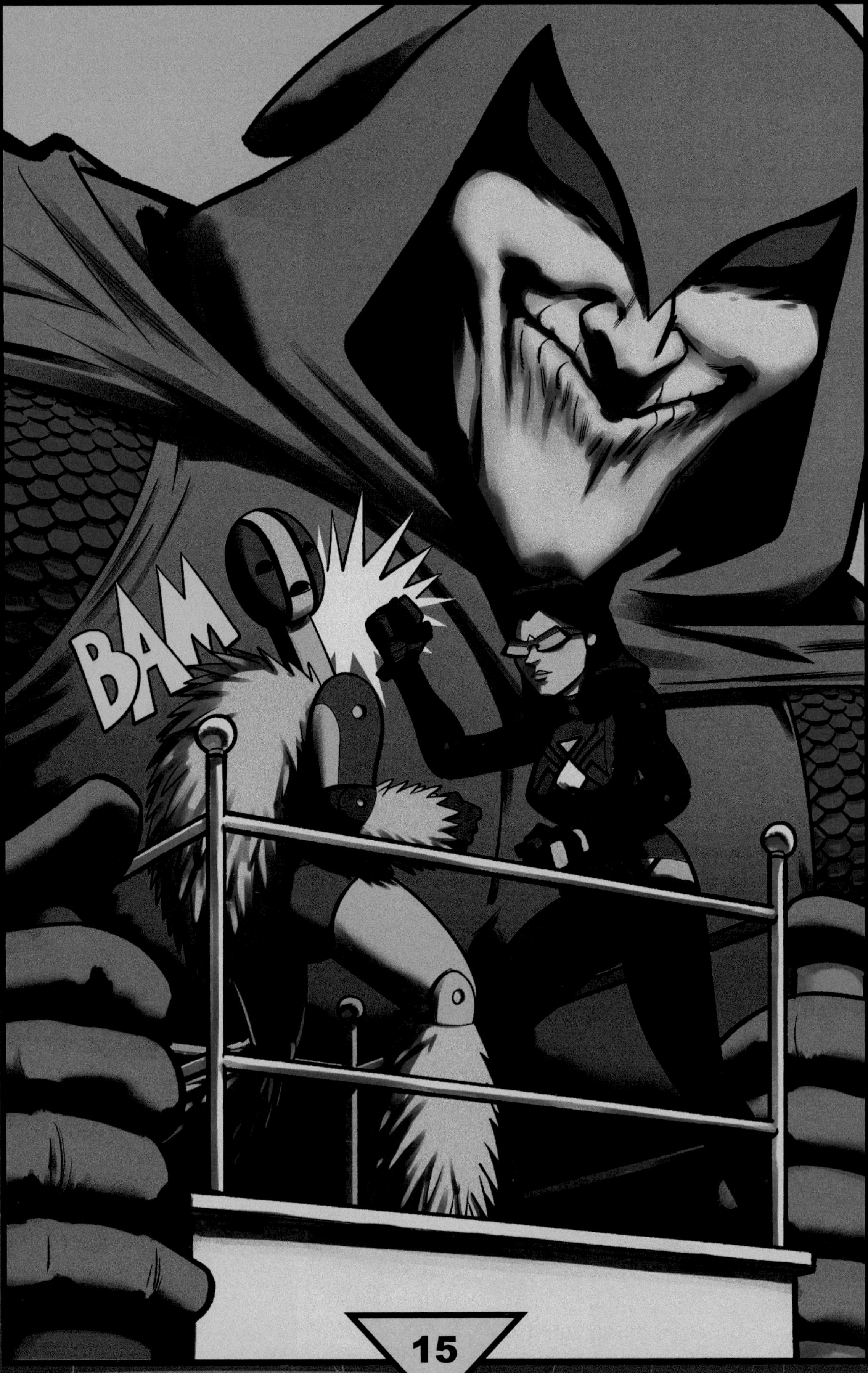
BAM

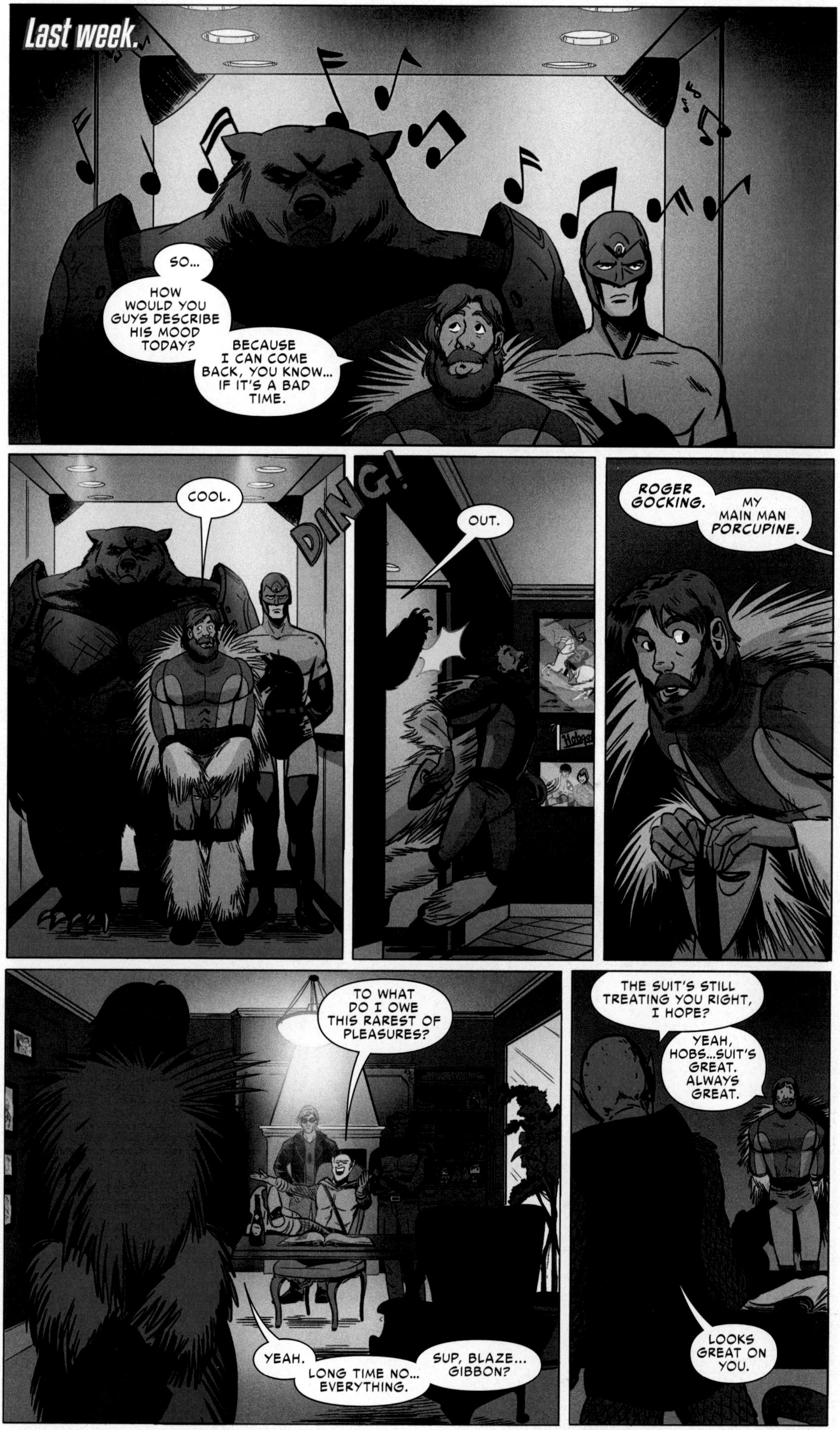
Last week.
SO...
HOW WOULD YOU GUYS DESCRIBE HIS MOOD TODAY?
BECAUSE I CAN COME BACK, YOU KNOW... IF IT'S A BAD TIME.
COOL.
DING!
OUT.
ROGER GOCKING.
MY MAIN MAN PORCUPINE.
TO WHAT DO I OWE THIS RAREST OF PLEASURES?
YEAH.
LONG TIME NO... EVERYTHING.
SUP, BLAZE... GIBBON?
THE SUIT'S STILL TREATING YOU RIGHT, I HOPE?
YEAH, HOBS...SUIT'S GREAT. ALWAYS GREAT.
LOOKS GREAT ON YOU.

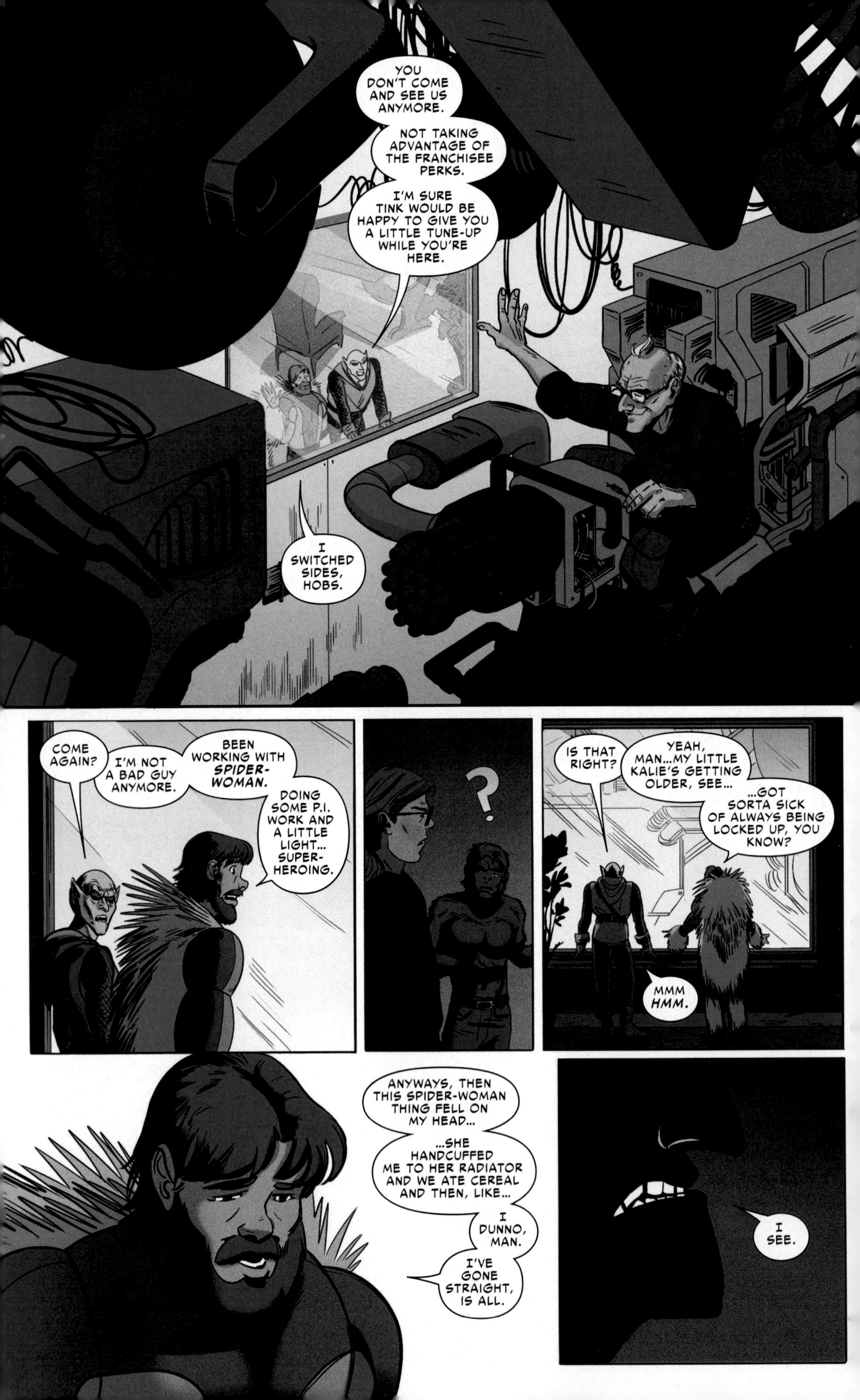
YOU DON'T COME AND SEE US ANYMORE.
NOT TAKING ADVANTAGE OF THE FRANCHISEE PERKS.
I'M SURE TINK WOULD BE HAPPY TO GIVE YOU A LITTLE TUNE-UP WHILE YOU'RE HERE.
I SWITCHED SIDES, HOBS.
COME AGAIN?
I'M NOT A BAD GUY ANYMORE.
BEEN WORKING WITH SPIDER-WOMAN.
DOING SOME P.I. WORK AND A LITTLE LIGHT... SUPER-HEROING.
?
IS THAT RIGHT?
YEAH, MAN...MY LITTLE KALIE'S GETTING OLDER, SEE...
...GOT SORTA SICK OF ALWAYS BEING LOCKED UP, YOU KNOW?
MMM HMM.
ANYWAYS, THEN THIS SPIDER-WOMAN THING FELL ON MY HEAD...
...SHE HANDCUFFED ME TO HER RADIATOR AND WE ATE CEREAL AND THEN, LIKE...
I DUNNO, MAN.
I'VE GONE STRAIGHT, IS ALL.
I SEE.

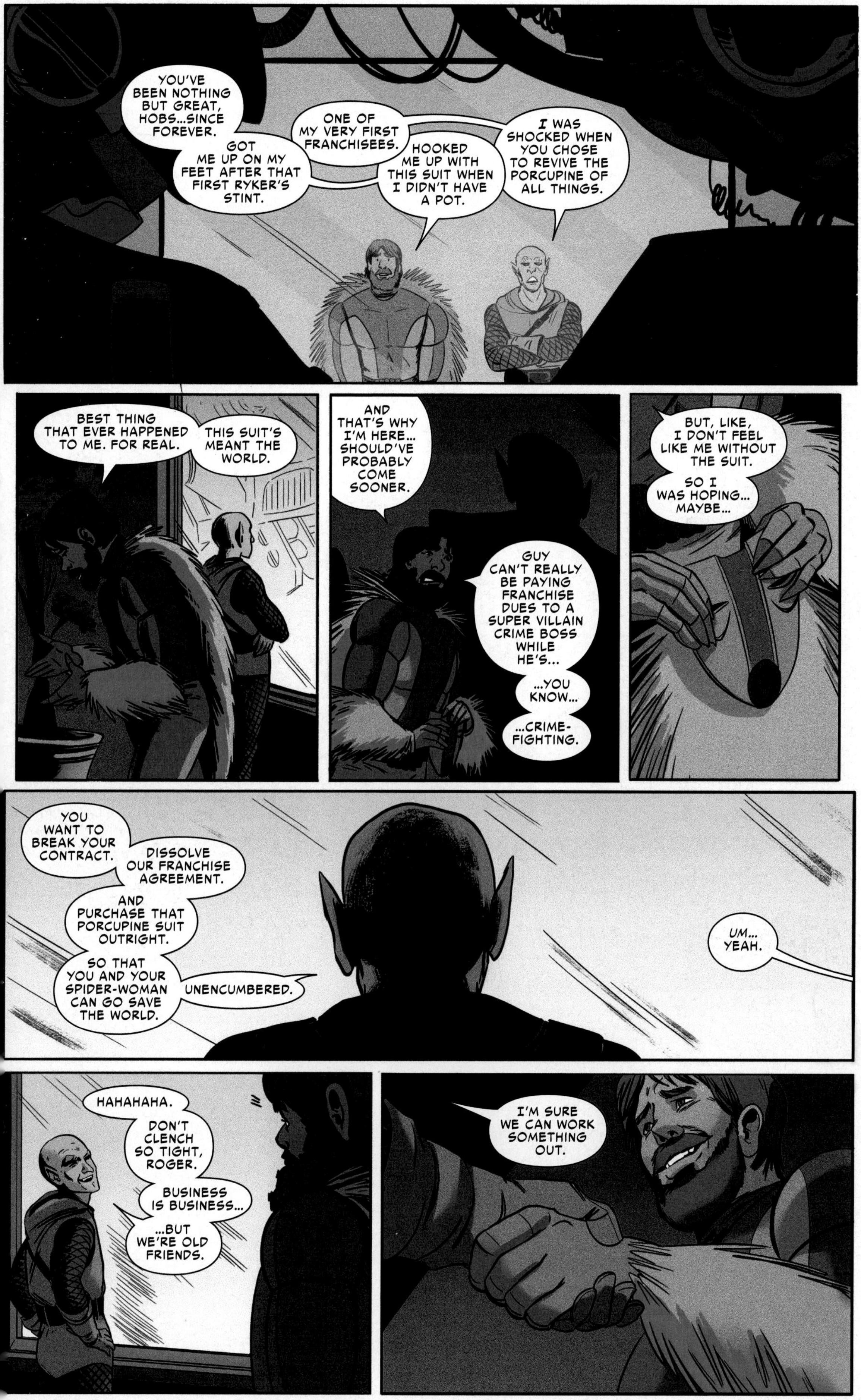
YOU'VE BEEN NOTHING BUT GREAT, HOBS...SINCE FOREVER.
GOT ME UP ON MY FEET AFTER THAT FIRST RYKER'S STINT.
ONE OF MY VERY FIRST FRANCHISEES.
HOOKED ME UP WITH THIS SUIT WHEN I DIDN'T HAVE A POT.
I WAS SHOCKED WHEN YOU CHOSE TO REVIVE THE PORCUPINE OF ALL THINGS.
BEST THING THAT EVER HAPPENED TO ME. FOR REAL.
THIS SUIT'S MEANT THE WORLD.
AND THAT'S WHY I'M HERE... SHOULD'VE PROBABLY COME SOONER.
GUY CAN'T REALLY BE PAYING FRANCHISE DUES TO A SUPER VILLAIN CRIME BOSS WHILE HE'S...
...YOU KNOW...
...CRIME-FIGHTING.
BUT, LIKE, I DON'T FEEL LIKE ME WITHOUT THE SUIT.
SO I WAS HOPING... MAYBE...
YOU WANT TO BREAK YOUR CONTRACT.
DISSOLVE OUR FRANCHISE AGREEMENT.
AND PURCHASE THAT PORCUPINE SUIT OUTRIGHT.
SO THAT YOU AND YOUR SPIDER-WOMAN CAN GO SAVE THE WORLD.
UNENCUMBERED.
UM... YEAH.
HAHAHAHA.
DON'T CLENCH SO TIGHT, ROGER.
BUSINESS IS BUSINESS...
...BUT WE'RE OLD FRIENDS.
I'M SURE WE CAN WORK SOMETHING OUT.

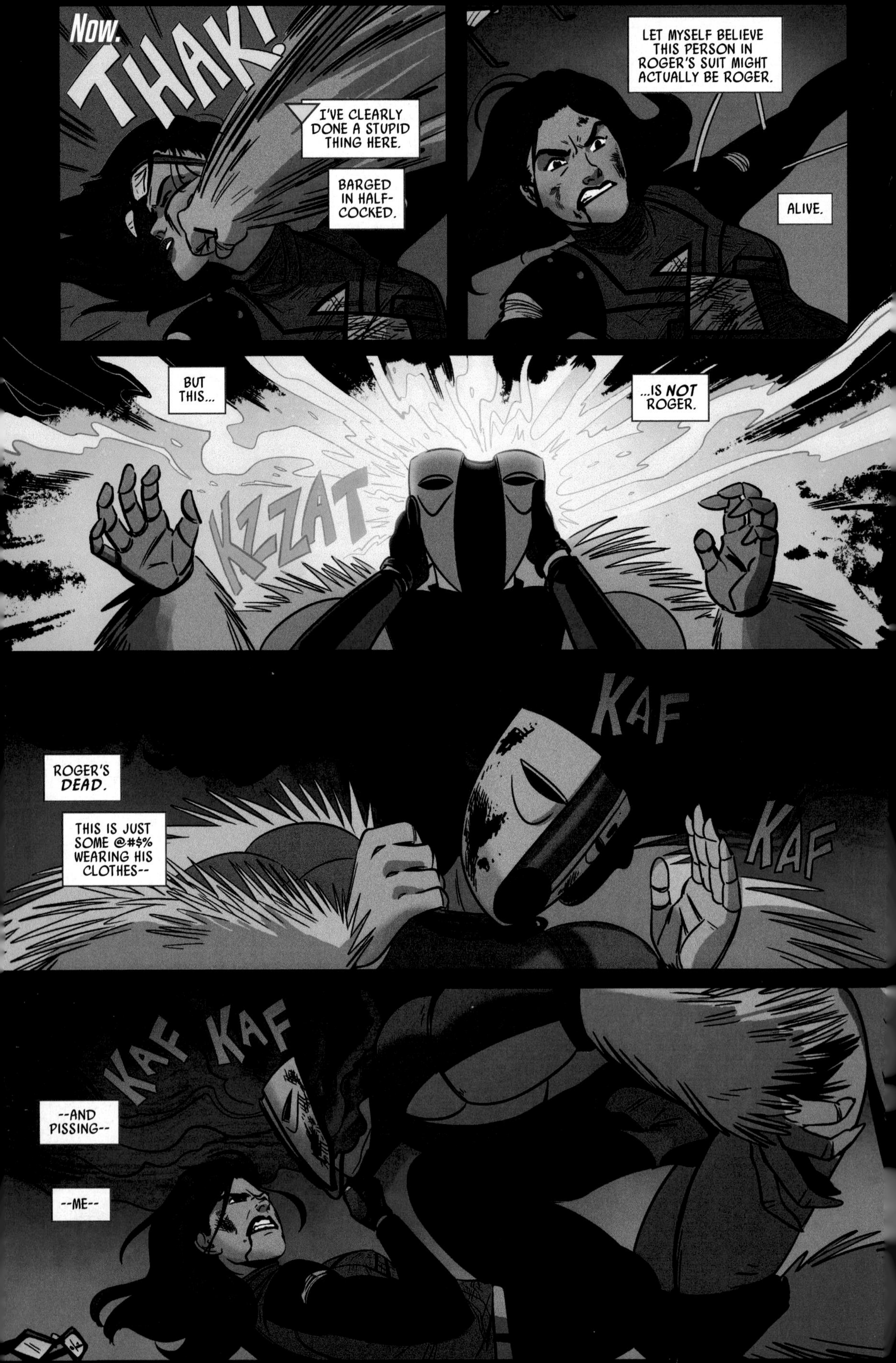
Now.
THAK!
I'VE CLEARLY DONE A STUPID THING HERE.
BARGED IN HALF-COCKED.
LET MYSELF BELIEVE THIS PERSON IN ROGER'S SUIT MIGHT ACTUALLY BE ROGER.
ALIVE.
BUT THIS...
...IS NOT ROGER.
KZZAT
ROGER'S DEAD.
THIS IS JUST SOME @#$% WEARING HIS CLOTHES--
KAF
KAF
KAF KAF
--AND PISSING--
--ME--

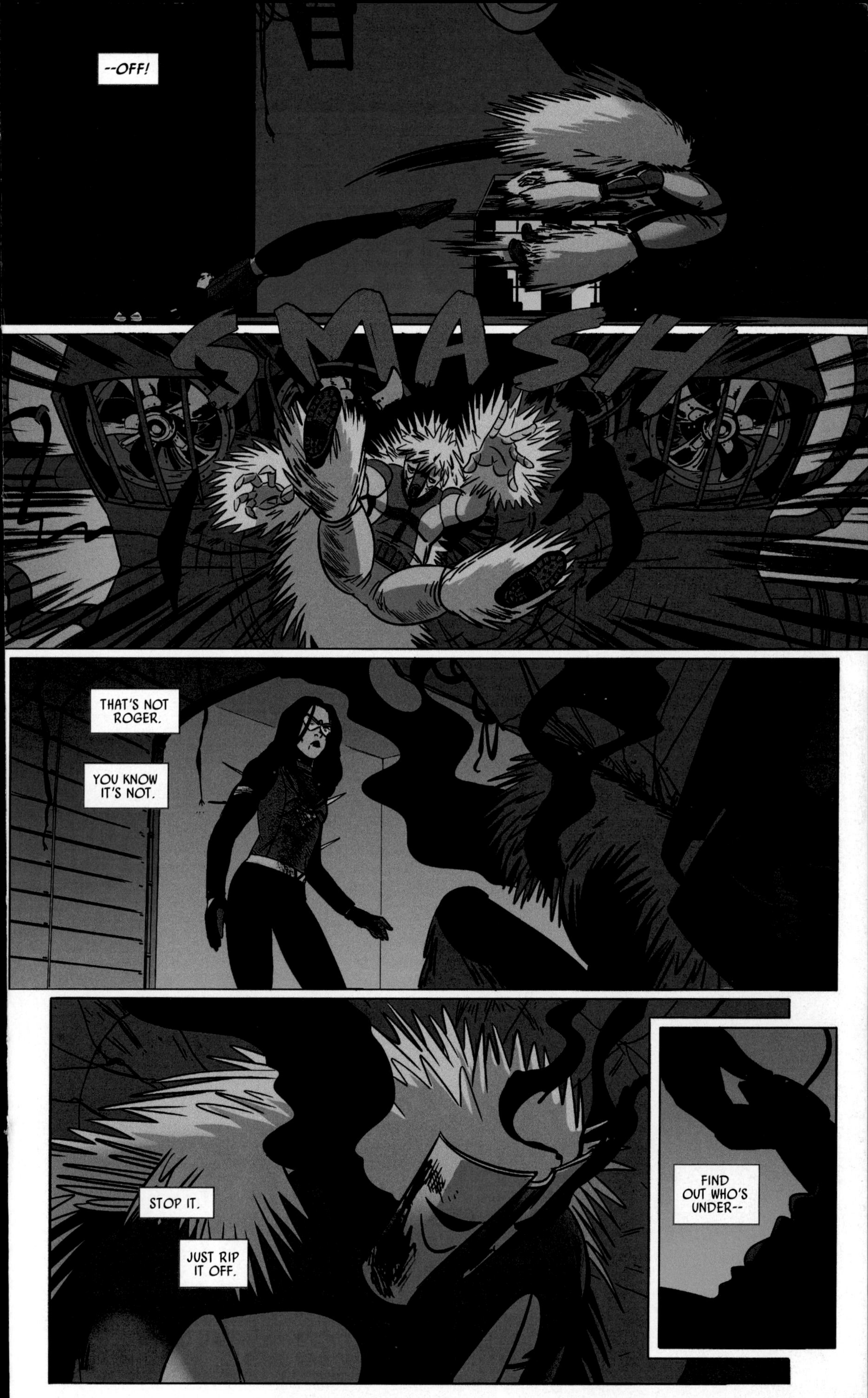
--OFF!
SMASH
THAT'S NOT ROGER.
YOU KNOW IT'S NOT.
STOP IT.
JUST RIP IT OFF.
FIND OUT WHO'S UNDER--

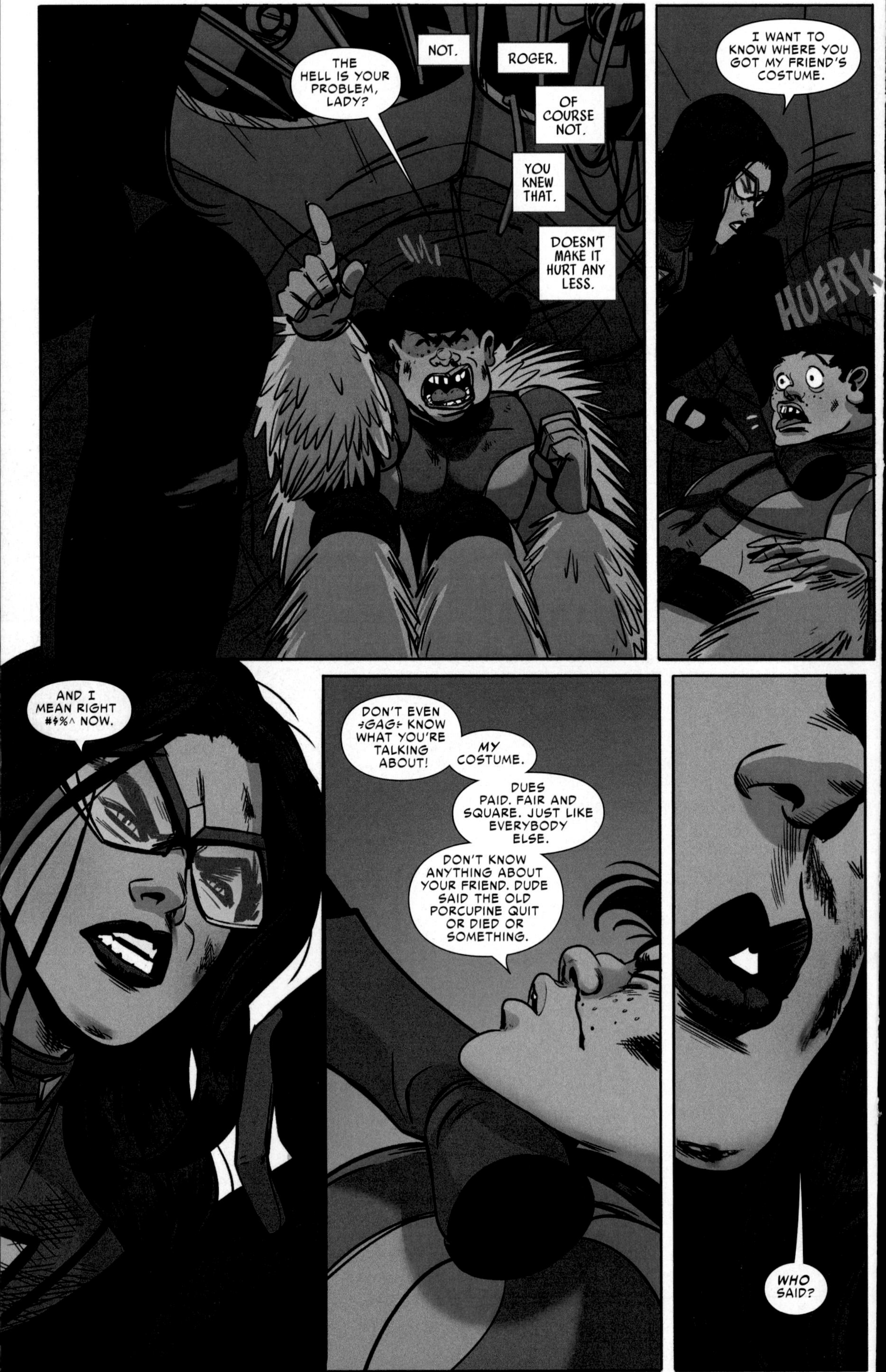

THE HELL IS YOUR PROBLEM, LADY?
NOT.
ROGER.
OF COURSE NOT.
YOU KNEW THAT.
DOESN'T MAKE IT HURT ANY LESS.
I WANT TO KNOW WHERE YOU GOT MY FRIEND'S COSTUME.
HUERK
AND I MEAN RIGHT #$%^ NOW.
DON'T EVEN ≑GAG≑ KNOW WHAT YOU'RE TALKING ABOUT!
MY COSTUME.
DUES PAID. FAIR AND SQUARE. JUST LIKE EVERYBODY ELSE.
DON'T KNOW ANYTHING ABOUT YOUR FRIEND. DUDE SAID THE OLD PORCUPINE QUIT OR DIED OR SOMETHING.
WHO SAID?

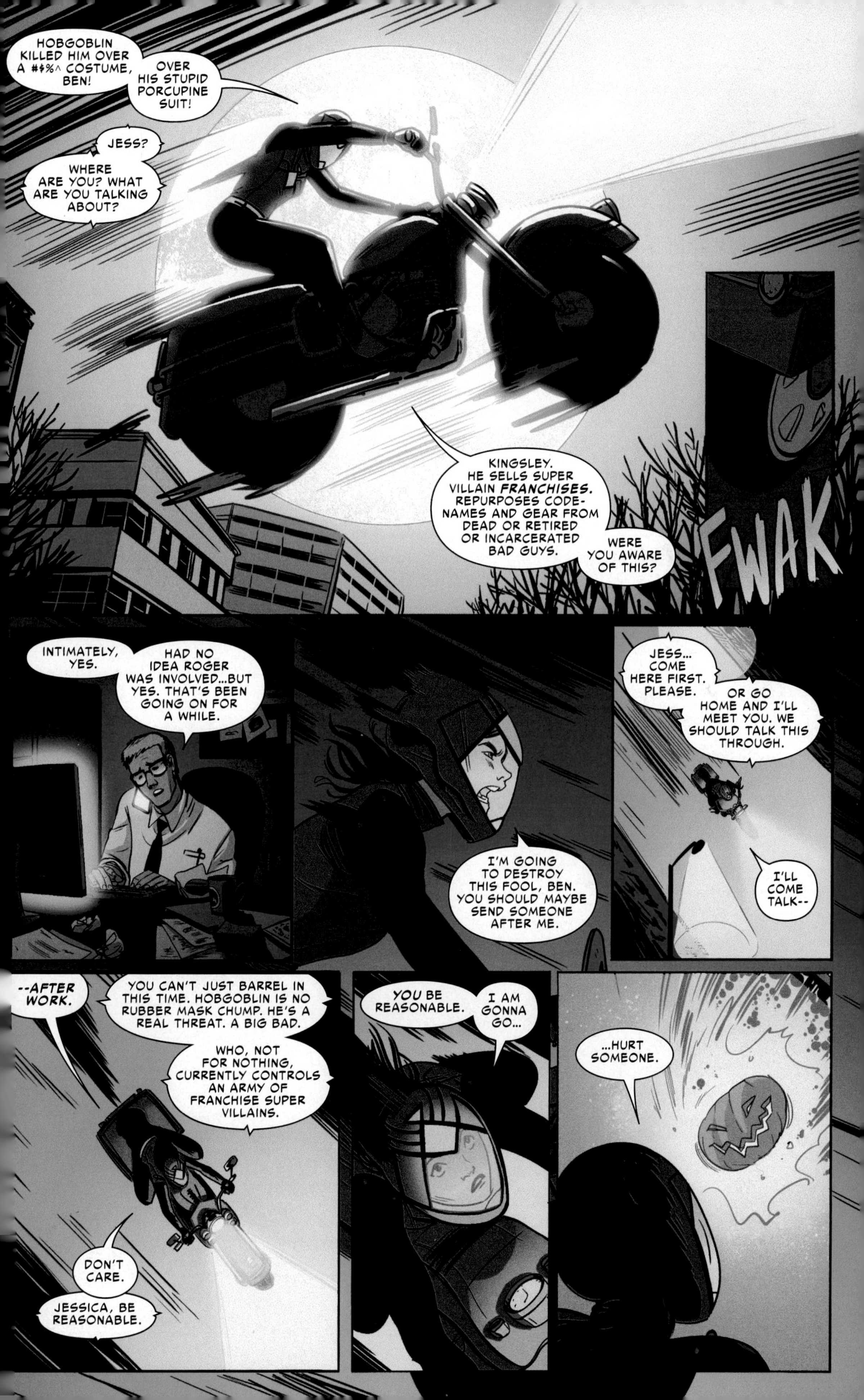
HOBGOBLIN KILLED HIM OVER A #$%^ COSTUME, BEN!
OVER HIS STUPID PORCUPINE SUIT!
JESS?
WHERE ARE YOU? WHAT ARE YOU TALKING ABOUT?
KINGSLEY. HE SELLS SUPER VILLAIN FRANCHISES. REPURPOSES CODE-NAMES AND GEAR FROM DEAD OR RETIRED OR INCARCERATED BAD GUYS.
WERE YOU AWARE OF THIS?
FWAK
INTIMATELY, YES.
HAD NO IDEA ROGER WAS INVOLVED...BUT YES. THAT'S BEEN GOING ON FOR A WHILE.
I'M GOING TO DESTROY THIS FOOL, BEN. YOU SHOULD MAYBE SEND SOMEONE AFTER ME.
JESS... COME HERE FIRST. PLEASE.
OR GO HOME AND I'LL MEET YOU. WE SHOULD TALK THIS THROUGH.
I'LL COME TALK--
--AFTER WORK.
YOU CAN'T JUST BARREL IN THIS TIME. HOBGOBLIN IS NO RUBBER MASK CHUMP. HE'S A REAL THREAT. A BIG BAD.
WHO, NOT FOR NOTHING, CURRENTLY CONTROLS AN ARMY OF FRANCHISE SUPER VILLAINS.
DON'T CARE.
JESSICA, BE REASONABLE.
YOU BE REASONABLE.
I AM GONNA GO...
...HURT SOMEONE.

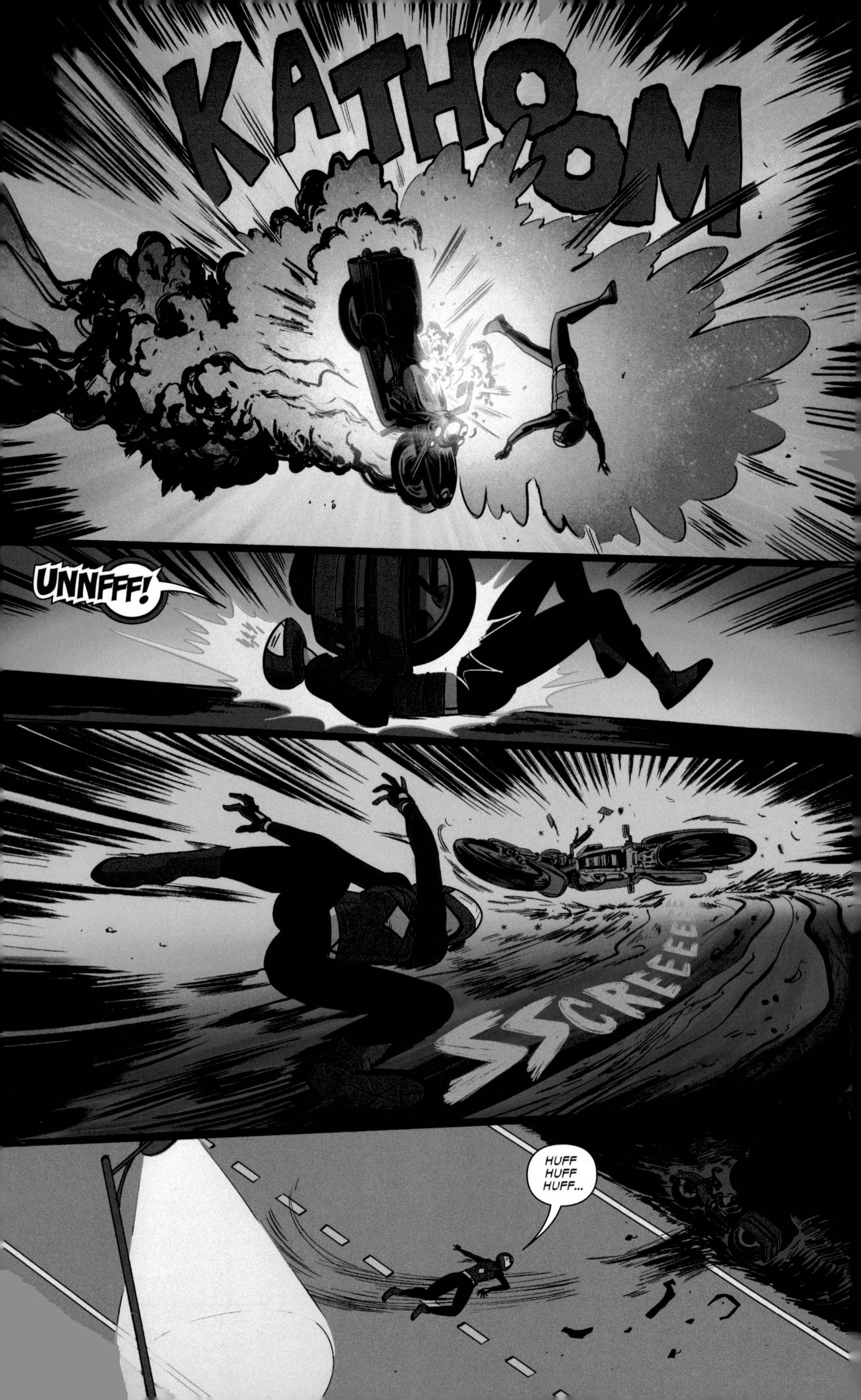
KATHOOM
UNNFFF!
SSCREEEE
HUFF
HUFF
HUFF...

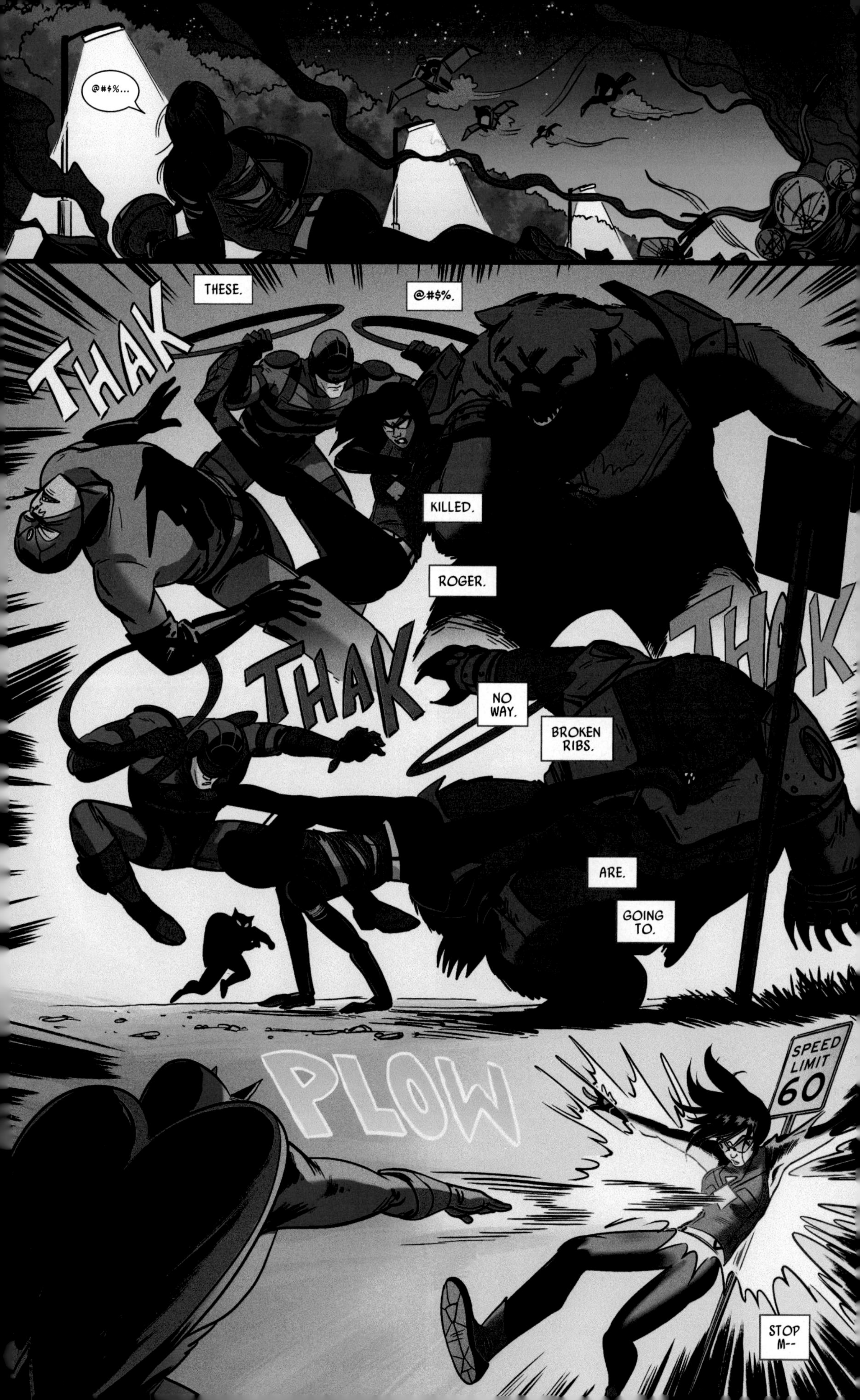
@#$%...
THESE.
@#$%.
THAK
KILLED.
ROGER.
THAK
THAK
NO WAY.
BROKEN RIBS.
ARE.
GOING TO.
PLOW
SPEED LIMIT 60
STOP M--

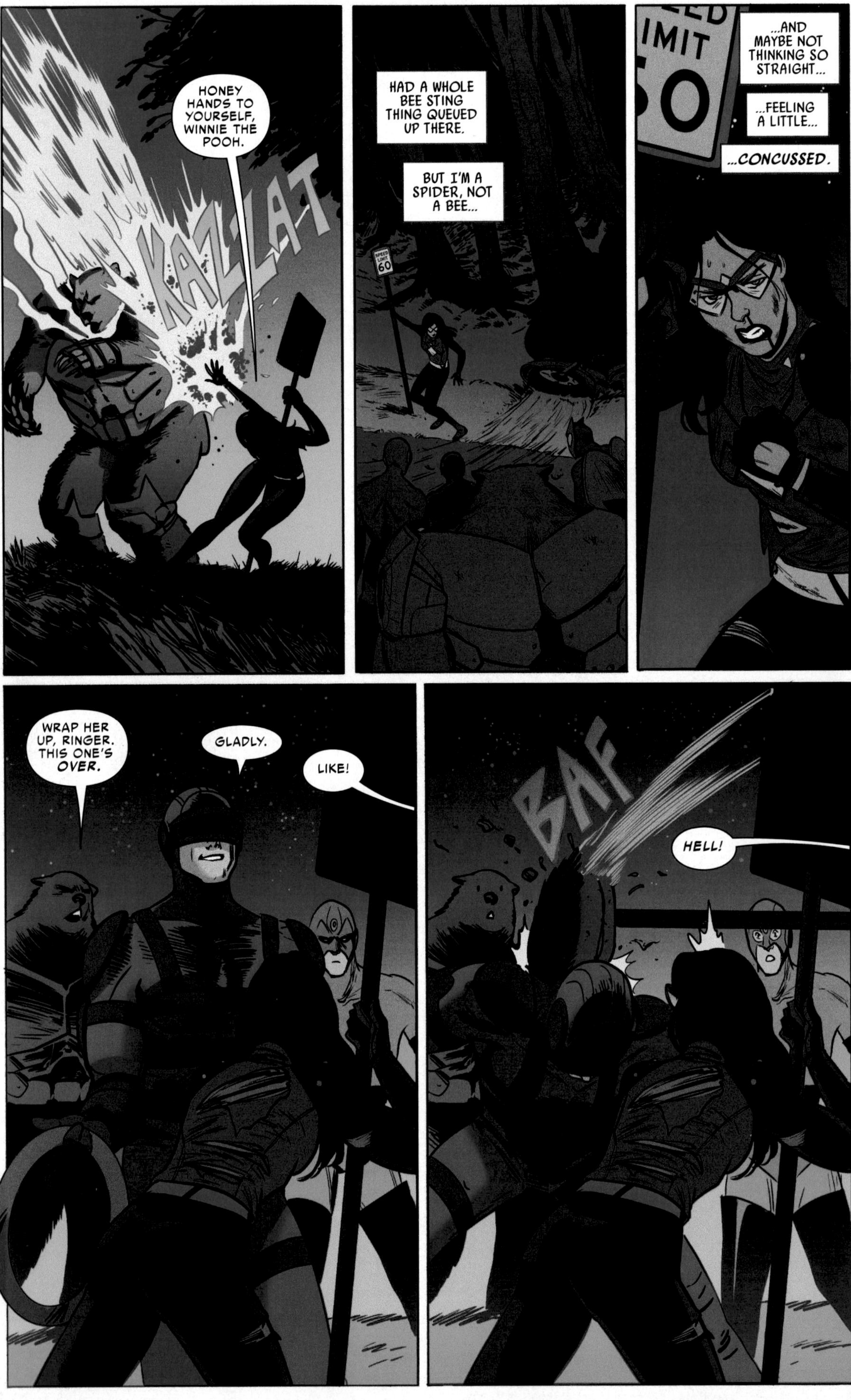
HONEY HANDS TO YOURSELF, WINNIE THE POOH.
KAZ-ZLAT
HAD A WHOLE BEE STING THING QUEUED UP THERE.
BUT I'M A SPIDER, NOT A BEE...
SPEED LIMIT 60
...AND MAYBE NOT THINKING SO STRAIGHT...
...FEELING A LITTLE...
...CONCUSSED.
WRAP HER UP, RINGER. THIS ONE'S OVER.
GLADLY.
LIKE!
BAF
HELL!

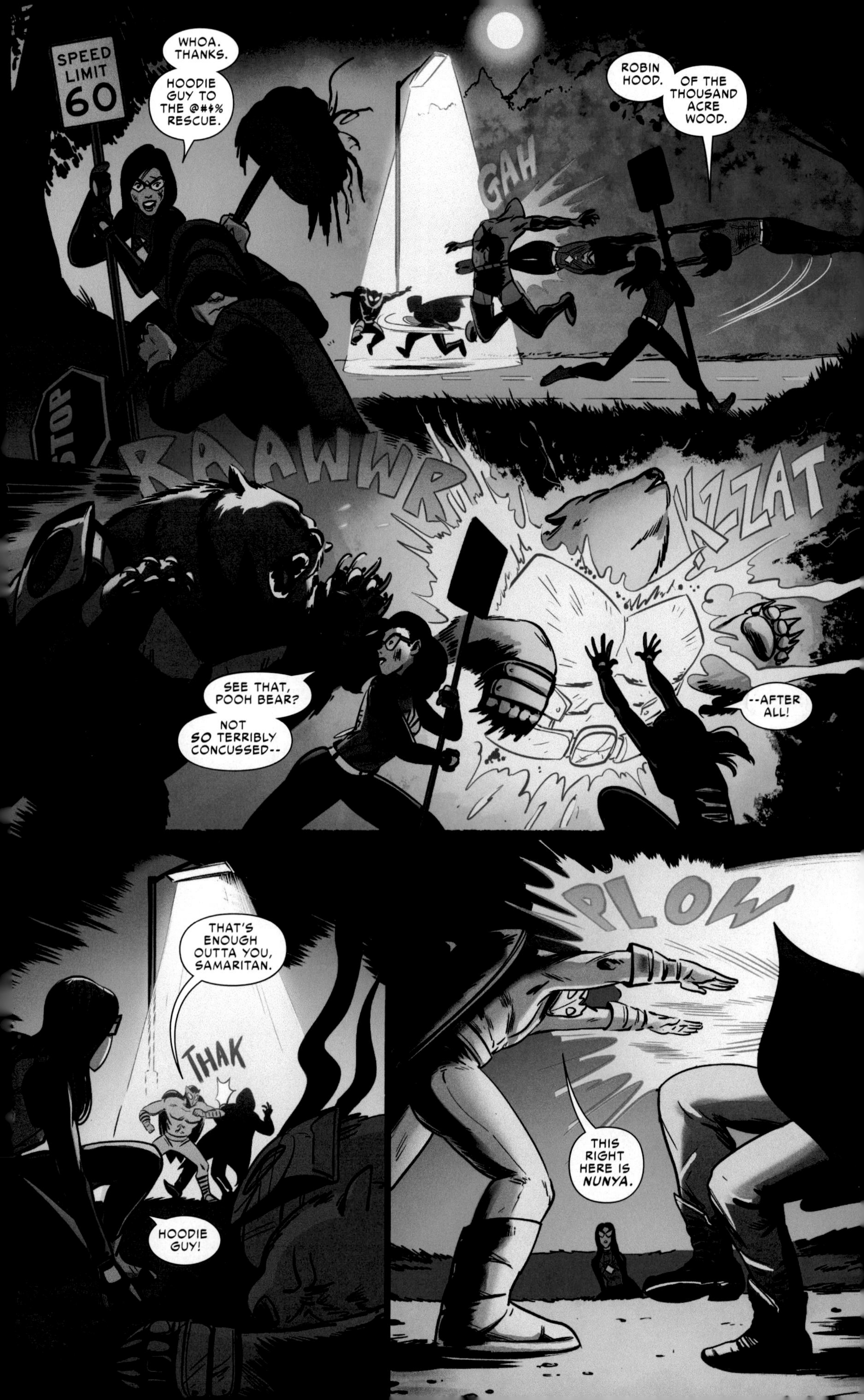
SPEED LIMIT 60
WHOA. THANKS.
HOODIE GUY TO THE @#$% RESCUE.
ROBIN HOOD.
OF THE THOUSAND ACRE WOOD.
GAH
STOP
RAAWWR
KZZZAT
SEE THAT, POOH BEAR?
NOT SO TERRIBLY CONCUSSED--
--AFTER ALL!
THAT'S ENOUGH OUTTA YOU, SAMARITAN.
THAK
HOODIE GUY!
PLOW
THIS RIGHT HERE IS *NUNYA*.

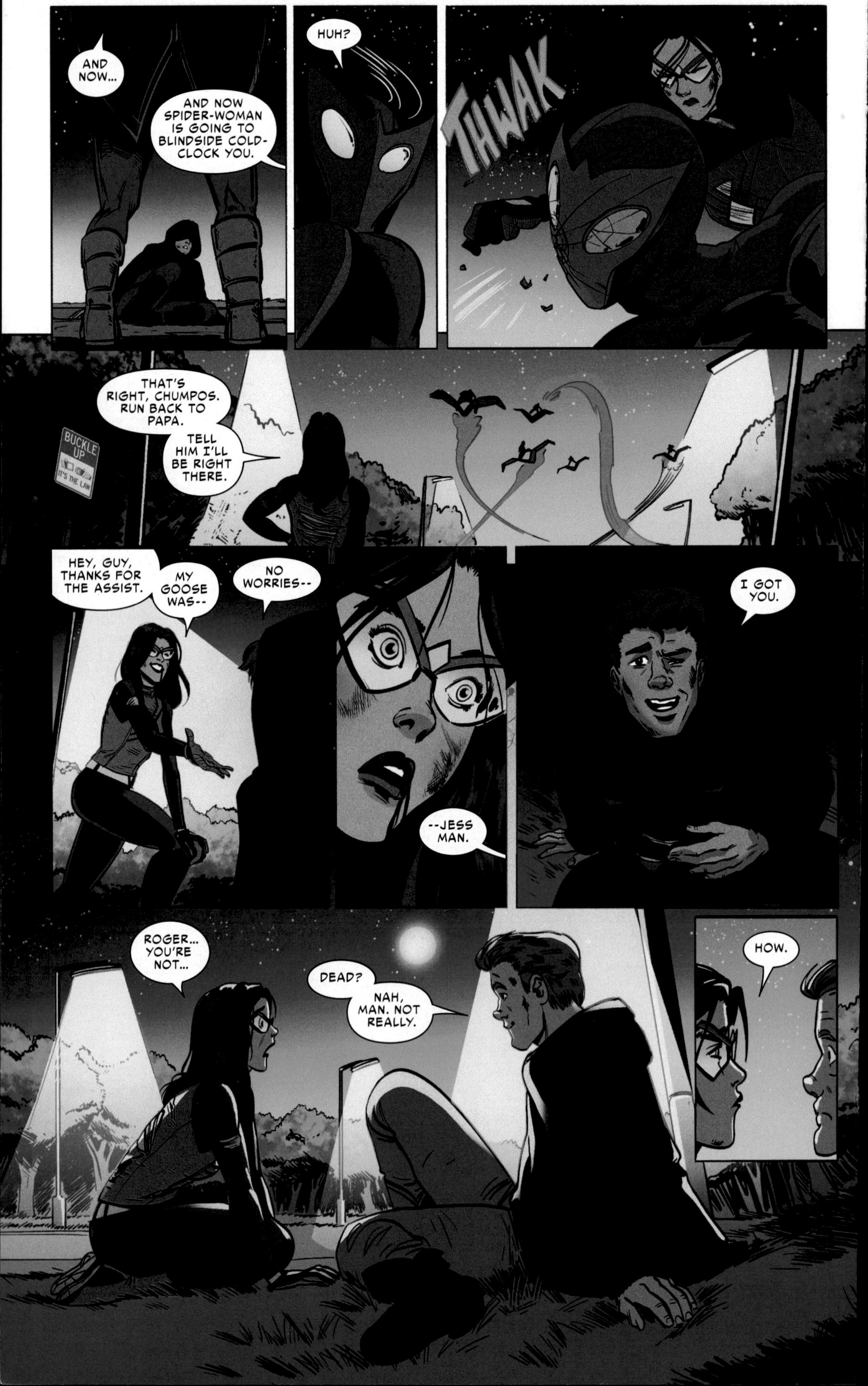
AND NOW...
AND NOW SPIDER-WOMAN IS GOING TO BLINDSIDE COLD-CLOCK YOU.
HUH?
THWAK
THAT'S RIGHT, CHUMPOS. RUN BACK TO PAPA.
TELL HIM I'LL BE RIGHT THERE.
BUCKLE UP
IT'S THE LAW
HEY, GUY, THANKS FOR THE ASSIST.
MY GOOSE WAS--
NO WORRIES--
--JESS MAN.
I GOT YOU.
ROGER... YOU'RE NOT...
DEAD?
NAH, MAN. NOT REALLY.
HOW.

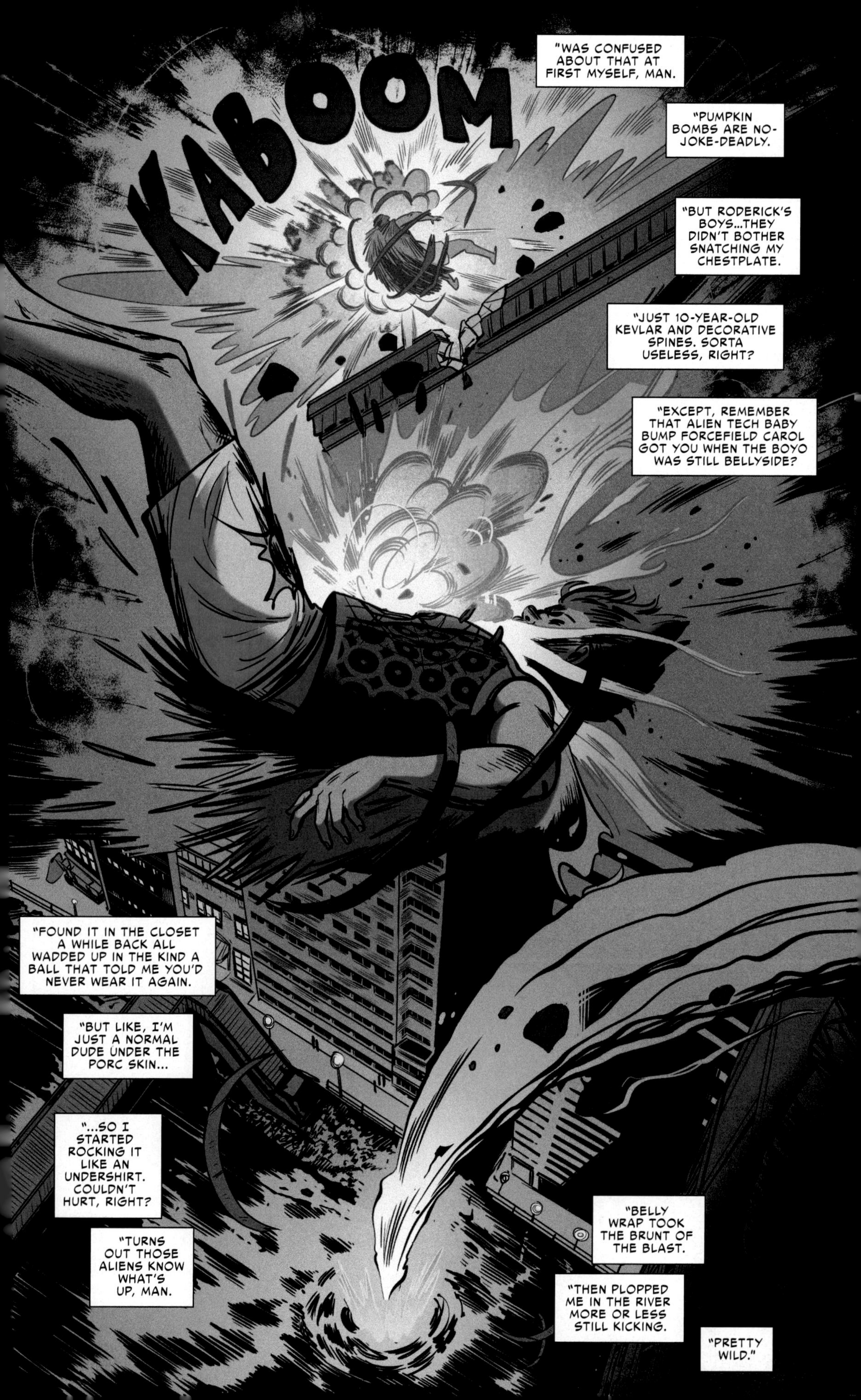
KABOOM
"WAS CONFUSED ABOUT THAT AT FIRST MYSELF, MAN.
"PUMPKIN BOMBS ARE NO-JOKE-DEADLY.
"BUT RODERICK'S BOYS...THEY DIDN'T BOTHER SNATCHING MY CHESTPLATE.
"JUST 10-YEAR-OLD KEVLAR AND DECORATIVE SPINES. SORTA USELESS, RIGHT?
"EXCEPT, REMEMBER THAT ALIEN TECH BABY BUMP FORCEFIELD CAROL GOT YOU WHEN THE BOYO WAS STILL BELLYSIDE?
"FOUND IT IN THE CLOSET A WHILE BACK ALL WADDED UP IN THE KIND A BALL THAT TOLD ME YOU'D NEVER WEAR IT AGAIN.
"BUT LIKE, I'M JUST A NORMAL DUDE UNDER THE PORC SKIN...
"...SO I STARTED ROCKING IT LIKE AN UNDERSHIRT. COULDN'T HURT, RIGHT?
"TURNS OUT THOSE ALIENS KNOW WHAT'S UP, MAN.
"BELLY WRAP TOOK THE BRUNT OF THE BLAST.
"THEN PLOPPED ME IN THE RIVER MORE OR LESS STILL KICKING.
"PRETTY WILD."

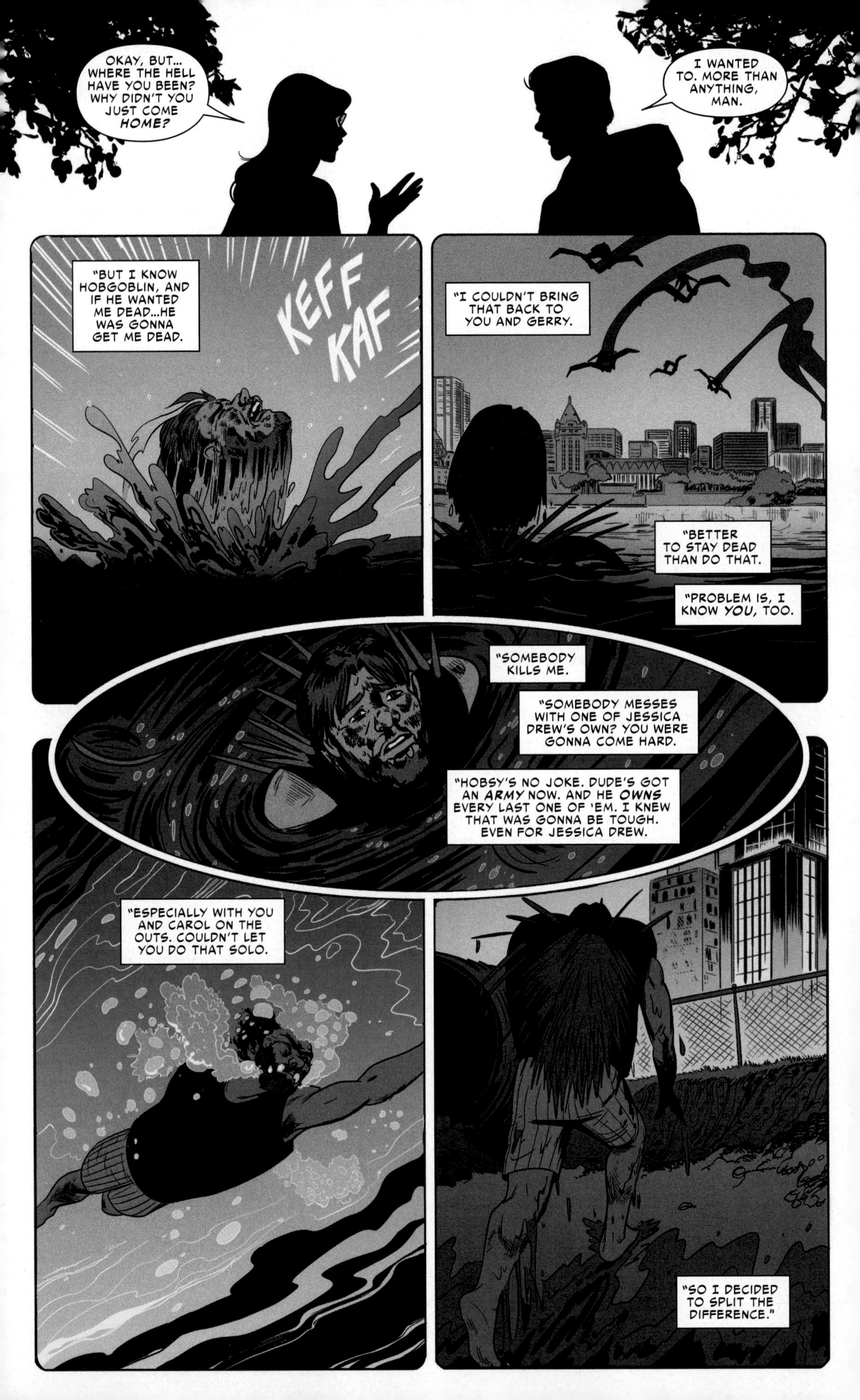
OKAY, BUT... WHERE THE HELL HAVE YOU BEEN? WHY DIDN'T YOU JUST COME HOME?
I WANTED TO. MORE THAN ANYTHING, MAN.
"BUT I KNOW HOBGOBLIN, AND IF HE WANTED ME DEAD...HE WAS GONNA GET ME DEAD.
KEFF KAF
"I COULDN'T BRING THAT BACK TO YOU AND GERRY.
"BETTER TO STAY DEAD THAN DO THAT.
"PROBLEM IS, I KNOW YOU, TOO.
"SOMEBODY KILLS ME.
"SOMEBODY MESSES WITH ONE OF JESSICA DREW'S OWN? YOU WERE GONNA COME HARD.
"HOBSY'S NO JOKE. DUDE'S GOT AN ARMY NOW. AND HE OWNS EVERY LAST ONE OF 'EM. I KNEW THAT WAS GONNA BE TOUGH. EVEN FOR JESSICA DREW.
"ESPECIALLY WITH YOU AND CAROL ON THE OUTS. COULDN'T LET YOU DO THAT SOLO.
"SO I DECIDED TO SPLIT THE DIFFERENCE."

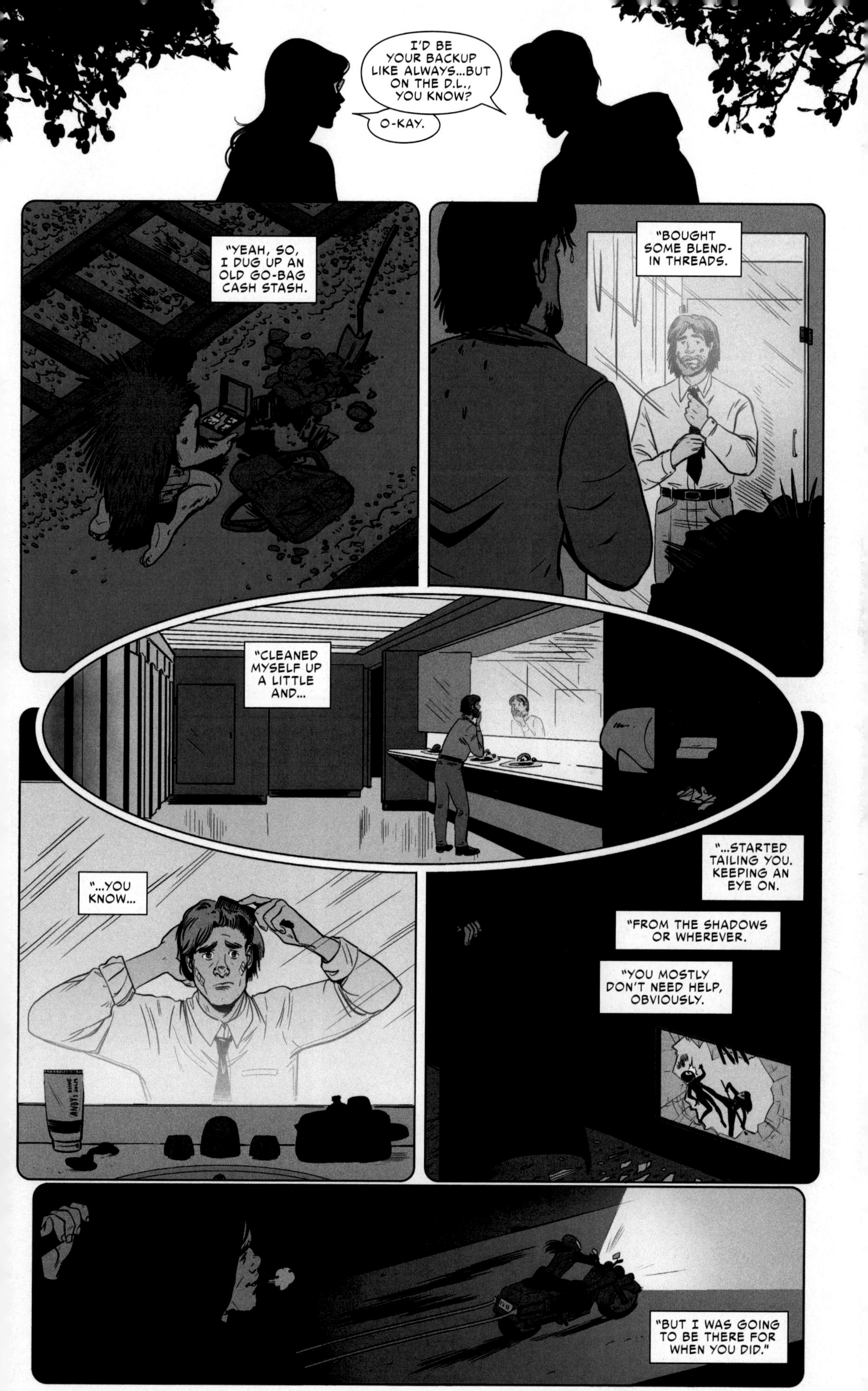
I'D BE YOUR BACKUP LIKE ALWAYS...BUT ON THE D.L., YOU KNOW?
O-KAY.
"YEAH, SO, I DUG UP AN OLD GO-BAG CASH STASH.
"BOUGHT SOME BLEND-IN THREADS.
"CLEANED MYSELF UP A LITTLE AND...
"...YOU KNOW...
"...STARTED TAILING YOU. KEEPING AN EYE ON.
"FROM THE SHADOWS OR WHEREVER.
"YOU MOSTLY DON'T NEED HELP, OBVIOUSLY.
"BUT I WAS GOING TO BE THERE FOR WHEN YOU DID."

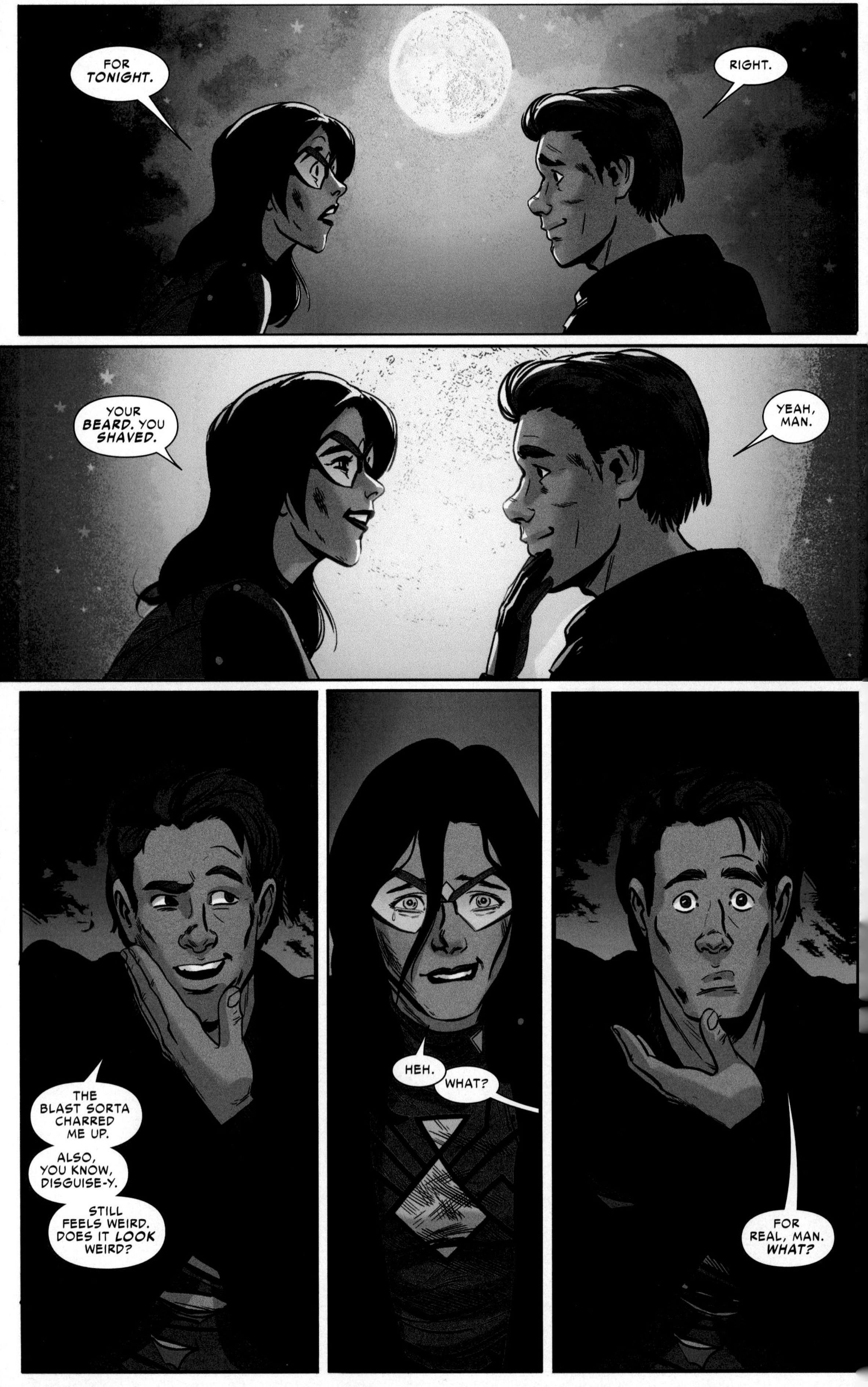
FOR *TONIGHT*.
RIGHT.
YOUR *BEARD*. YOU *SHAVED*.
YEAH, MAN.
THE BLAST SORTA CHARRED ME UP.
ALSO, YOU KNOW, DISGUISE-Y.
STILL FEELS WEIRD. DOES IT *LOOK* WEIRD?
HEH.
WHAT?
FOR REAL, MAN. *WHAT?*

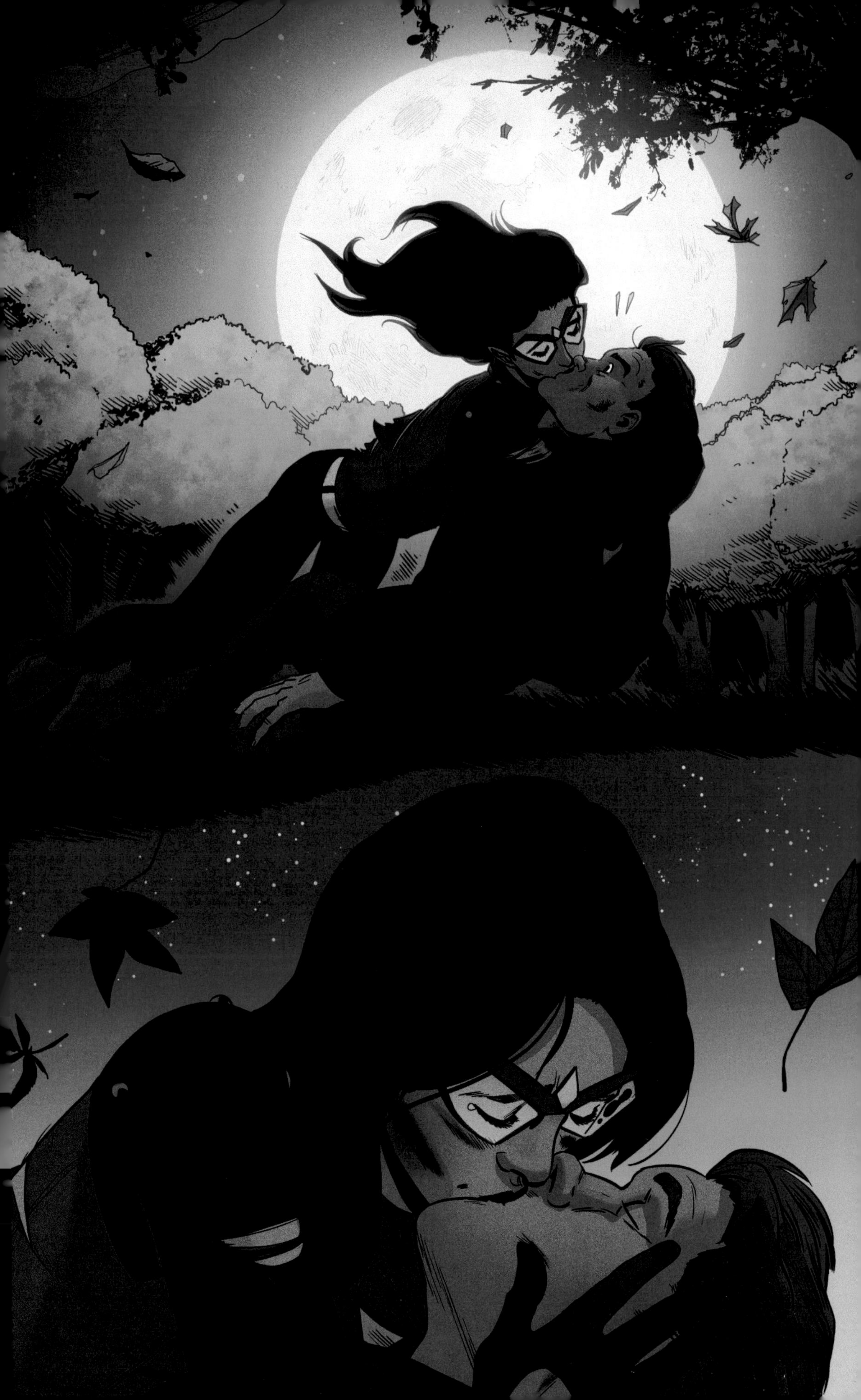
!!

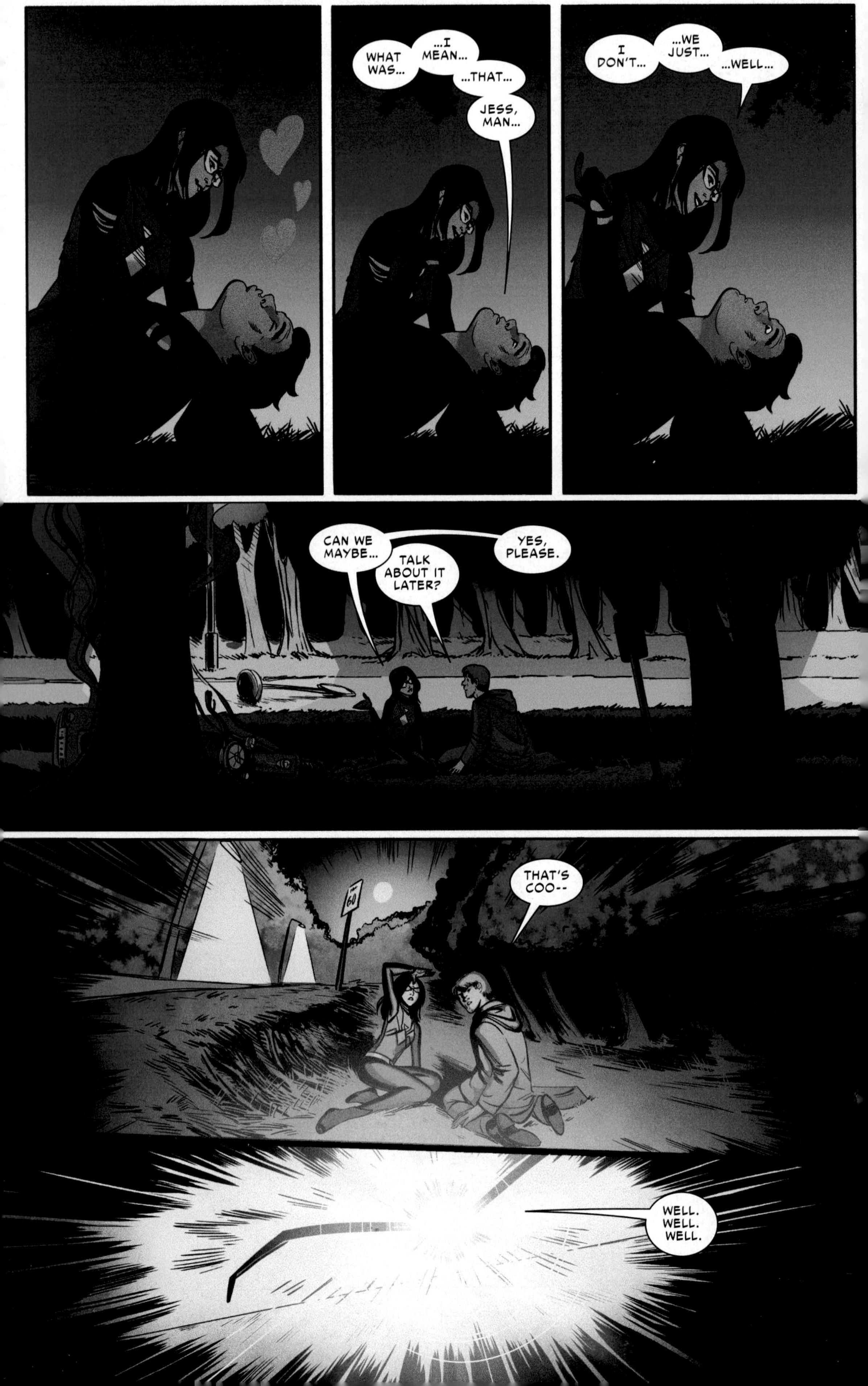
WHAT WAS...
...I MEAN...
...THAT...
JESS, MAN...
I DON'T...
...WE JUST...
...WELL...
CAN WE MAYBE...
TALK ABOUT IT LATER?
YES, PLEASE.
60
THAT'S COO--
WELL. WELL. WELL.

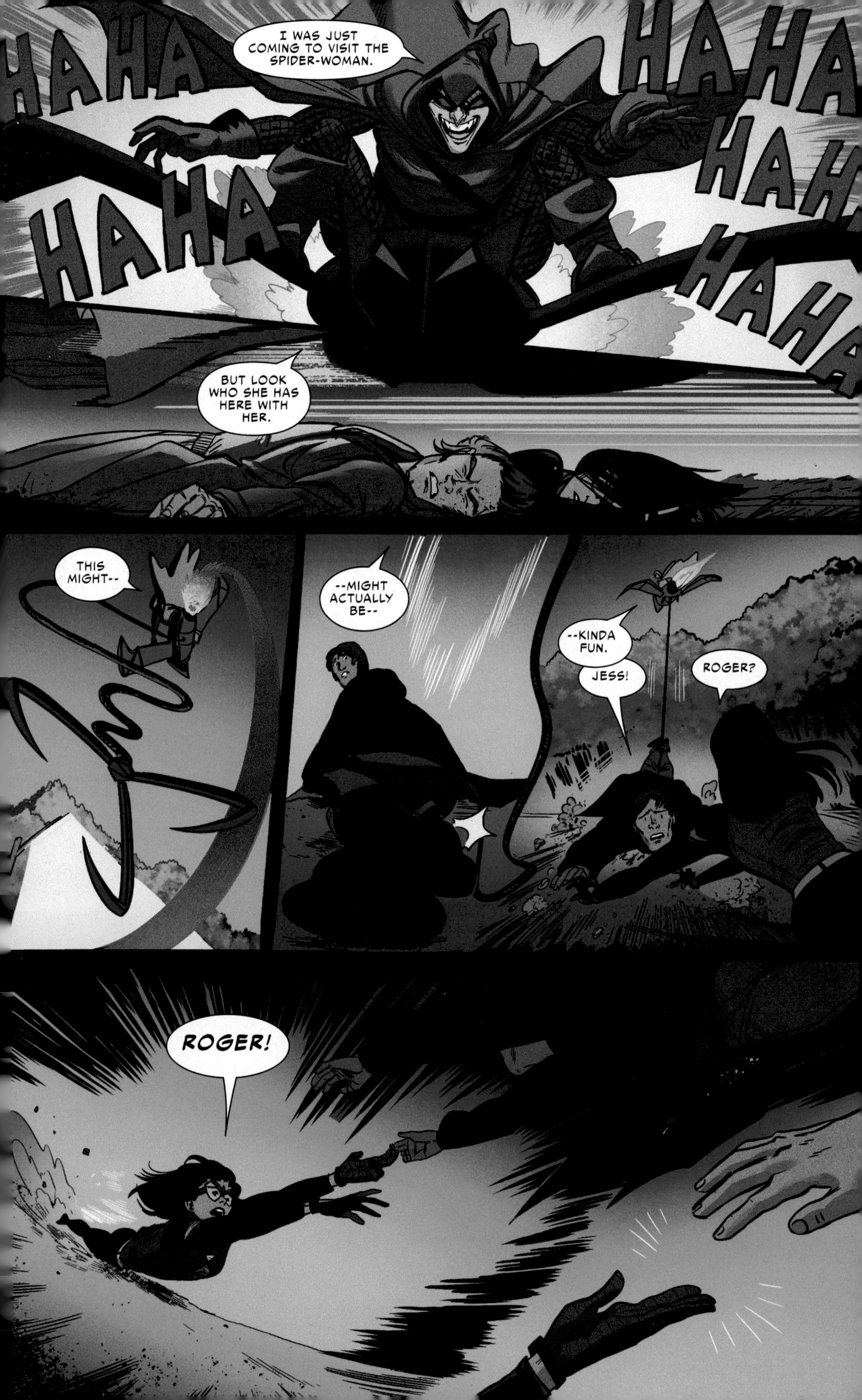
HAHA
I WAS JUST COMING TO VISIT THE SPIDER-WOMAN.
HAHA
HAHA
HAHA
HAHA
BUT LOOK WHO SHE HAS HERE WITH HER.
THIS MIGHT--
--MIGHT ACTUALLY BE--
--KINDA FUN.
JESS!
ROGER?
ROGER!

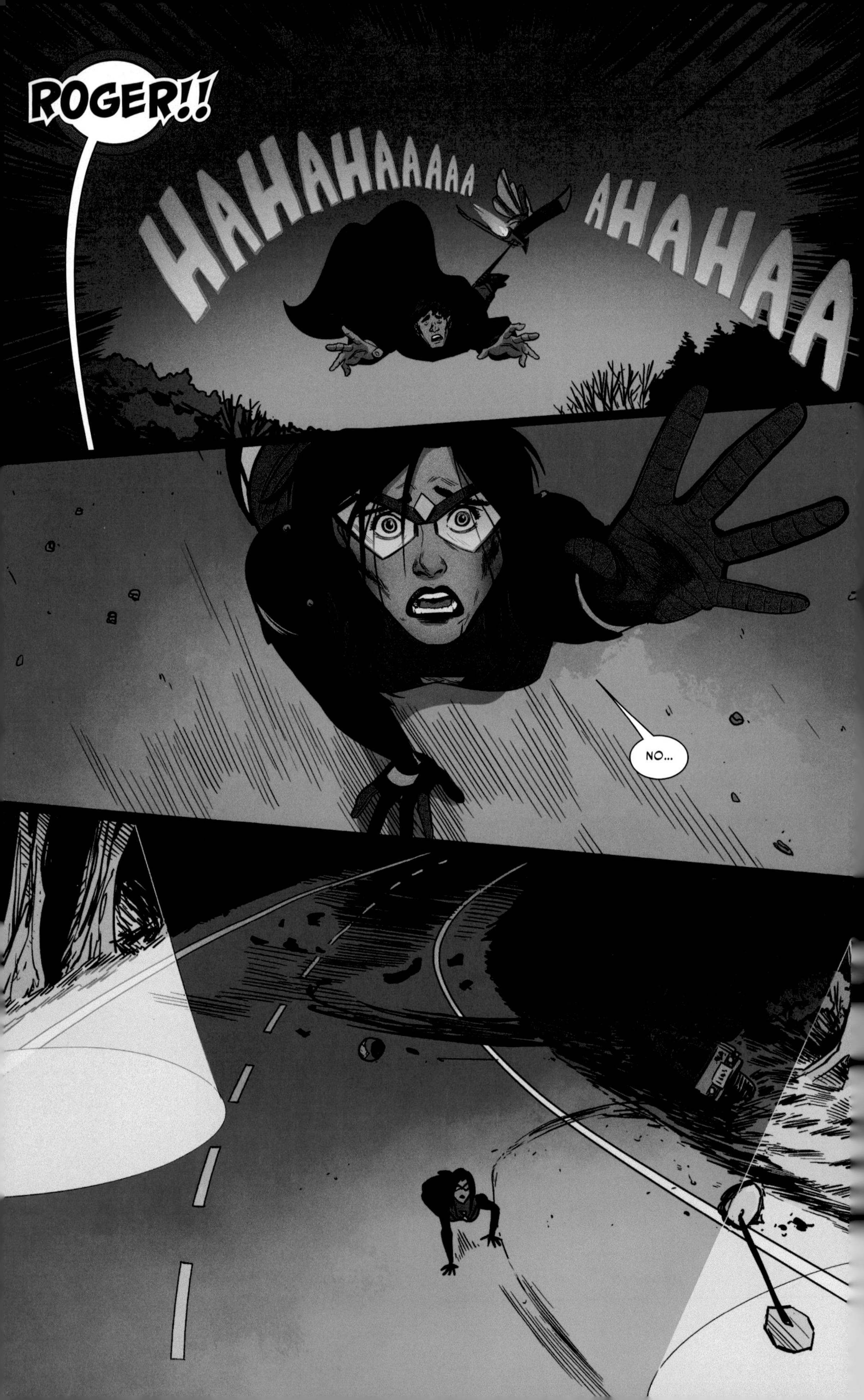
ROGER!!
HAHAHAAAAA AHAHAA
NO...

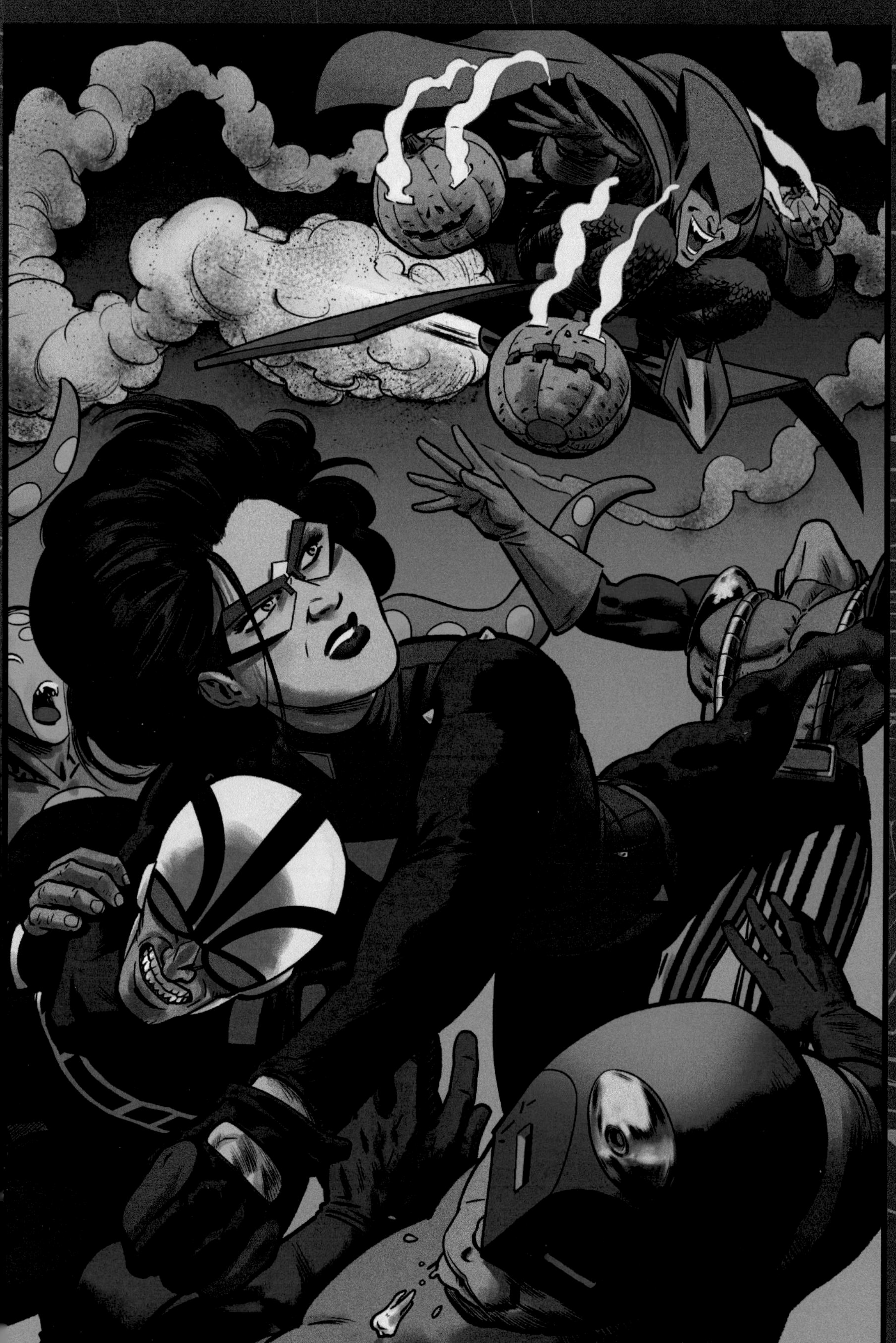

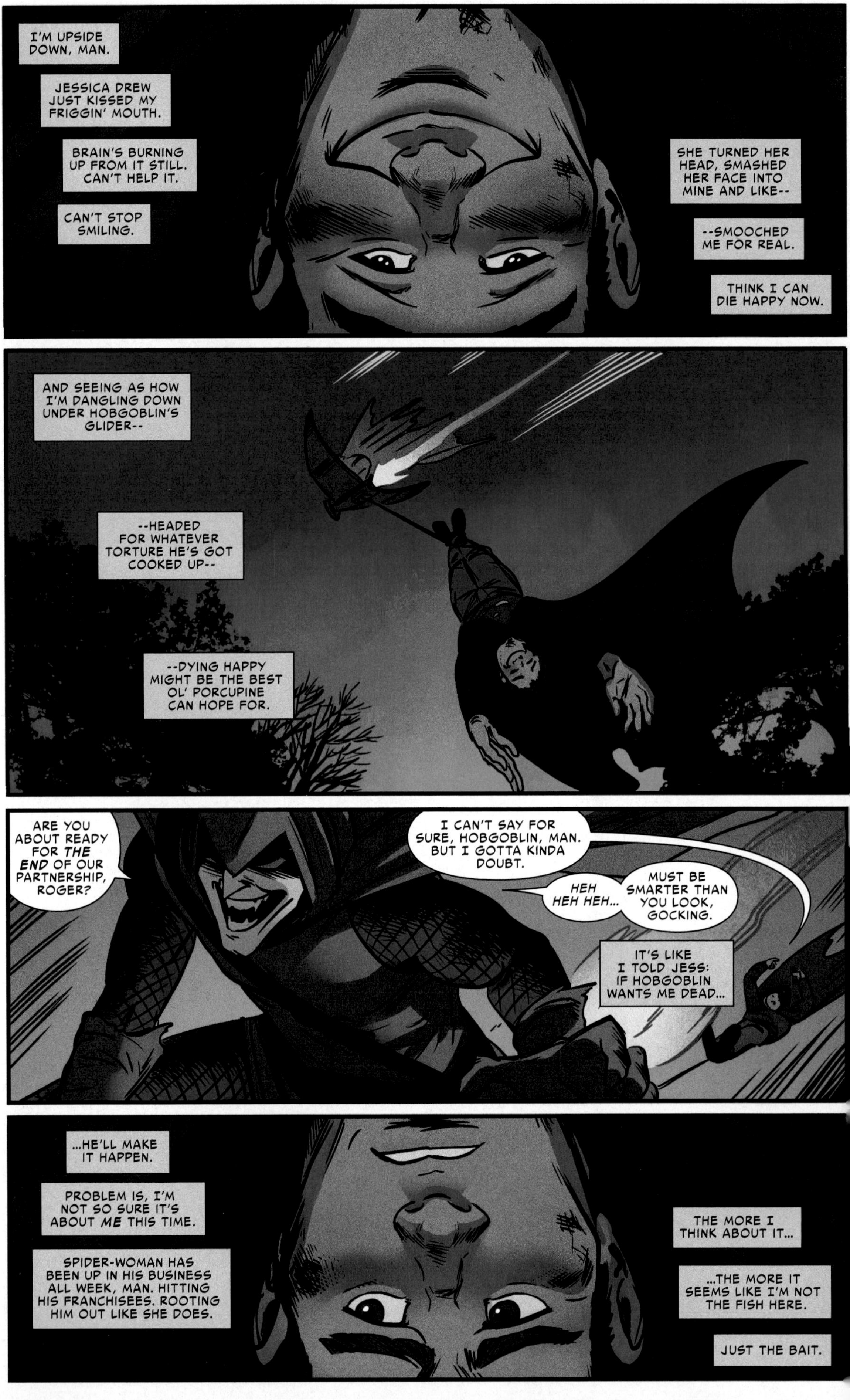

I'M UPSIDE DOWN, MAN.
JESSICA DREW JUST KISSED MY FRIGGIN' MOUTH.
BRAIN'S BURNING UP FROM IT STILL. CAN'T HELP IT.
CAN'T STOP SMILING.
SHE TURNED HER HEAD, SMASHED HER FACE INTO MINE AND LIKE--
--SMOOCHED ME FOR REAL.
THINK I CAN DIE HAPPY NOW.
AND SEEING AS HOW I'M DANGLING DOWN UNDER HOBGOBLIN'S GLIDER--
--HEADED FOR WHATEVER TORTURE HE'S GOT COOKED UP--
--DYING HAPPY MIGHT BE THE BEST OL' PORCUPINE CAN HOPE FOR.
ARE YOU ABOUT READY FOR *THE END* OF OUR PARTNERSHIP, ROGER?
I CAN'T SAY FOR SURE, HOBGOBLIN, MAN. BUT I GOTTA KINDA DOUBT.
HEH HEH HEH...
MUST BE SMARTER THAN YOU LOOK, GOCKING.
IT'S LIKE I TOLD JESS: IF HOBGOBLIN WANTS ME DEAD...
...HE'LL MAKE IT HAPPEN.
PROBLEM IS, I'M NOT SO SURE IT'S ABOUT *ME* THIS TIME.
SPIDER-WOMAN HAS BEEN UP IN HIS BUSINESS ALL WEEK, MAN. HITTING HIS FRANCHISEES. ROOTING HIM OUT LIKE SHE DOES.
THE MORE I THINK ABOUT IT...
...THE MORE IT SEEMS LIKE I'M NOT THE FISH HERE.
JUST THE BAIT.

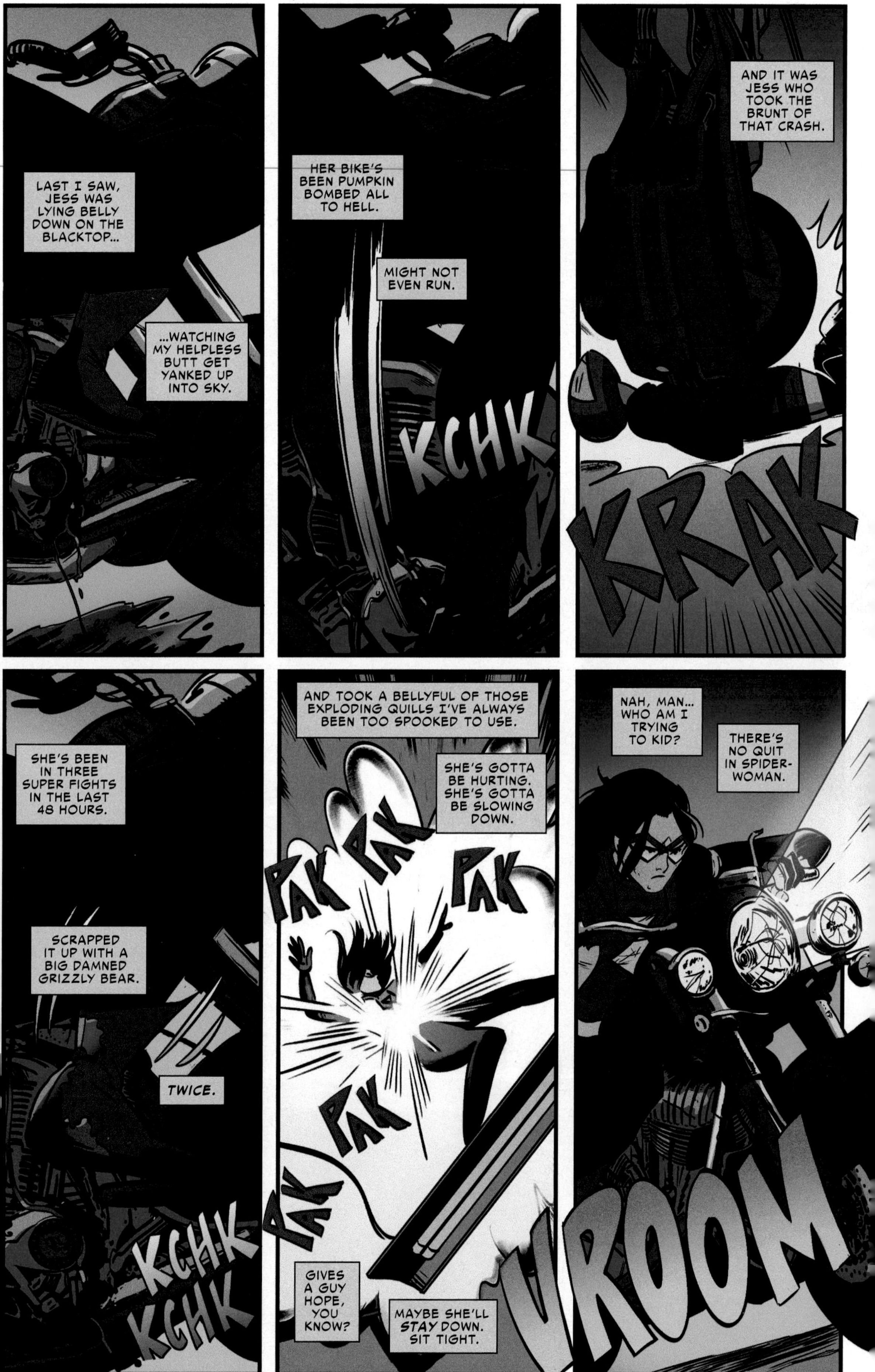
LAST I SAW, JESS WAS LYING BELLY DOWN ON THE BLACKTOP...
...WATCHING MY HELPLESS BUTT GET YANKED UP INTO SKY.
HER BIKE'S BEEN PUMPKIN BOMBED ALL TO HELL.
MIGHT NOT EVEN RUN.
KCHK
AND IT WAS JESS WHO TOOK THE BRUNT OF THAT CRASH.
KRAK
SHE'S BEEN IN THREE SUPER FIGHTS IN THE LAST 48 HOURS.
SCRAPPED IT UP WITH A BIG DAMNED GRIZZLY BEAR.
TWICE.
KCHK
KCHK
AND TOOK A BELLYFUL OF THOSE EXPLODING QUILLS I'VE ALWAYS BEEN TOO SPOOKED TO USE.
SHE'S GOTTA BE HURTING. SHE'S GOTTA BE SLOWING DOWN.
PAK PAK PAK
PAK
PAK
PAK
GIVES A GUY HOPE, YOU KNOW?
MAYBE SHE'LL STAY DOWN. SIT TIGHT.
NAH, MAN... WHO AM I TRYING TO KID?
THERE'S NO QUIT IN SPIDER-WOMAN.
VROOM

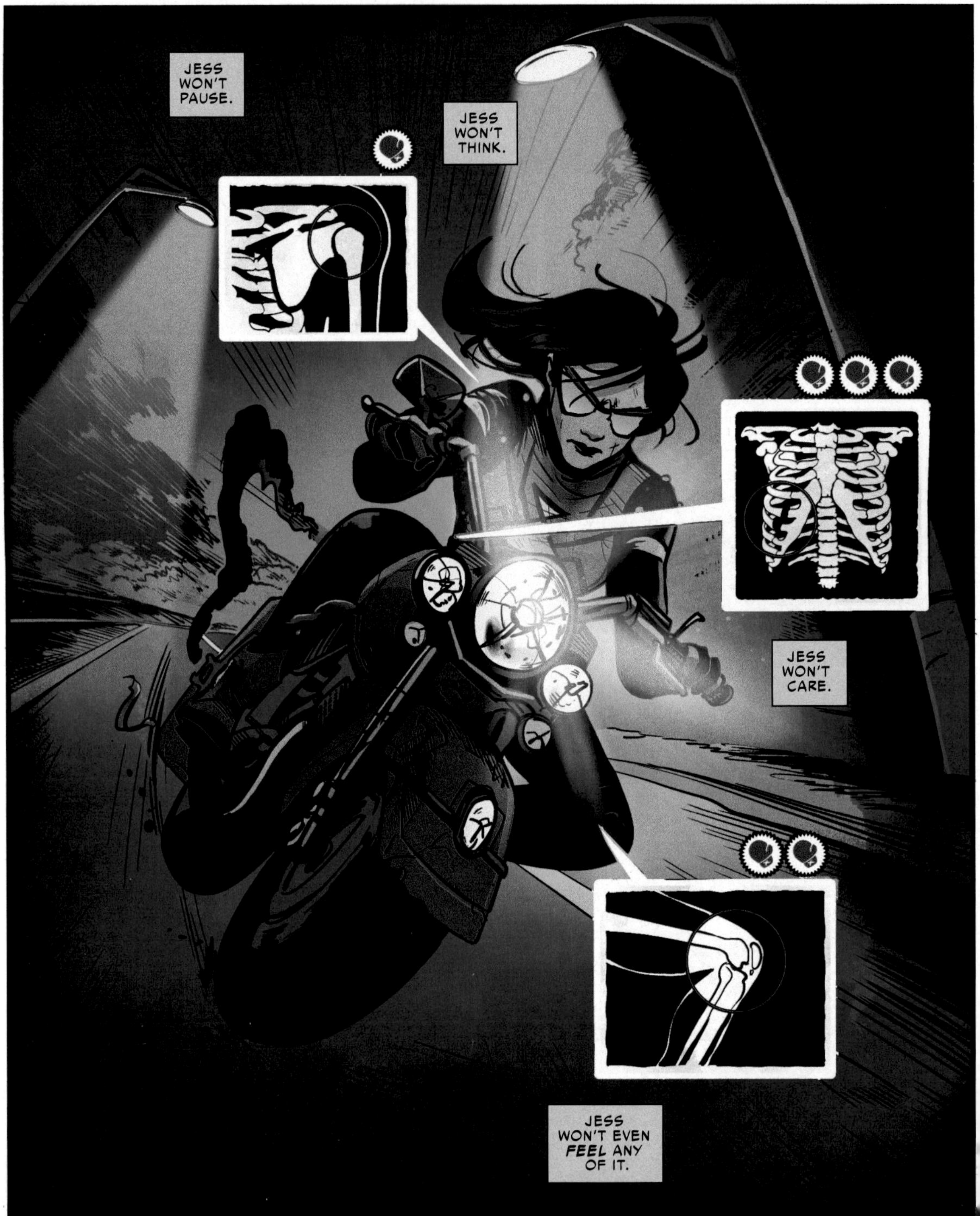
JESS WON'T PAUSE.
JESS WON'T THINK.
JESS WON'T CARE.
JESS WON'T EVEN *FEEL* ANY OF IT.

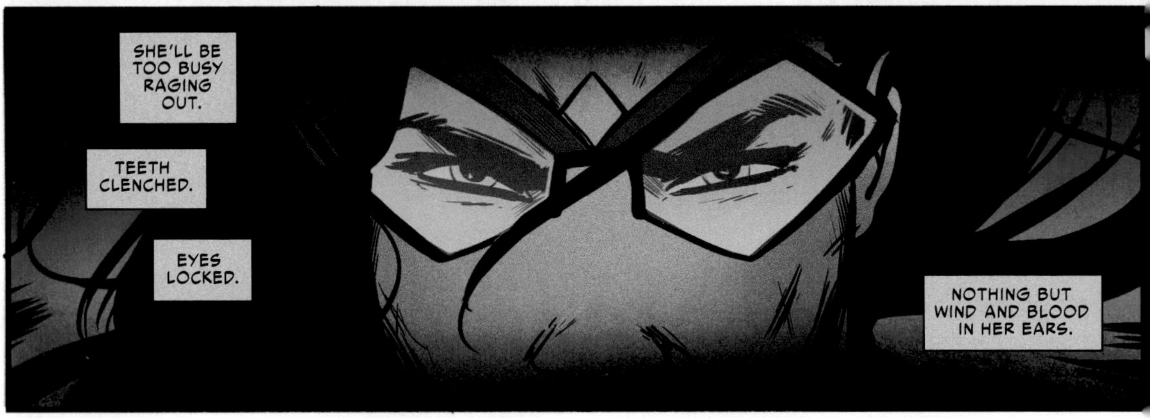
SHE'LL BE TOO BUSY RAGING OUT.
TEETH CLENCHED.
EYES LOCKED.
NOTHING BUT WIND AND BLOOD IN HER EARS.

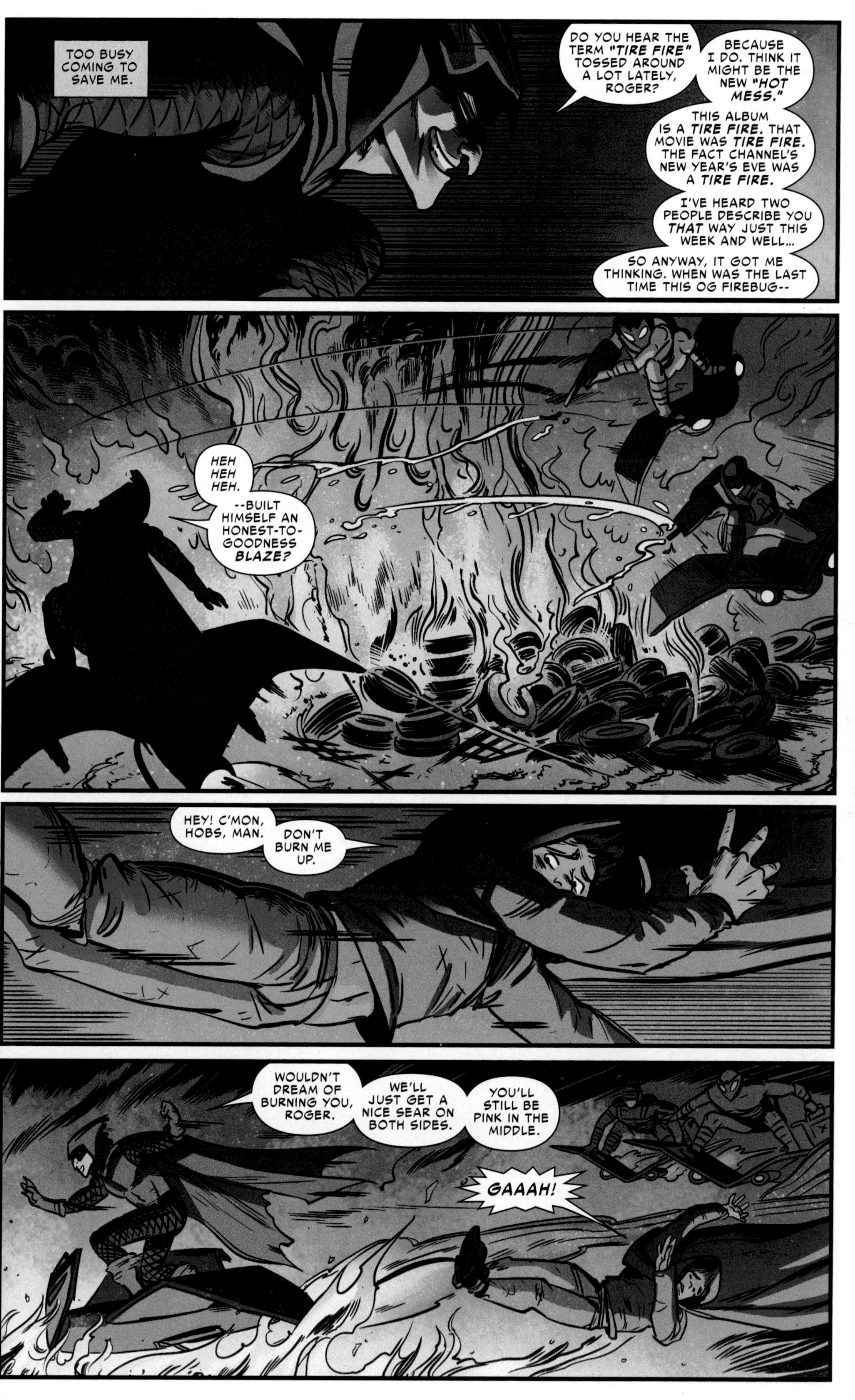

TOO BUSY COMING TO SAVE ME.
DO YOU HEAR THE TERM "TIRE FIRE" TOSSED AROUND A LOT LATELY, ROGER?
BECAUSE I DO. THINK IT MIGHT BE THE NEW "HOT MESS."
THIS ALBUM IS A TIRE FIRE. THAT MOVIE WAS TIRE FIRE. THE FACT CHANNEL'S NEW YEAR'S EVE WAS A TIRE FIRE.
I'VE HEARD TWO PEOPLE DESCRIBE YOU THAT WAY JUST THIS WEEK AND WELL...
SO ANYWAY, IT GOT ME THINKING. WHEN WAS THE LAST TIME THIS OG FIREBUG--
HEH HEH HEH.
--BUILT HIMSELF AN HONEST-TO-GOODNESS BLAZE?
HEY! C'MON, HOBS, MAN.
DON'T BURN ME UP.
WOULDN'T DREAM OF BURNING YOU, ROGER.
WE'LL JUST GET A NICE SEAR ON BOTH SIDES.
YOU'LL STILL BE PINK IN THE MIDDLE.
GAAAH!

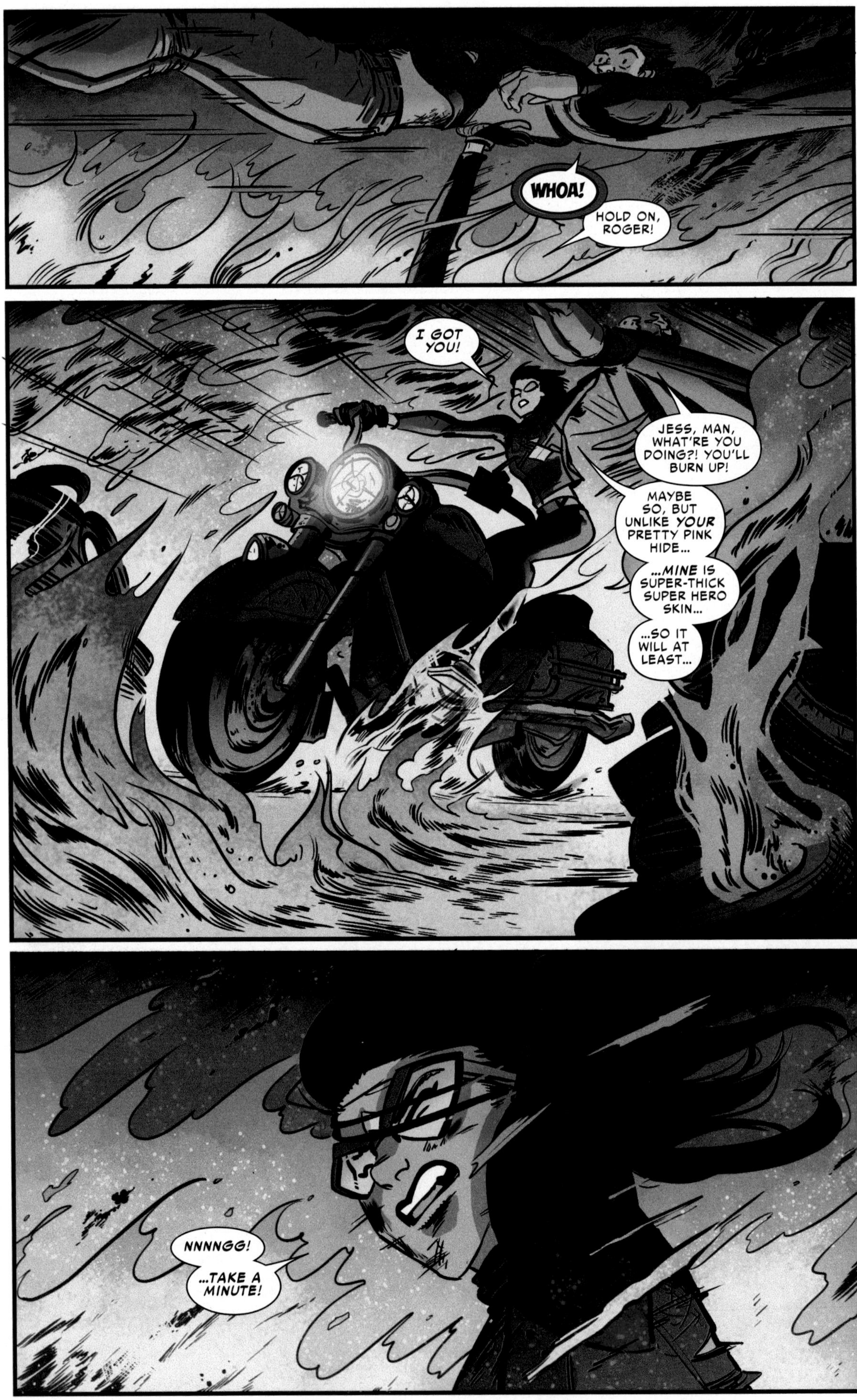
WHOA!
HOLD ON, ROGER!
I GOT YOU!
JESS, MAN, WHAT'RE YOU DOING?! YOU'LL BURN UP!
MAYBE SO, BUT UNLIKE YOUR PRETTY PINK HIDE...
...MINE IS SUPER-THICK SUPER HERO SKIN...
...SO IT WILL AT LEAST...
NNNNGG!
...TAKE A MINUTE!

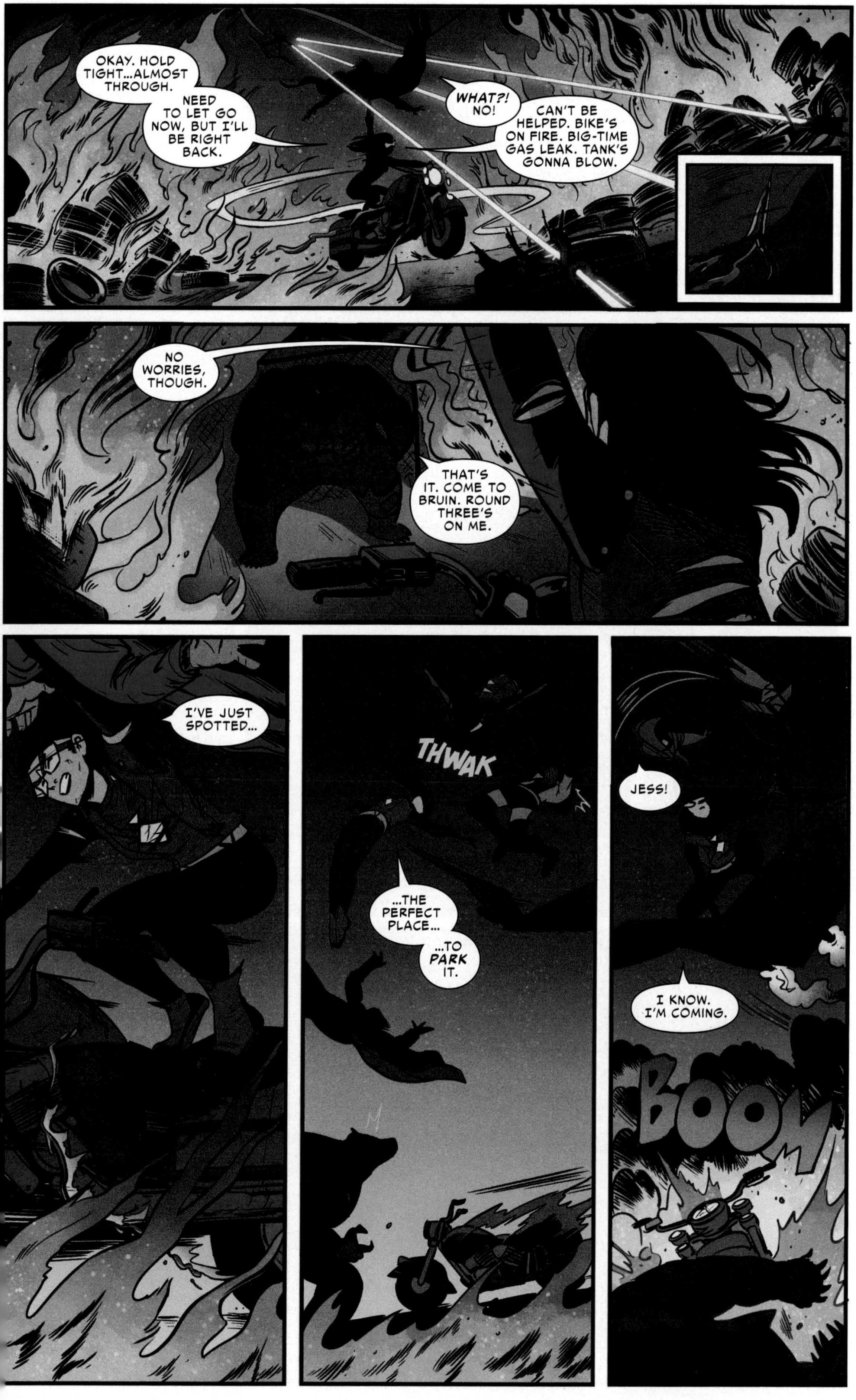
OKAY. HOLD TIGHT...ALMOST THROUGH.
NEED TO LET GO NOW, BUT I'LL BE RIGHT BACK.
WHAT?! NO!
CAN'T BE HELPED. BIKE'S ON FIRE. BIG-TIME GAS LEAK. TANK'S GONNA BLOW.
NO WORRIES, THOUGH.
THAT'S IT. COME TO BRUIN. ROUND THREE'S ON ME.
I'VE JUST SPOTTED...
THWAK
...THE PERFECT PLACE...
...TO PARK IT.
JESS!
I KNOW. I'M COMING.
BOOM

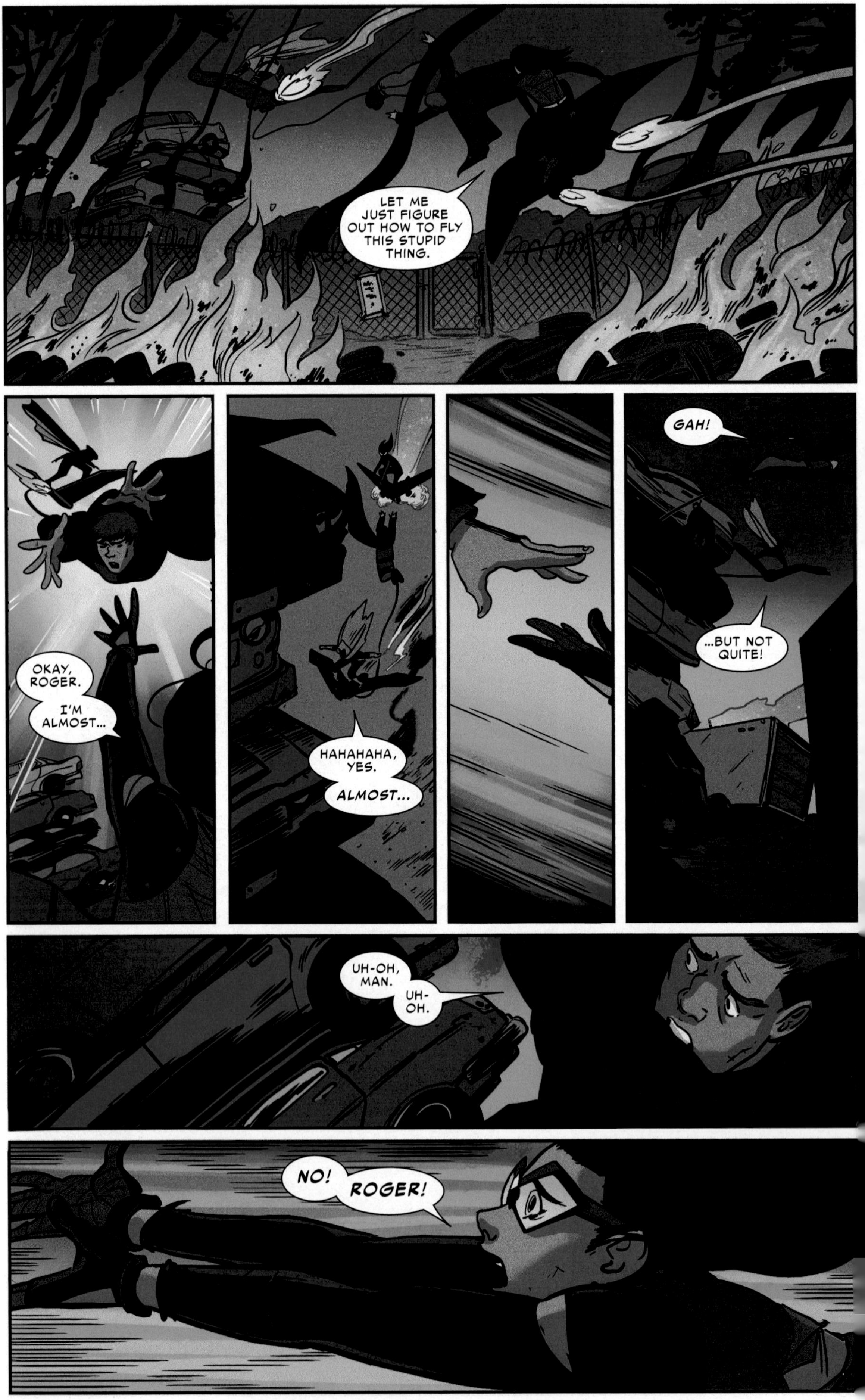
LET ME JUST FIGURE OUT HOW TO FLY THIS STUPID THING.
OKAY, ROGER.
I'M ALMOST...
HAHAHAHA, YES.
ALMOST...
GAH!
...BUT NOT QUITE!
UH-OH, MAN.
UH-OH.
NO!
ROGER!

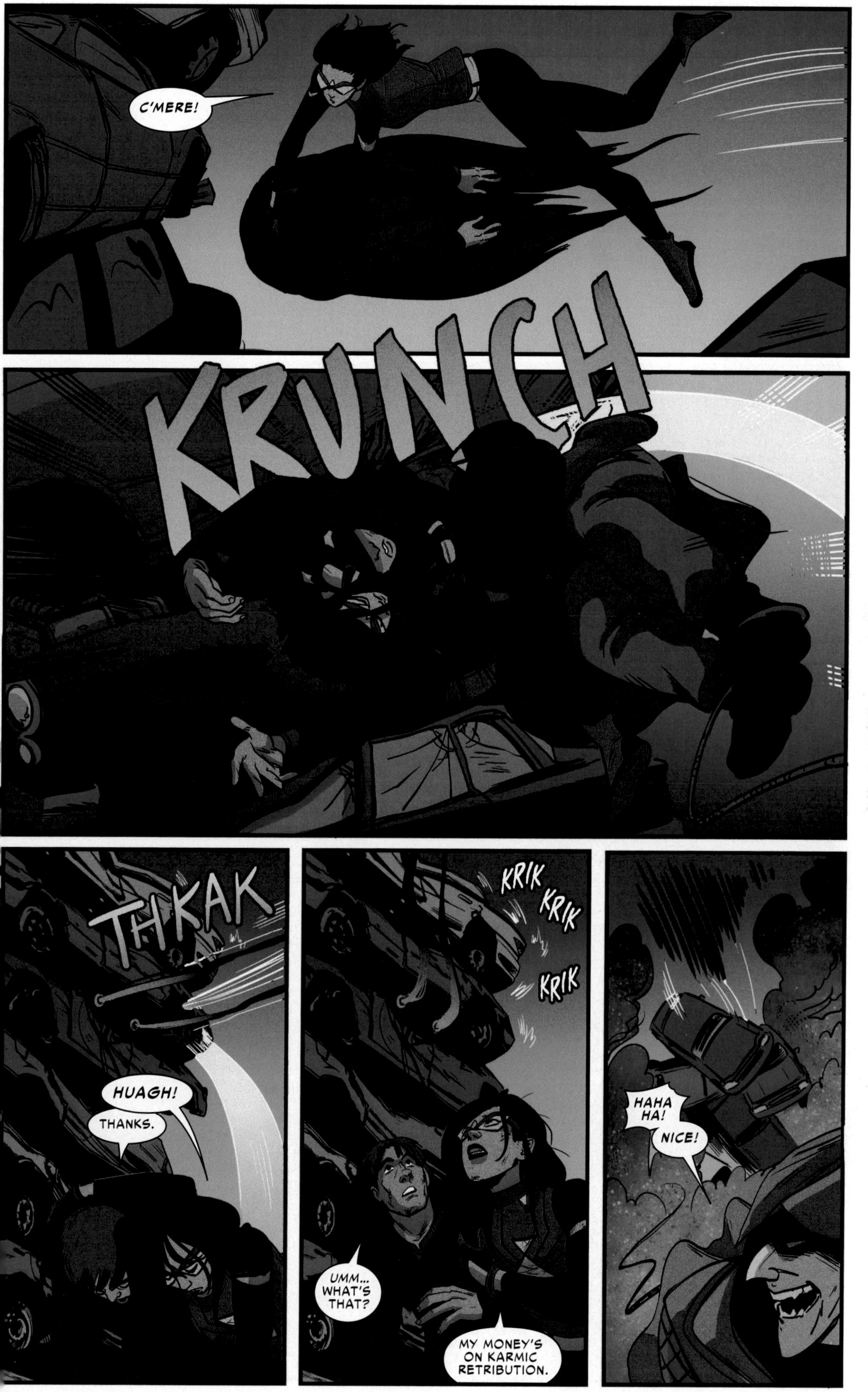
C'MERE!
KRUNCH
THKAK
HUAGH!
THANKS.
KRIK
KRIK
KRIK
UMM... WHAT'S THAT?
MY MONEY'S ON KARMIC RETRIBUTION.
HAHA HA!
NICE!

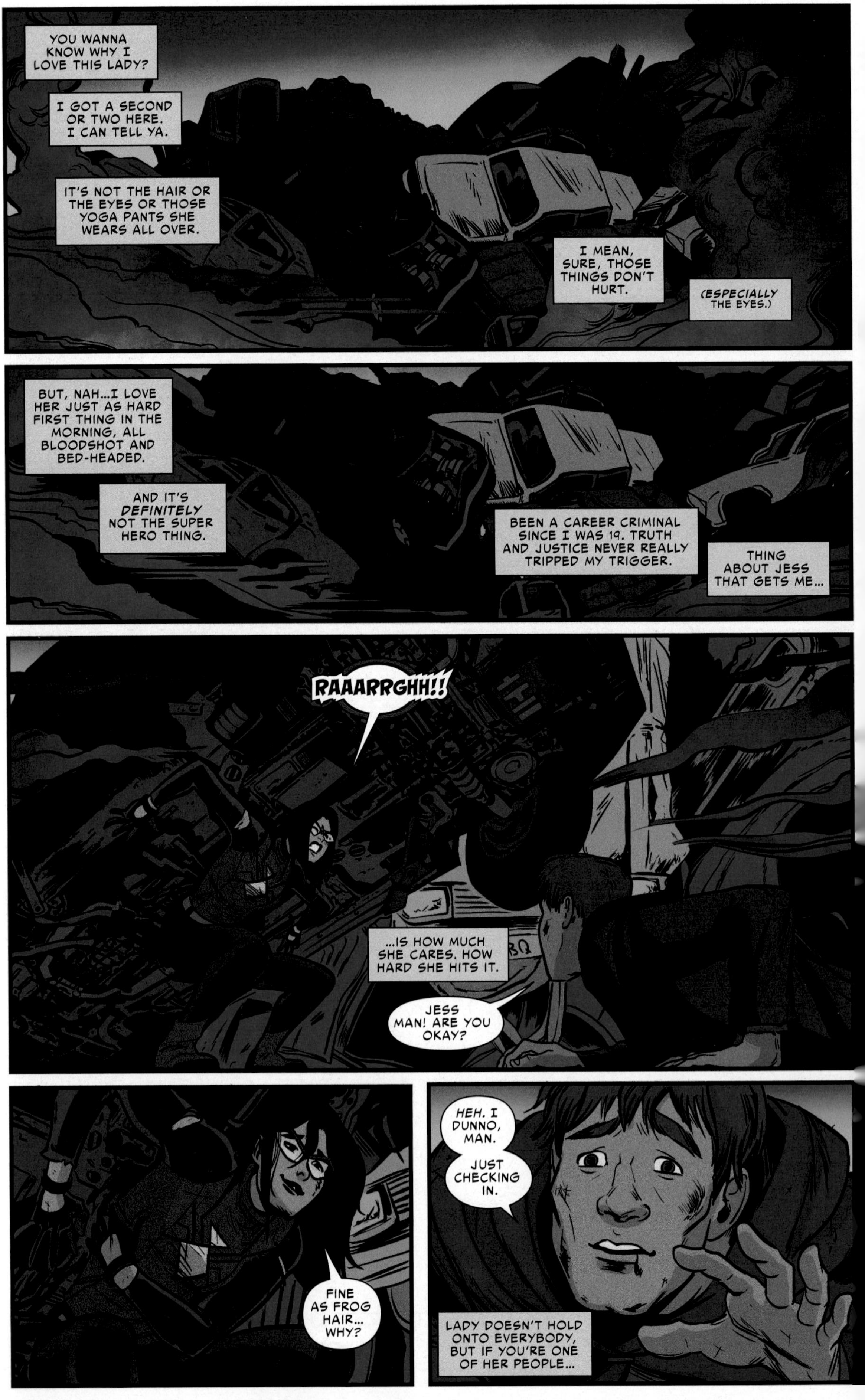
YOU WANNA KNOW WHY I LOVE THIS LADY?
I GOT A SECOND OR TWO HERE. I CAN TELL YA.
IT'S NOT THE HAIR OR THE EYES OR THOSE YOGA PANTS SHE WEARS ALL OVER.
I MEAN, SURE, THOSE THINGS DON'T HURT.
(ESPECIALLY THE EYES.)
BUT, NAH...I LOVE HER JUST AS HARD FIRST THING IN THE MORNING, ALL BLOODSHOT AND BED-HEADED.
AND IT'S *DEFINITELY* NOT THE SUPER HERO THING.
BEEN A CAREER CRIMINAL SINCE I WAS 19. TRUTH AND JUSTICE NEVER REALLY TRIPPED MY TRIGGER.
THING ABOUT JESS THAT GETS ME...
RAAARRGHH!!
...IS HOW MUCH SHE CARES. HOW HARD SHE HITS IT.
JESS MAN! ARE YOU OKAY?
FINE AS FROG HAIR... WHY?
HEH. I DUNNO, MAN.
JUST CHECKING IN.
LADY DOESN'T HOLD ONTO EVERYBODY, BUT IF YOU'RE ONE OF HER PEOPLE...

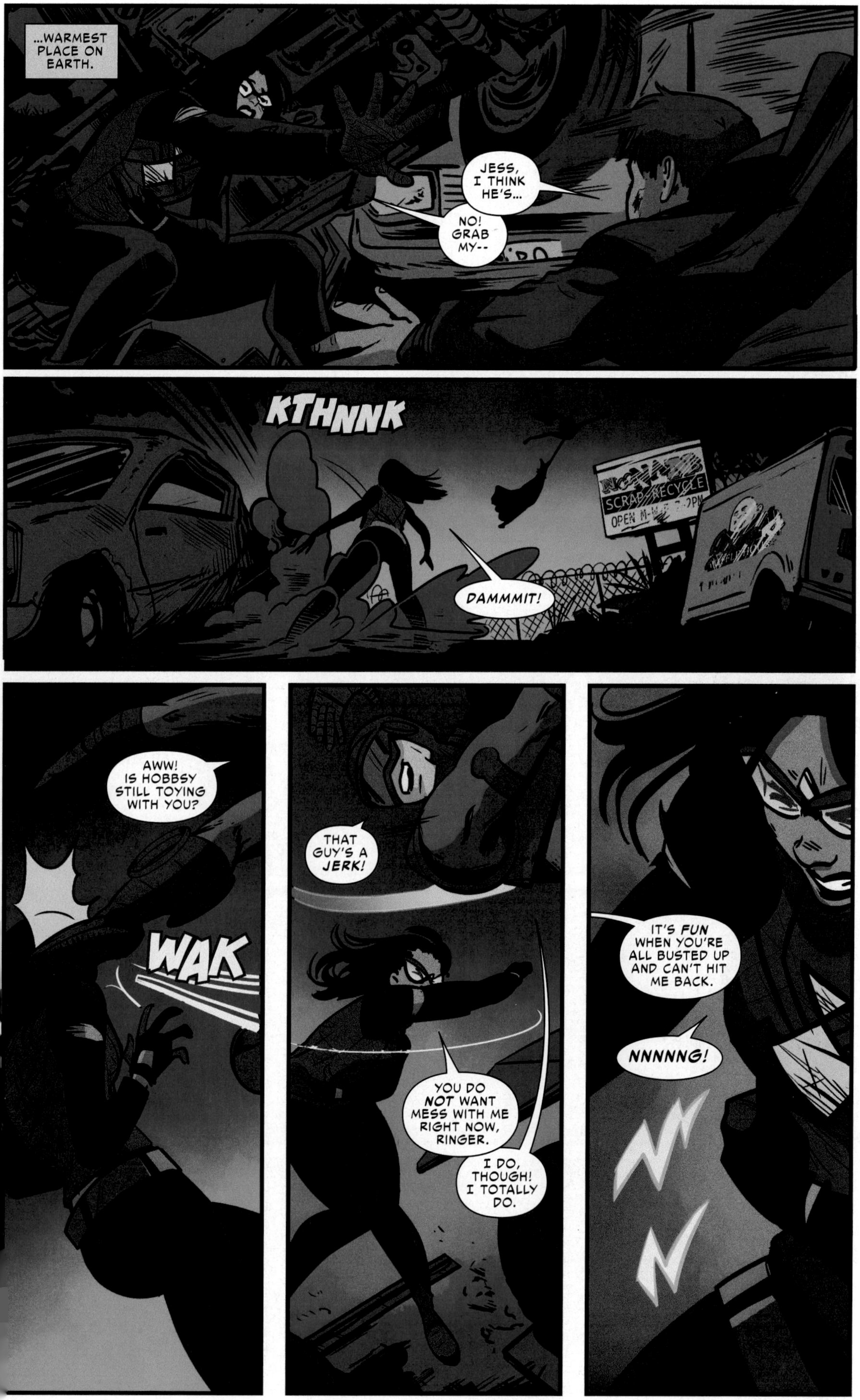
...WARMEST PLACE ON EARTH.
JESS, I THINK HE'S...
NO! GRAB MY--
KTHNNK
SCRAP RECYCLE
OPEN M-
DAMMMIT!
AWW! IS HOBBSY STILL TOYING WITH YOU?
WAK
THAT GUY'S A JERK!
YOU DO NOT WANT MESS WITH ME RIGHT NOW, RINGER.
I DO, THOUGH! I TOTALLY DO.
IT'S FUN WHEN YOU'RE ALL BUSTED UP AND CAN'T HIT ME BACK.
NNNNNG!

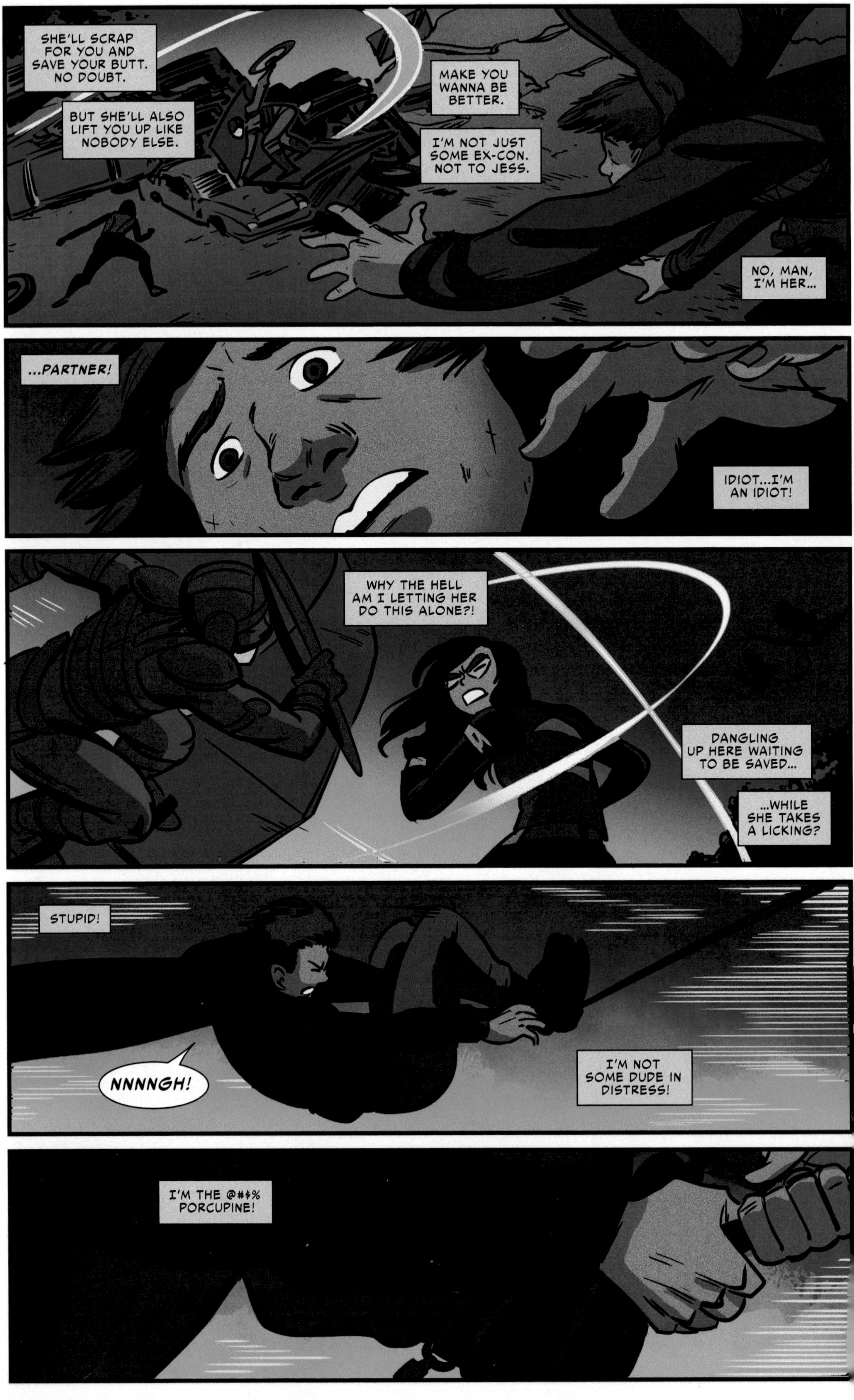
SHE'LL SCRAP FOR YOU AND SAVE YOUR BUTT. NO DOUBT.
BUT SHE'LL ALSO LIFT YOU UP LIKE NOBODY ELSE.
MAKE YOU WANNA BE BETTER.
I'M NOT JUST SOME EX-CON. NOT TO JESS.
NO, MAN, I'M HER...
...PARTNER!
IDIOT...I'M AN IDIOT!
WHY THE HELL AM I LETTING HER DO THIS ALONE?!
DANGLING UP HERE WAITING TO BE SAVED...
...WHILE SHE TAKES A LICKING?
STUPID!
NNNNGH!
I'M NOT SOME DUDE IN DISTRESS!
I'M THE @#$% PORCUPINE!

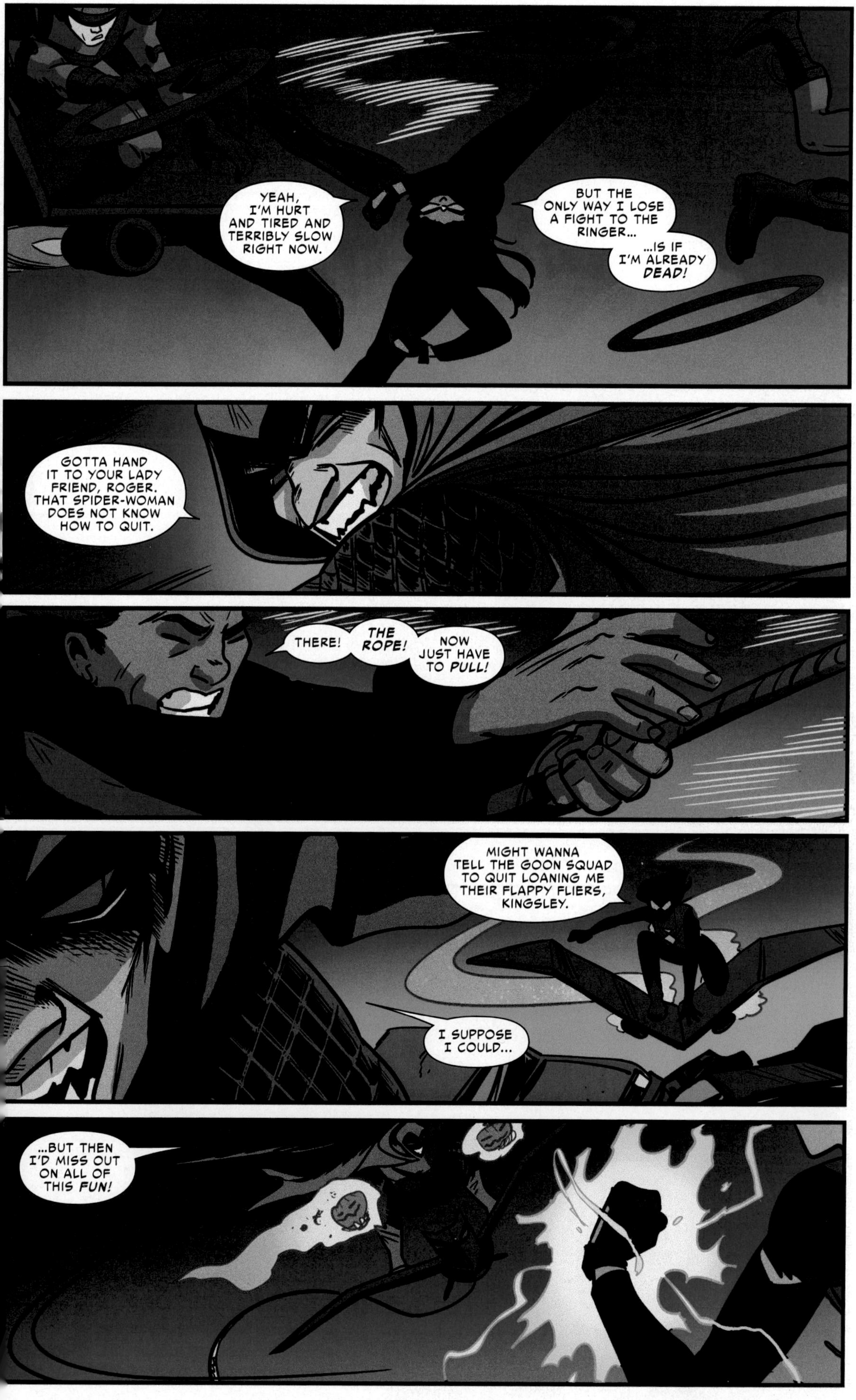
YEAH, I'M HURT AND TIRED AND TERRIBLY SLOW RIGHT NOW.
BUT THE ONLY WAY I LOSE A FIGHT TO THE RINGER...
...IS IF I'M ALREADY DEAD!
GOTTA HAND IT TO YOUR LADY FRIEND, ROGER. THAT SPIDER-WOMAN DOES NOT KNOW HOW TO QUIT.
THERE!
THE ROPE!
NOW JUST HAVE TO PULL!
MIGHT WANNA TELL THE GOON SQUAD TO QUIT LOANING ME THEIR FLAPPY FLIERS, KINGSLEY.
I SUPPOSE I COULD...
...BUT THEN I'D MISS OUT ON ALL OF THIS FUN!

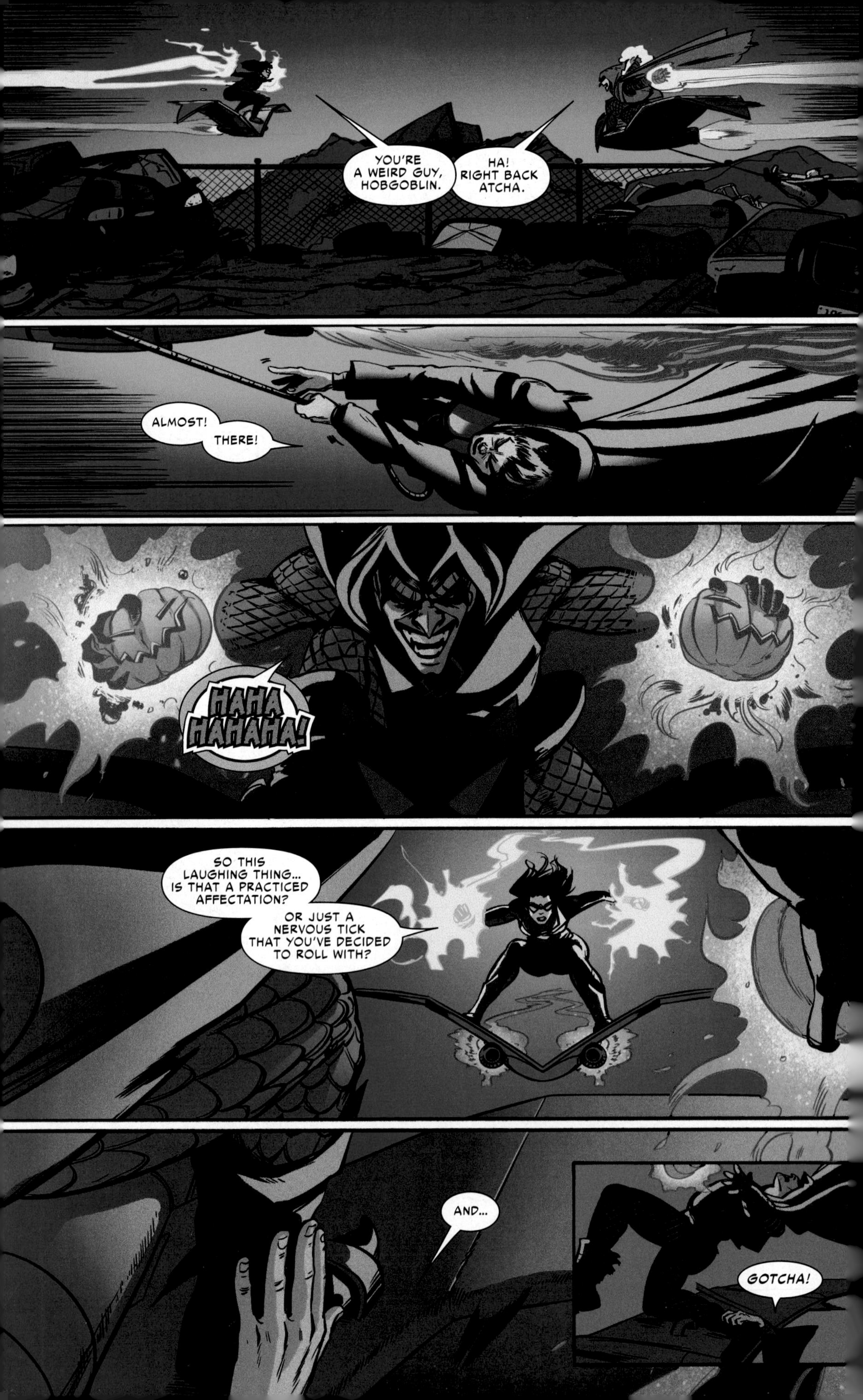
YOU'RE A WEIRD GUY, HOBGOBLIN.
HA! RIGHT BACK ATCHA.
ALMOST!
THERE!
HAHA HAHAHA!
SO THIS LAUGHING THING... IS THAT A PRACTICED AFFECTATION?
OR JUST A NERVOUS TICK THAT YOU'VE DECIDED TO ROLL WITH?
AND...
GOTCHA!

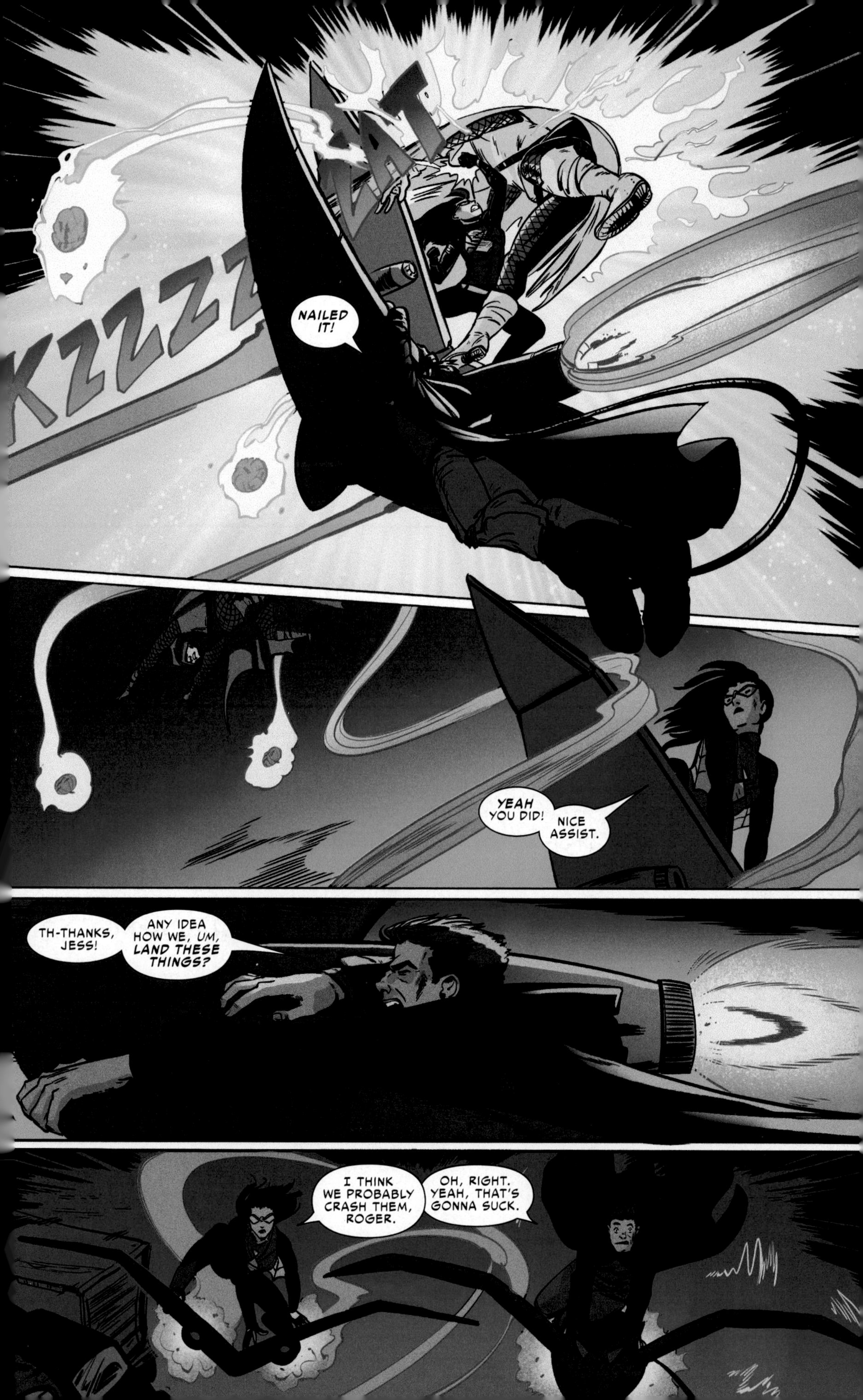
ZAT
KZZZZ
NAILED IT!
YEAH YOU DID!
NICE ASSIST.
TH-THANKS, JESS!
ANY IDEA HOW WE, UM, LAND THESE THINGS?
I THINK WE PROBABLY CRASH THEM, ROGER.
OH, RIGHT. YEAH, THAT'S GONNA SUCK.

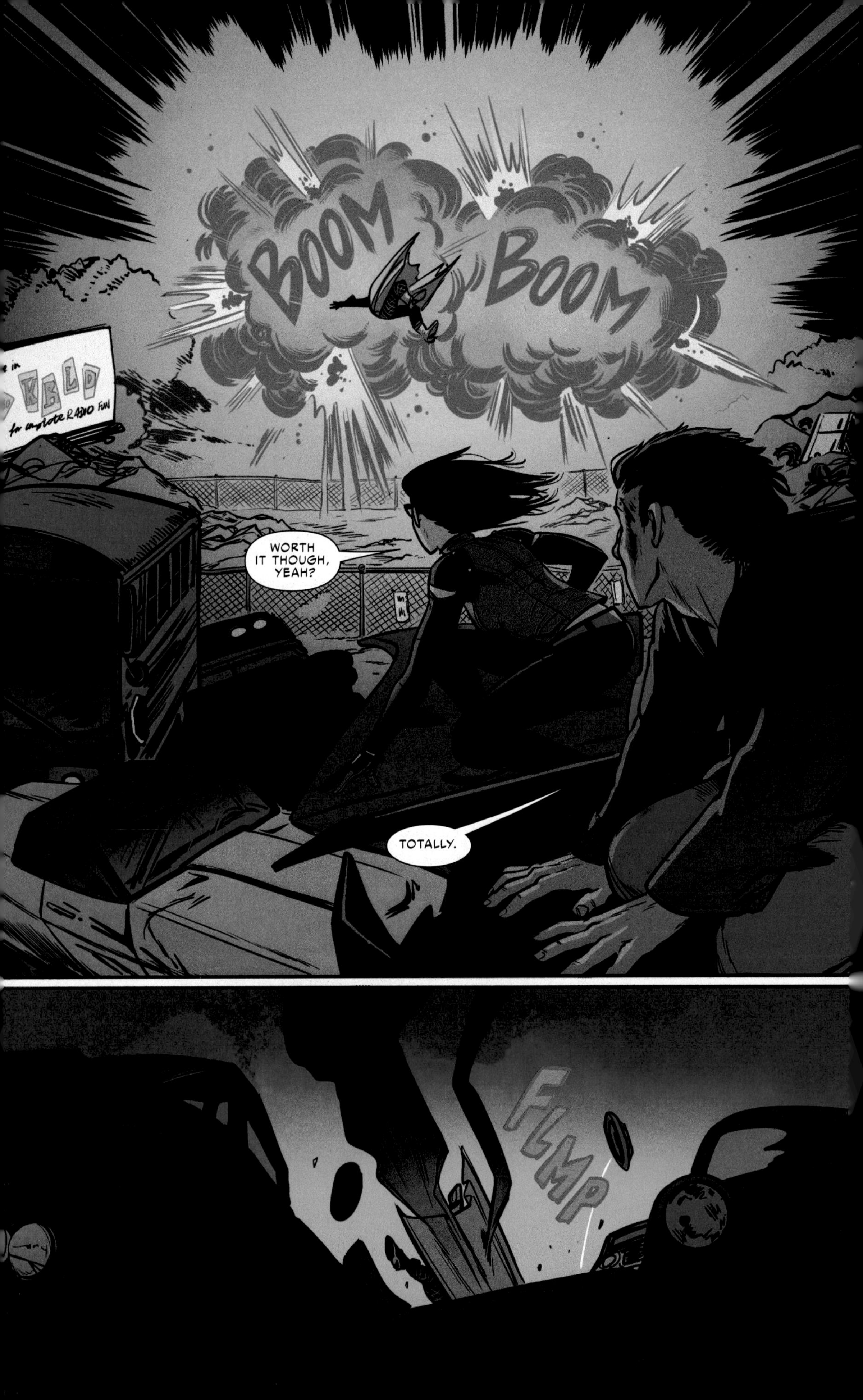
BOOM
BOOM
KBLD
WORTH IT THOUGH, YEAH?
TOTALLY.
FLMP.

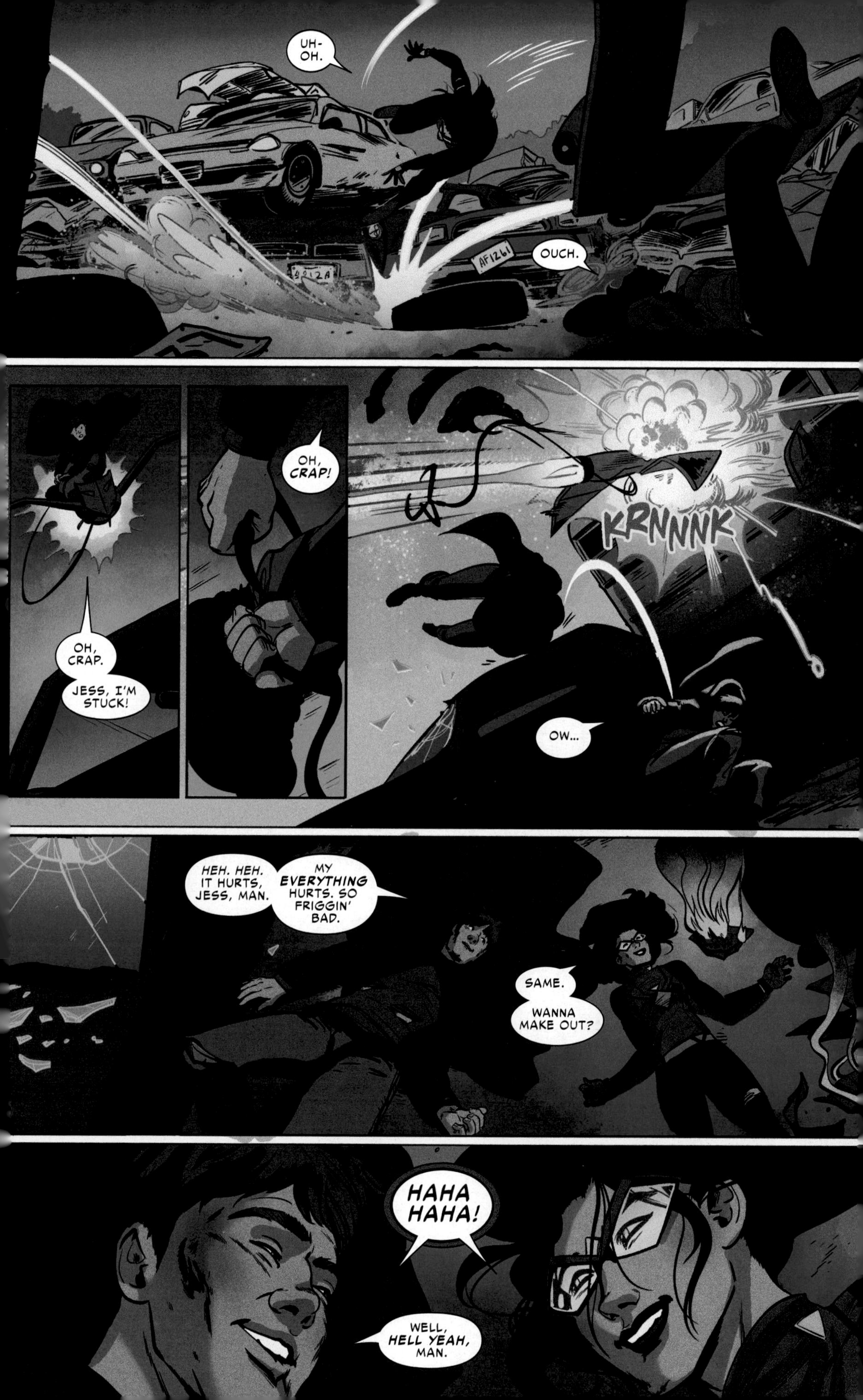
UH-OH.
OUCH.
AF1261
OH, CRAP.
JESS, I'M STUCK!
OH, CRAP!
KRNNNK
OW...
HEH. HEH. IT HURTS, JESS, MAN.
MY EVERYTHING HURTS. SO FRIGGIN' BAD.
SAME.
WANNA MAKE OUT?
HAHA HAHA!
WELL, HELL YEAH, MAN.

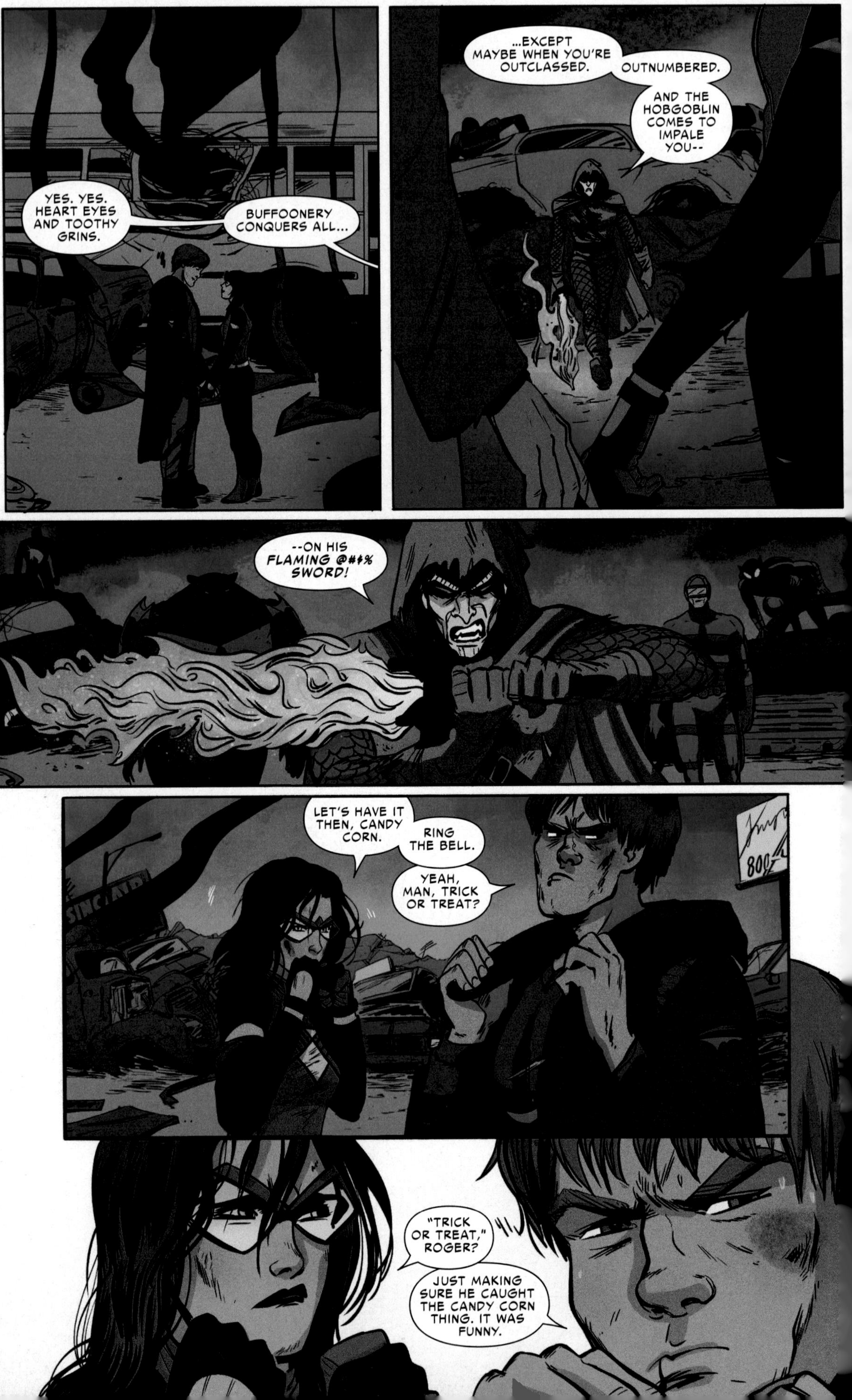
YES. YES. HEART EYES AND TOOTHY GRINS.
BUFFOONERY CONQUERS ALL...
...EXCEPT MAYBE WHEN YOU'RE OUTCLASSED.
OUTNUMBERED.
AND THE HOBGOBLIN COMES TO IMPALE YOU--
--ON HIS FLAMING @#$% SWORD!
LET'S HAVE IT THEN, CANDY CORN.
RING THE BELL.
YEAH, MAN, TRICK OR TREAT?
"TRICK OR TREAT," ROGER?
JUST MAKING SURE HE CAUGHT THE CANDY CORN THING. IT WAS FUNNY.

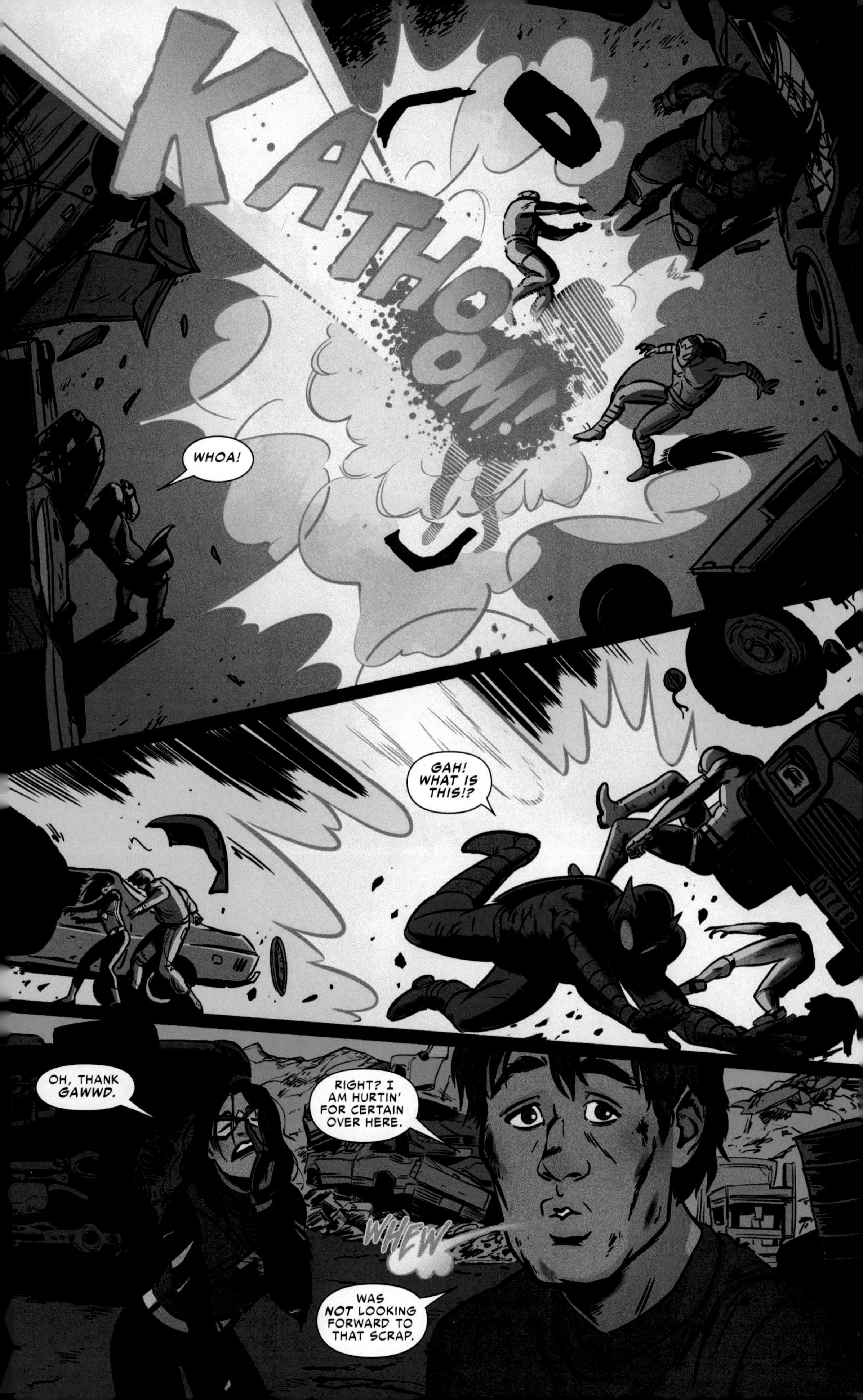
KATHOOM!
WHOA!
GAH! WHAT IS THIS!?
OH, THANK GAWWD.
RIGHT? I AM HURTIN' FOR CERTAIN OVER HERE.
WHEW
WAS NOT LOOKING FORWARD TO THAT SCRAP.

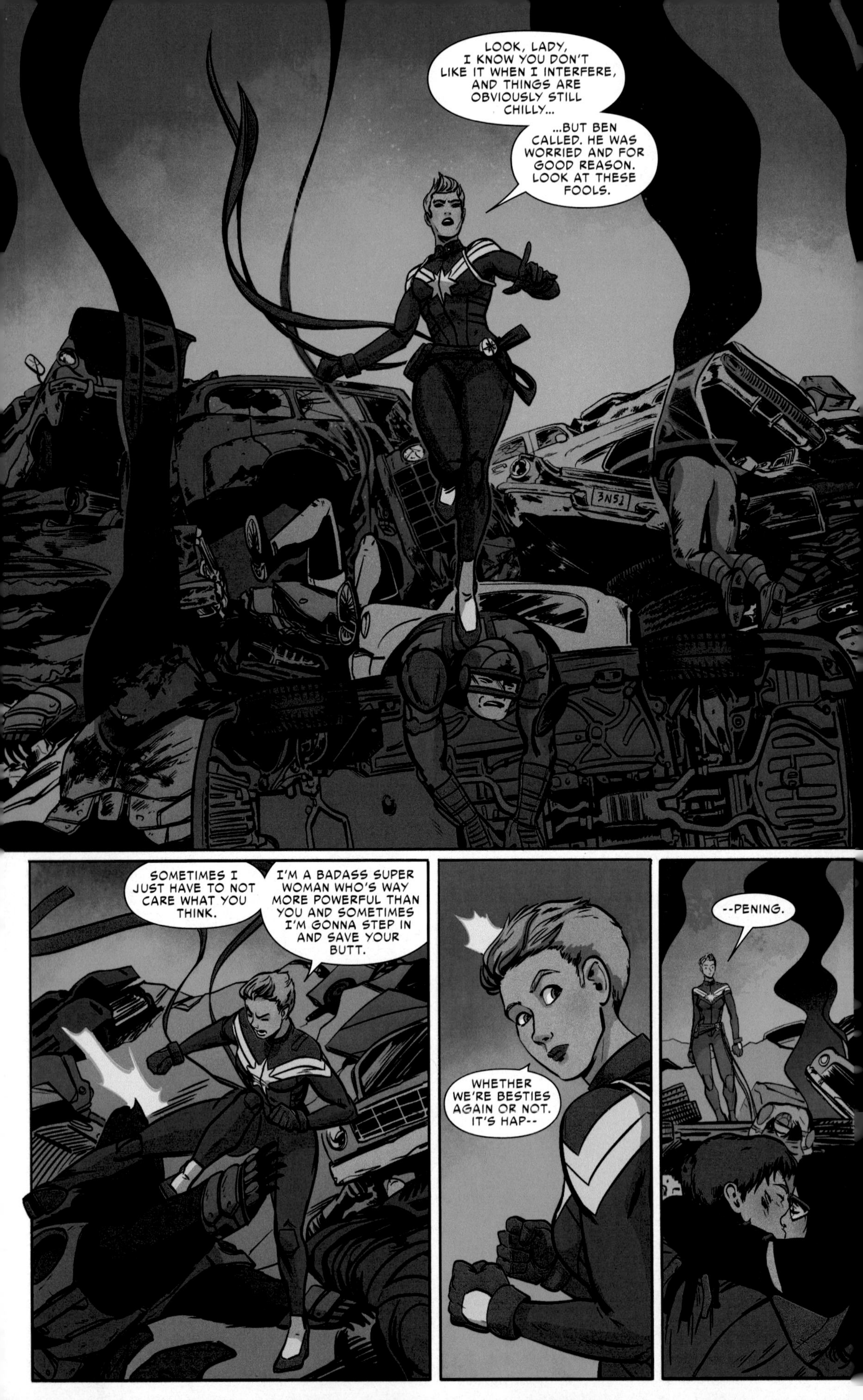
LOOK, LADY, I KNOW YOU DON'T LIKE IT WHEN I INTERFERE, AND THINGS ARE OBVIOUSLY STILL CHILLY...
...BUT BEN CALLED. HE WAS WORRIED AND FOR GOOD REASON. LOOK AT THESE FOOLS.
SOMETIMES I JUST HAVE TO NOT CARE WHAT YOU THINK.
I'M A BADASS SUPER WOMAN WHO'S WAY MORE POWERFUL THAN YOU AND SOMETIMES I'M GONNA STEP IN AND SAVE YOUR BUTT.
WHETHER WE'RE BESTIES AGAIN OR NOT. IT'S HAP--
--PENING.

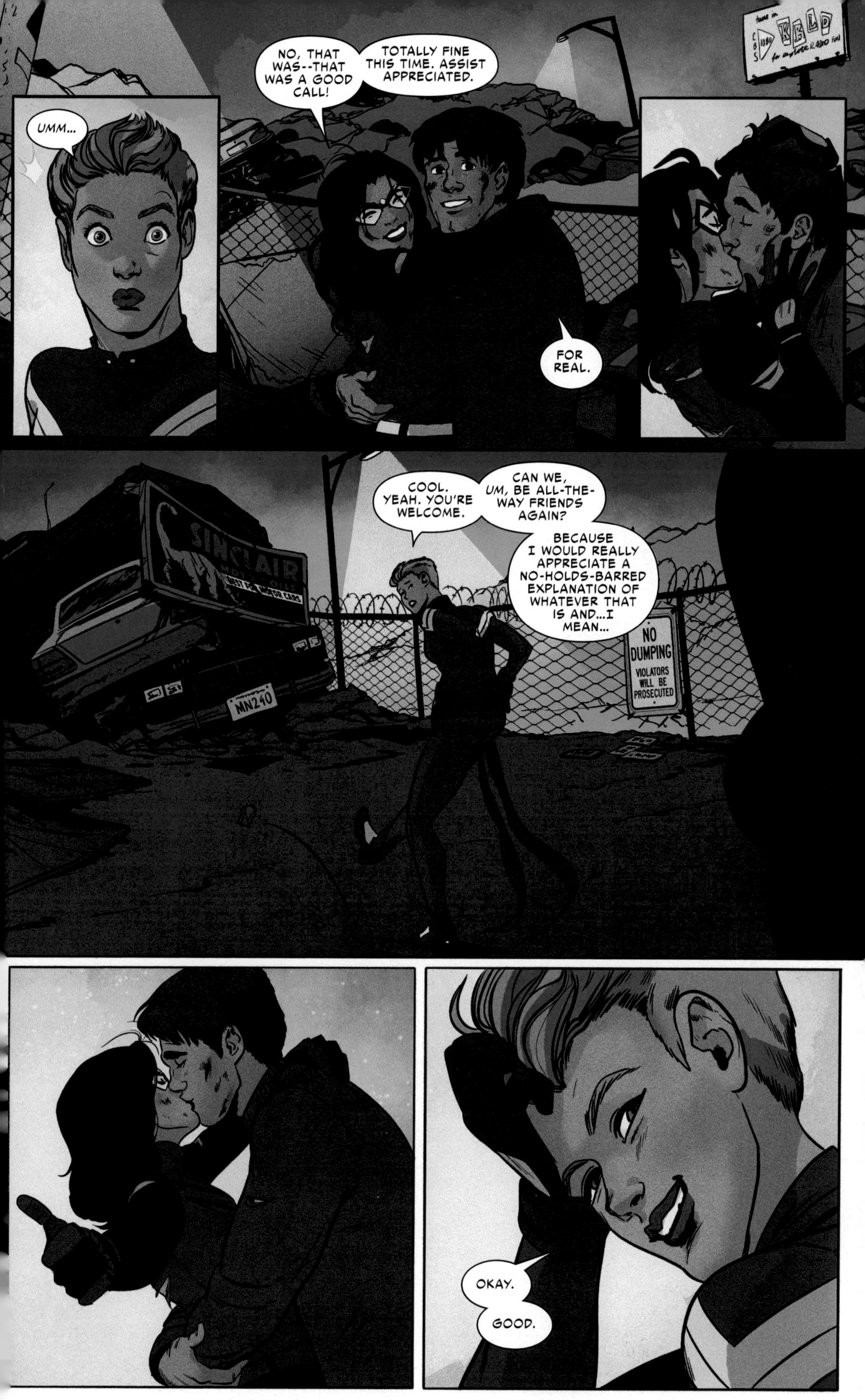
UMM...
NO, THAT WAS--THAT WAS A GOOD CALL!
TOTALLY FINE THIS TIME. ASSIST APPRECIATED.
FOR REAL.
SINCLAIR
MN240
COOL. YEAH. YOU'RE WELCOME.
CAN WE, UM, BE ALL-THE-WAY FRIENDS AGAIN?
BECAUSE I WOULD REALLY APPRECIATE A NO-HOLDS-BARRED EXPLANATION OF WHATEVER THAT IS AND...I MEAN...
NO DUMPING
VIOLATORS WILL BE PROSECUTED
OKAY.
GOOD.

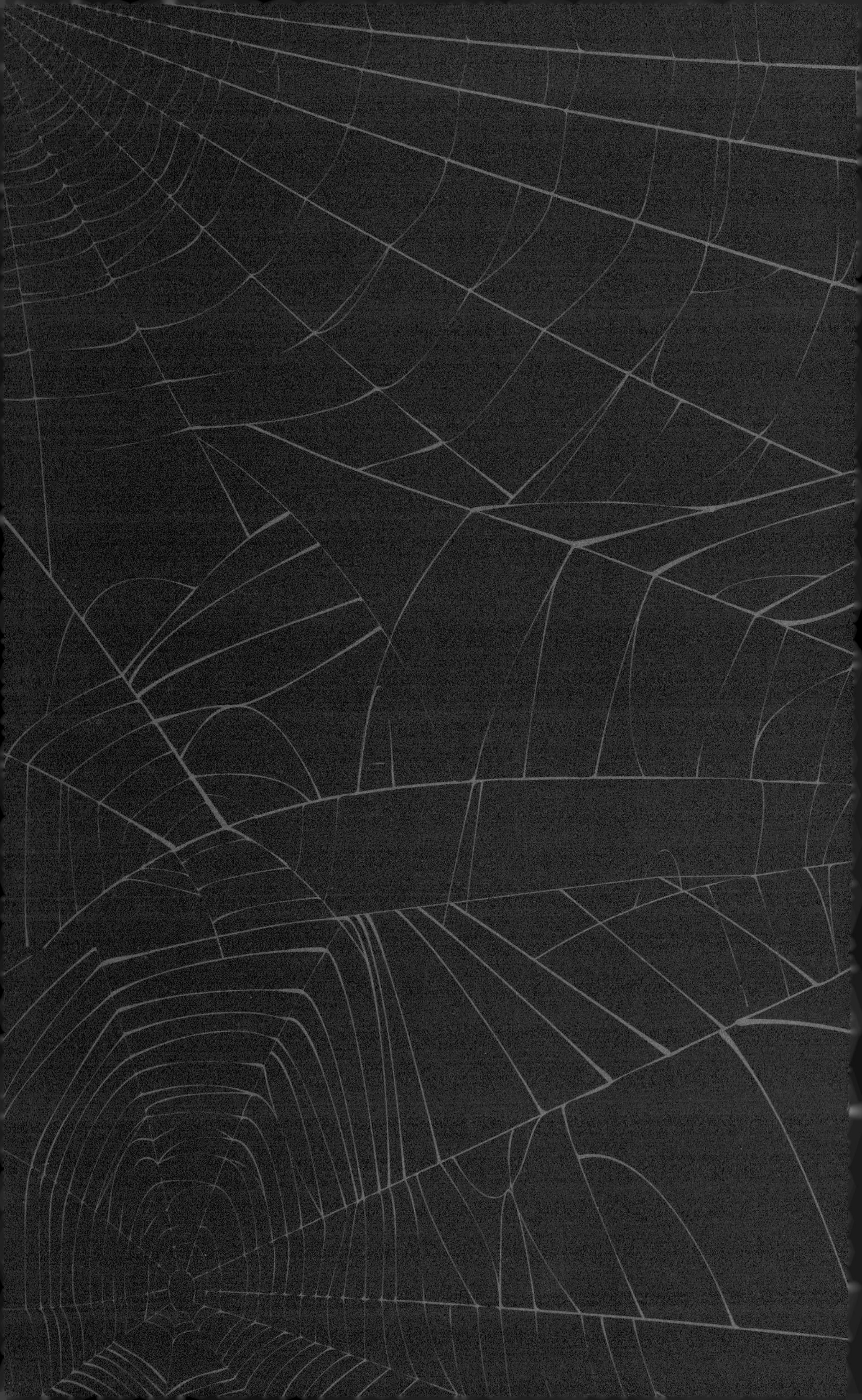

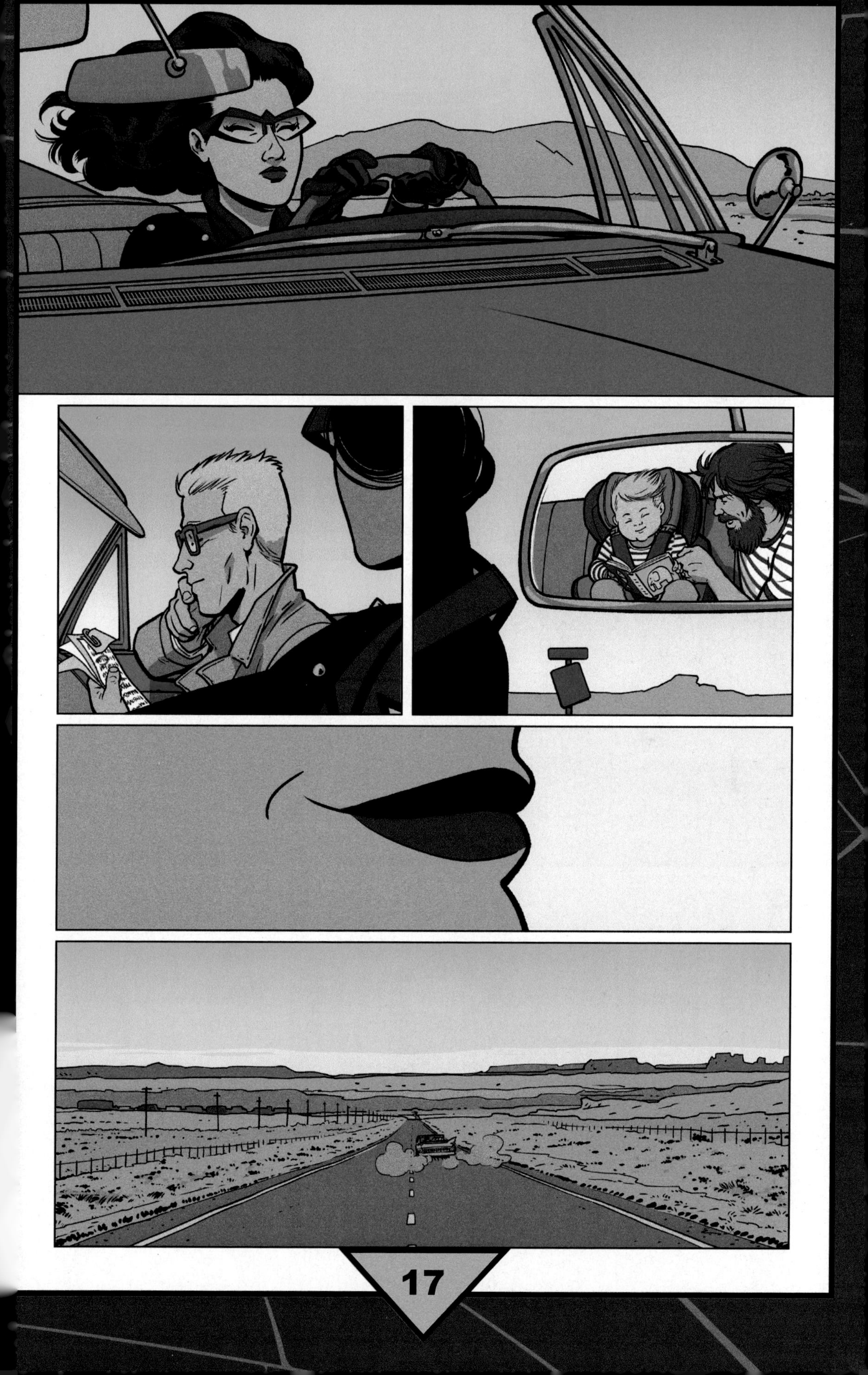

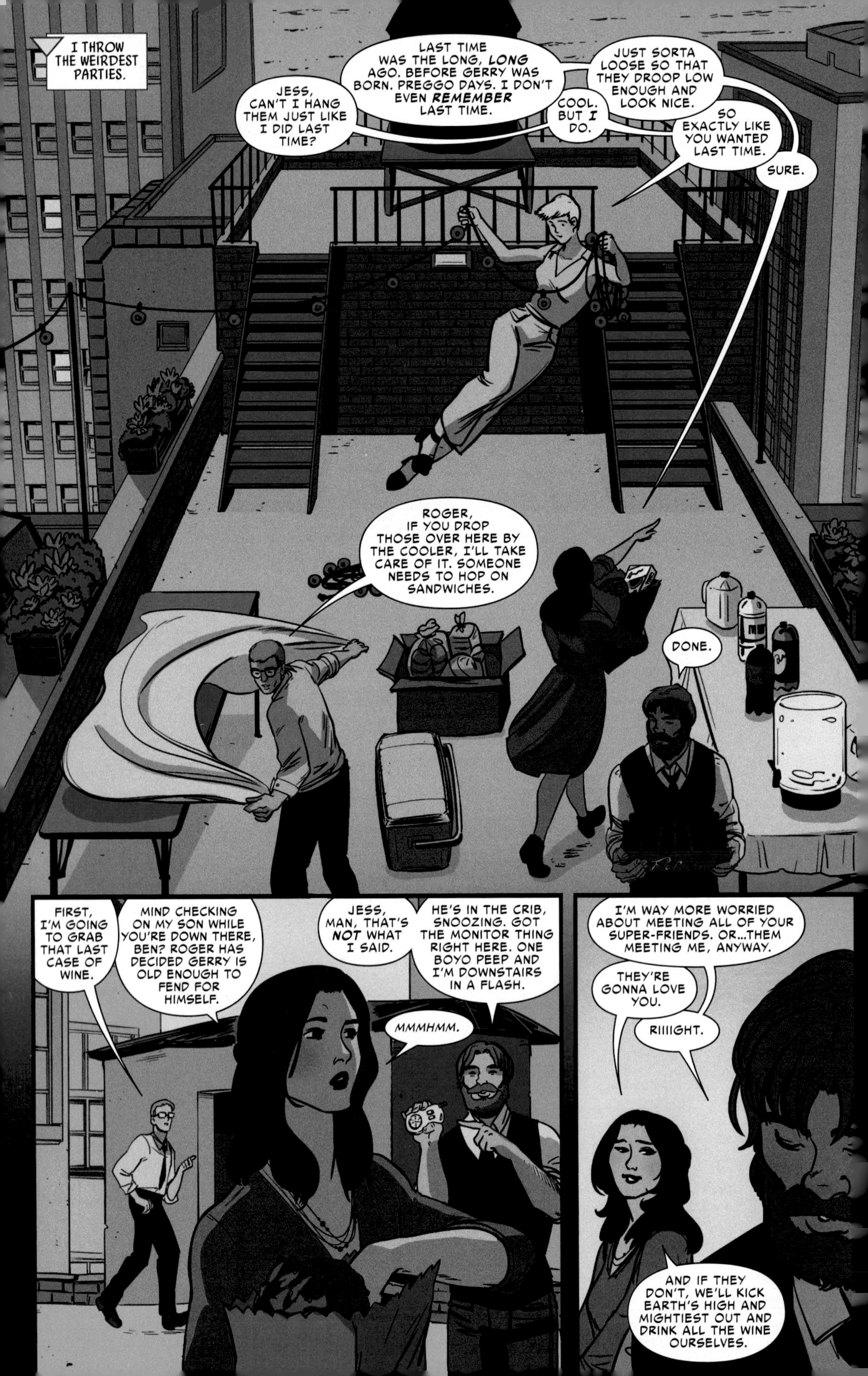
I THROW THE WEIRDEST PARTIES.
JESS, CAN'T I HANG THEM JUST LIKE I DID LAST TIME?
LAST TIME WAS THE LONG, *LONG* AGO. BEFORE GERRY WAS BORN. PREGGO DAYS. I DON'T EVEN *REMEMBER* LAST TIME.
JUST SORTA LOOSE SO THAT THEY DROOP LOW ENOUGH AND LOOK NICE.
COOL. BUT *I* DO.
SO EXACTLY LIKE YOU WANTED LAST TIME.
SURE.
ROGER, IF YOU DROP THOSE OVER HERE BY THE COOLER, I'LL TAKE CARE OF IT. SOMEONE NEEDS TO HOP ON SANDWICHES.
DONE.
FIRST, I'M GOING TO GRAB THAT LAST CASE OF WINE.
MIND CHECKING ON MY SON WHILE YOU'RE DOWN THERE, BEN? ROGER HAS DECIDED GERRY IS OLD ENOUGH TO FEND FOR HIMSELF.
JESS, MAN, THAT'S *NOT* WHAT I SAID.
HE'S IN THE CRIB, SNOOZING. GOT THE MONITOR THING RIGHT HERE. ONE BOYO PEEP AND I'M DOWNSTAIRS IN A FLASH.
MMMHMM.
I'M WAY MORE WORRIED ABOUT MEETING ALL OF YOUR SUPER-FRIENDS. OR...THEM MEETING ME, ANYWAY.
THEY'RE GONNA LOVE YOU.
RIIIIGHT.
AND IF THEY DON'T, WE'LL KICK EARTH'S HIGH AND MIGHTIEST OUT AND DRINK ALL THE WINE OURSELVES.

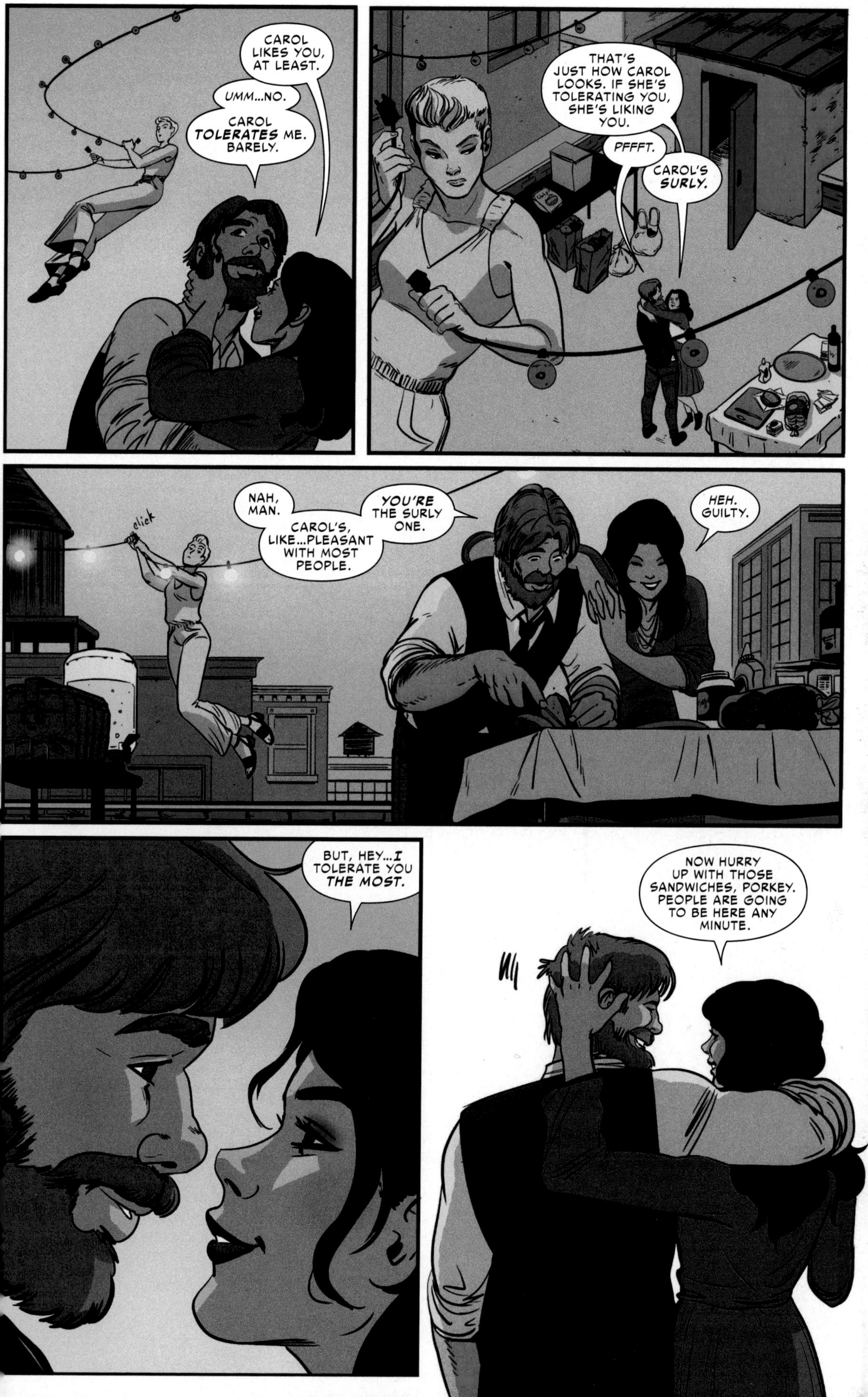
CAROL LIKES YOU, AT LEAST.
UMM...NO.
CAROL TOLERATES ME. BARELY.
THAT'S JUST HOW CAROL LOOKS. IF SHE'S TOLERATING YOU, SHE'S LIKING YOU.
PFFFT.
CAROL'S SURLY.
click
NAH, MAN.
CAROL'S, LIKE...PLEASANT WITH MOST PEOPLE.
YOU'RE THE SURLY ONE.
HEH. GUILTY.
BUT, HEY...I TOLERATE YOU THE MOST.
NOW HURRY UP WITH THOSE SANDWICHES, PORKEY. PEOPLE ARE GOING TO BE HERE ANY MINUTE.

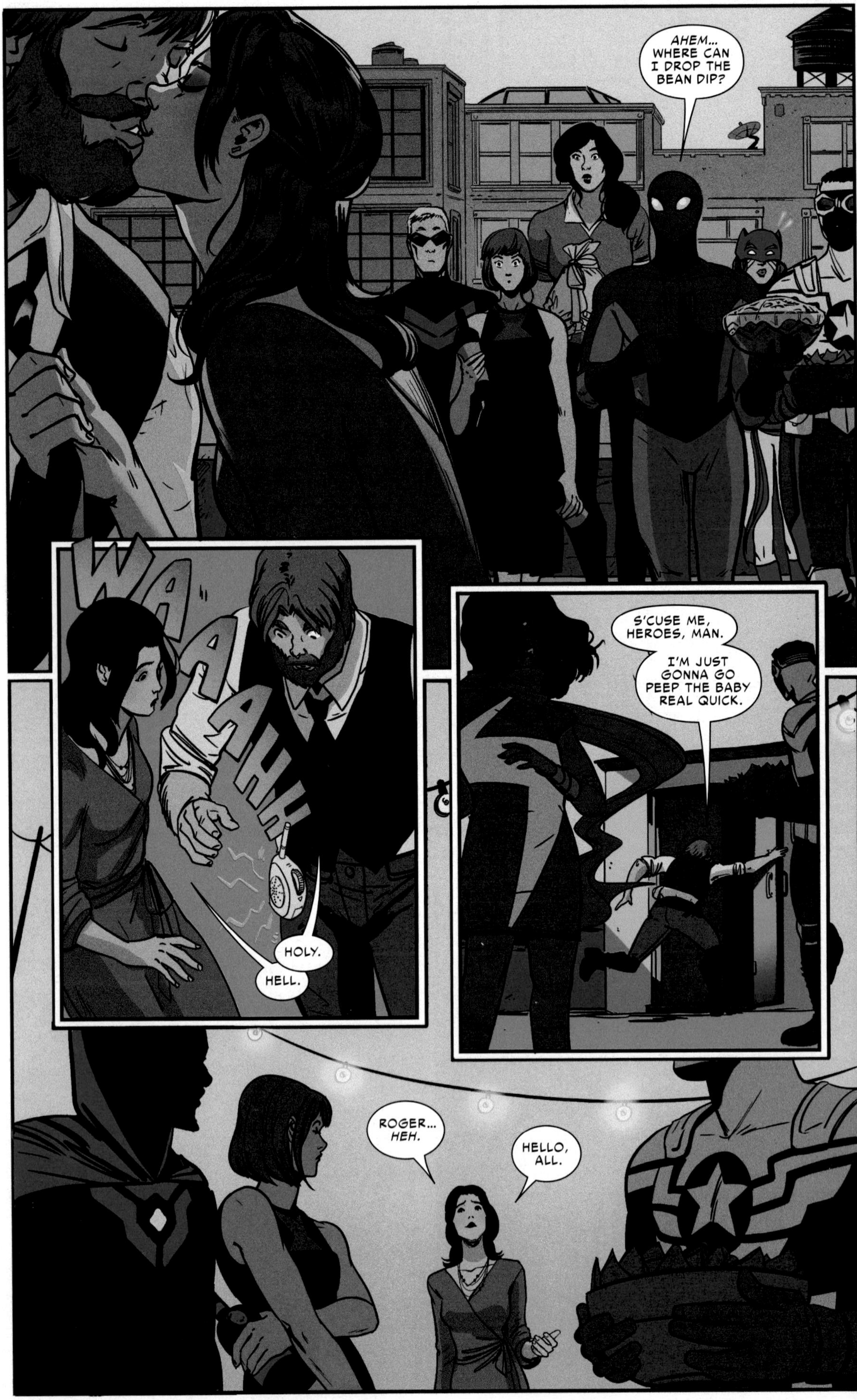
AHEM... WHERE CAN I DROP THE BEAN DIP?
WAAAAHH
HOLY.
HELL.
S'CUSE ME, HEROES, MAN.
I'M JUST GONNA GO PEEP THE BABY REAL QUICK.
ROGER... HEH.
HELLO, ALL.

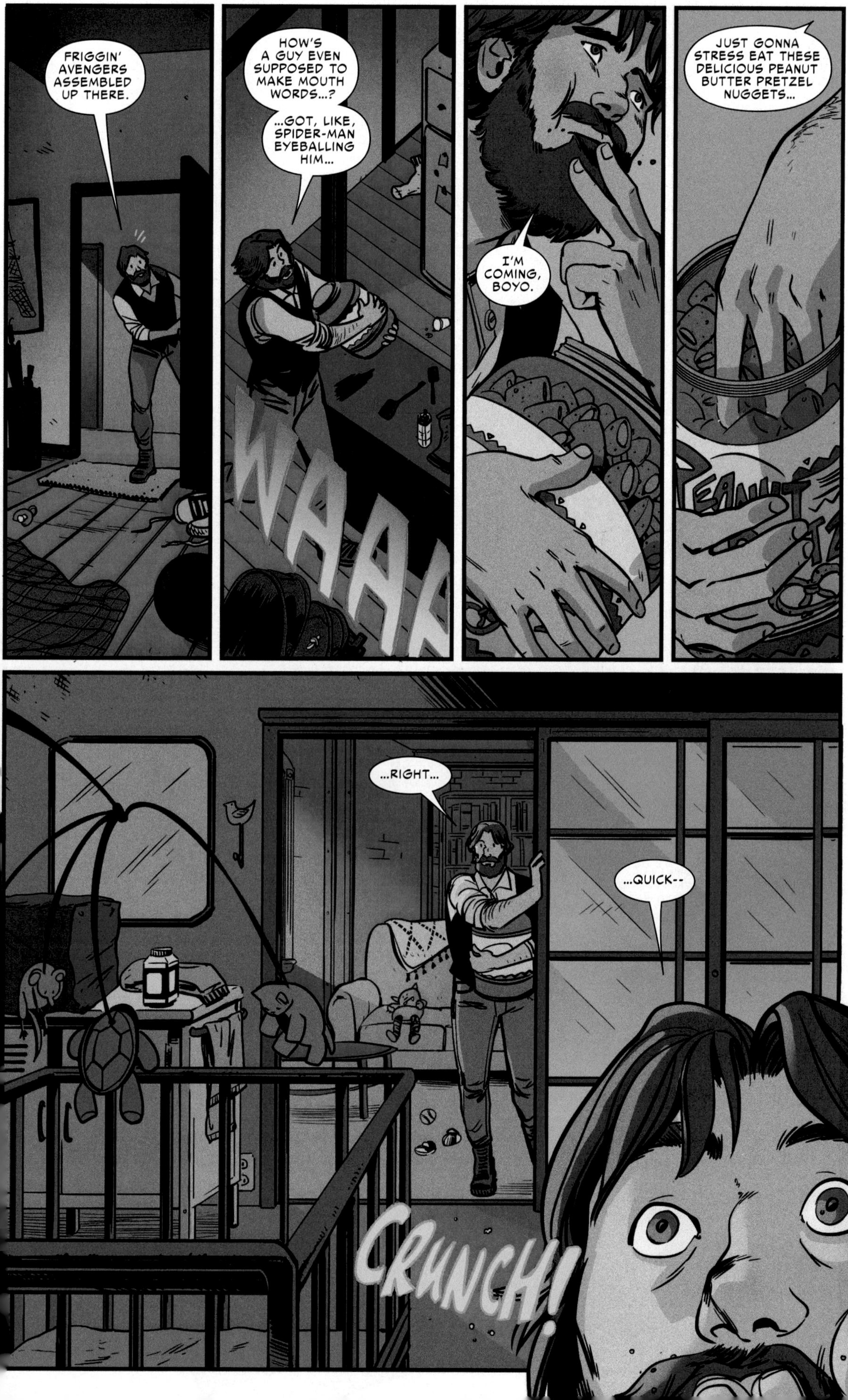
FRIGGIN' AVENGERS ASSEMBLED UP THERE.
HOW'S A GUY EVEN SUPPOSED TO MAKE MOUTH WORDS...?
...GOT, LIKE, SPIDER-MAN EYEBALLING HIM...
WAAA
I'M COMING, BOYO.
JUST GONNA STRESS EAT THESE DELICIOUS PEANUT BUTTER PRETZEL NUGGETS...
...RIGHT...
...QUICK--
CRUNCH!

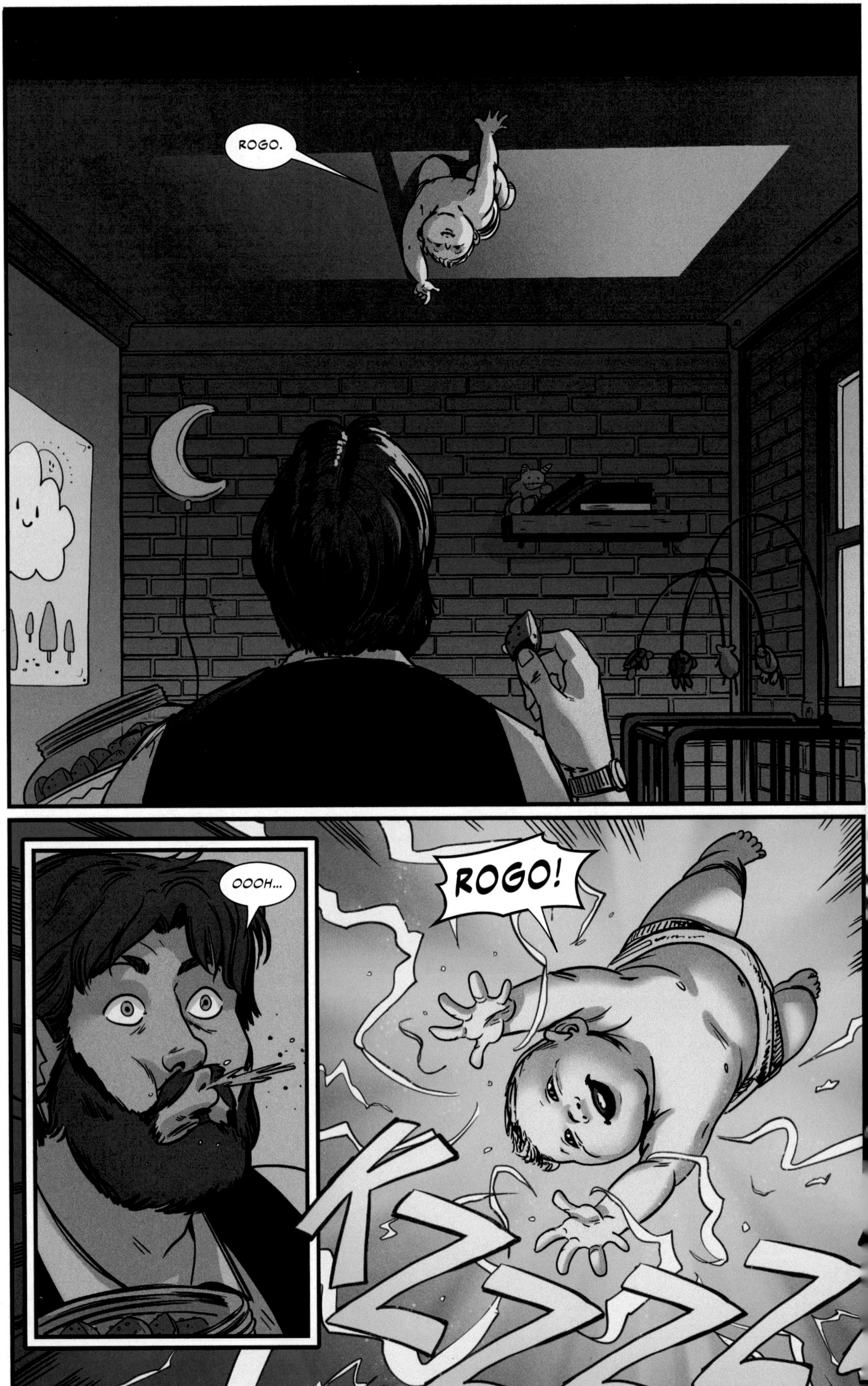
ROGO.
OOOH...
ROGO!
KZZZZ

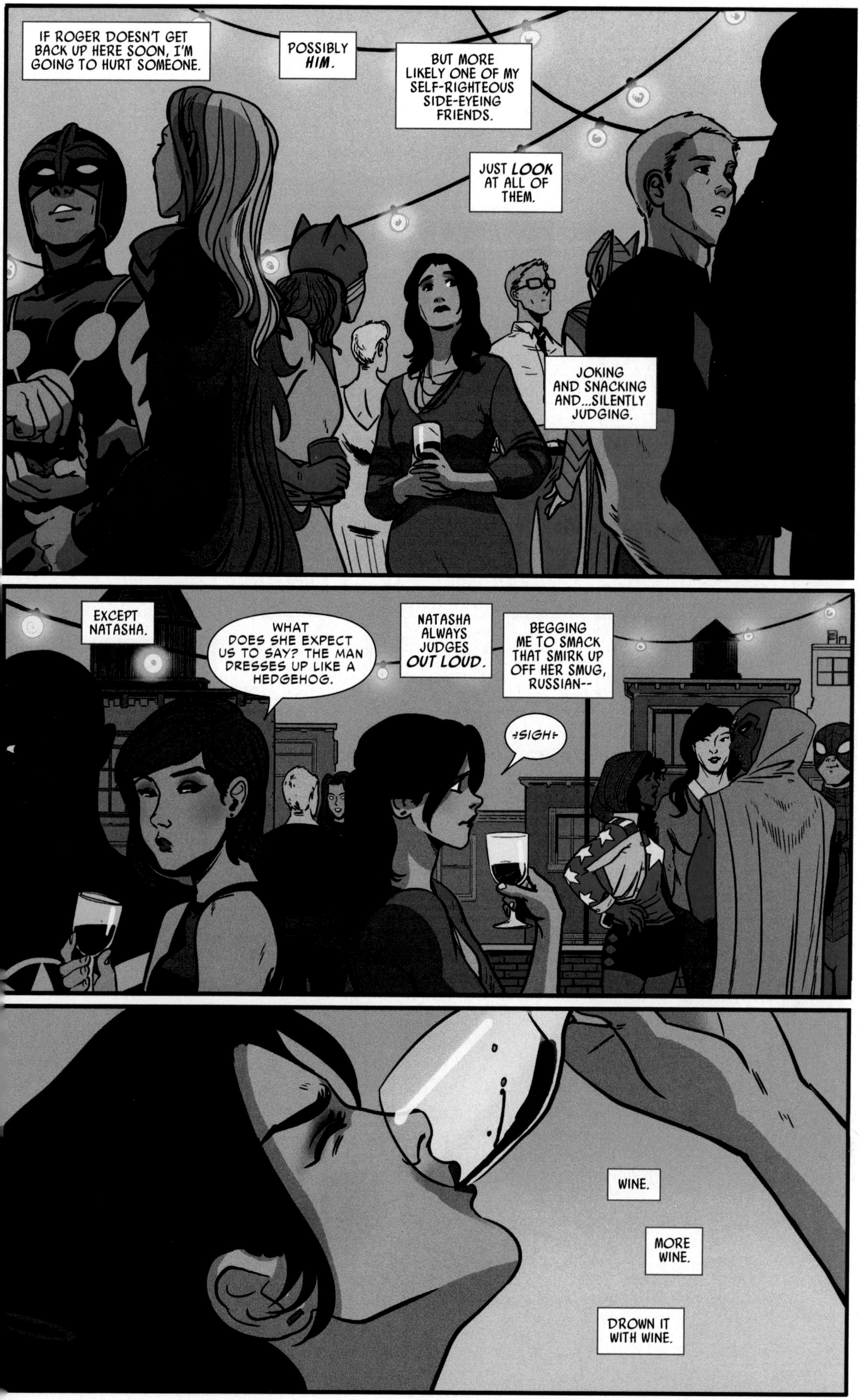
IF ROGER DOESN'T GET BACK UP HERE SOON, I'M GOING TO HURT SOMEONE.
POSSIBLY *HIM.*
BUT MORE LIKELY ONE OF MY SELF-RIGHTEOUS SIDE-EYEING FRIENDS.
JUST *LOOK* AT ALL OF THEM.
JOKING AND SNACKING AND...SILENTLY JUDGING.
EXCEPT NATASHA.
WHAT DOES SHE EXPECT US TO SAY? THE MAN DRESSES UP LIKE A HEDGEHOG.
NATASHA ALWAYS JUDGES *OUT LOUD.*
BEGGING ME TO SMACK THAT SMIRK UP OFF HER SMUG, RUSSIAN--
SIGH
WINE.
MORE WINE.
DROWN IT WITH WINE.

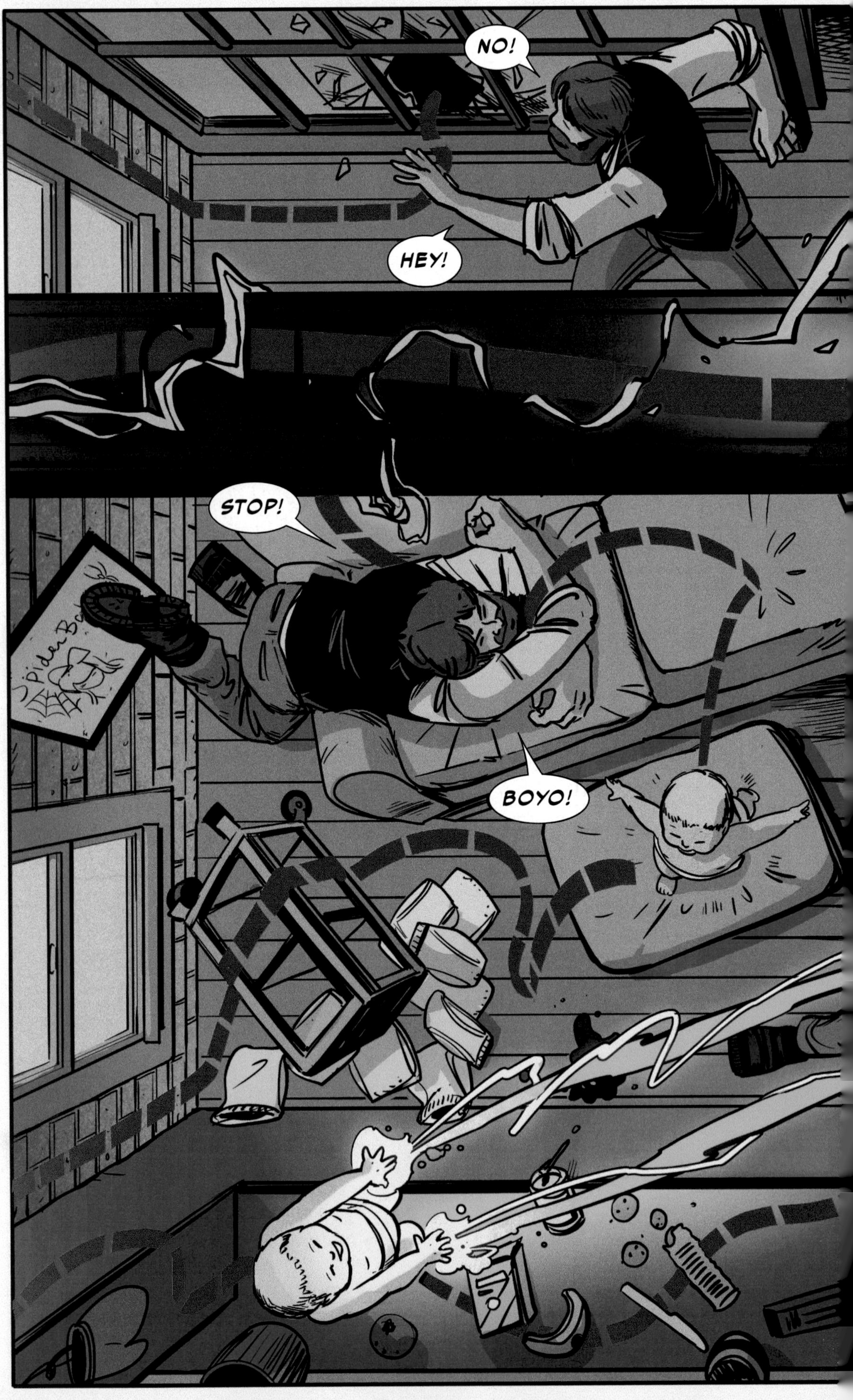
NO!
HEY!
STOP!
BOYO!

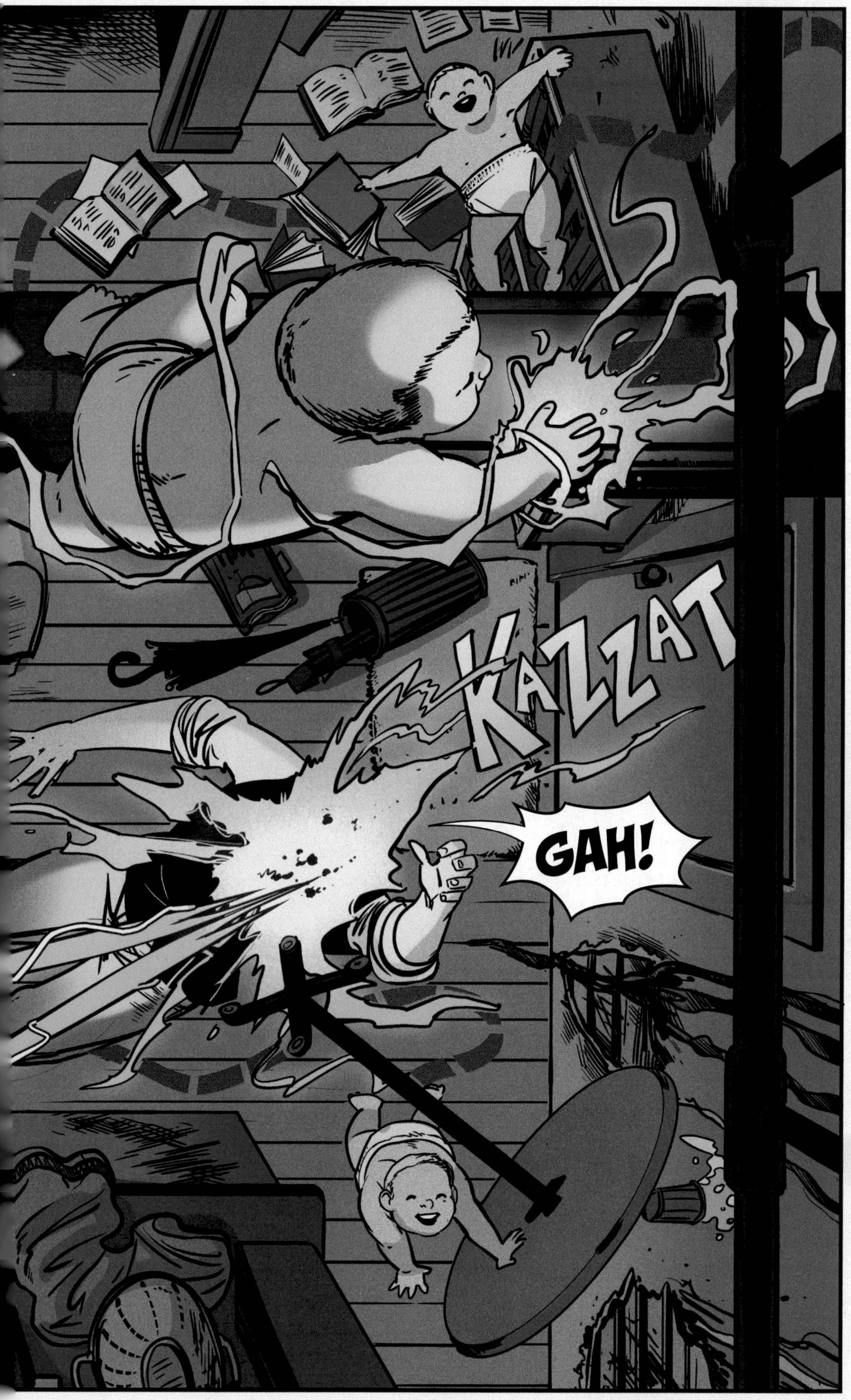
KAZZAT
GAH!

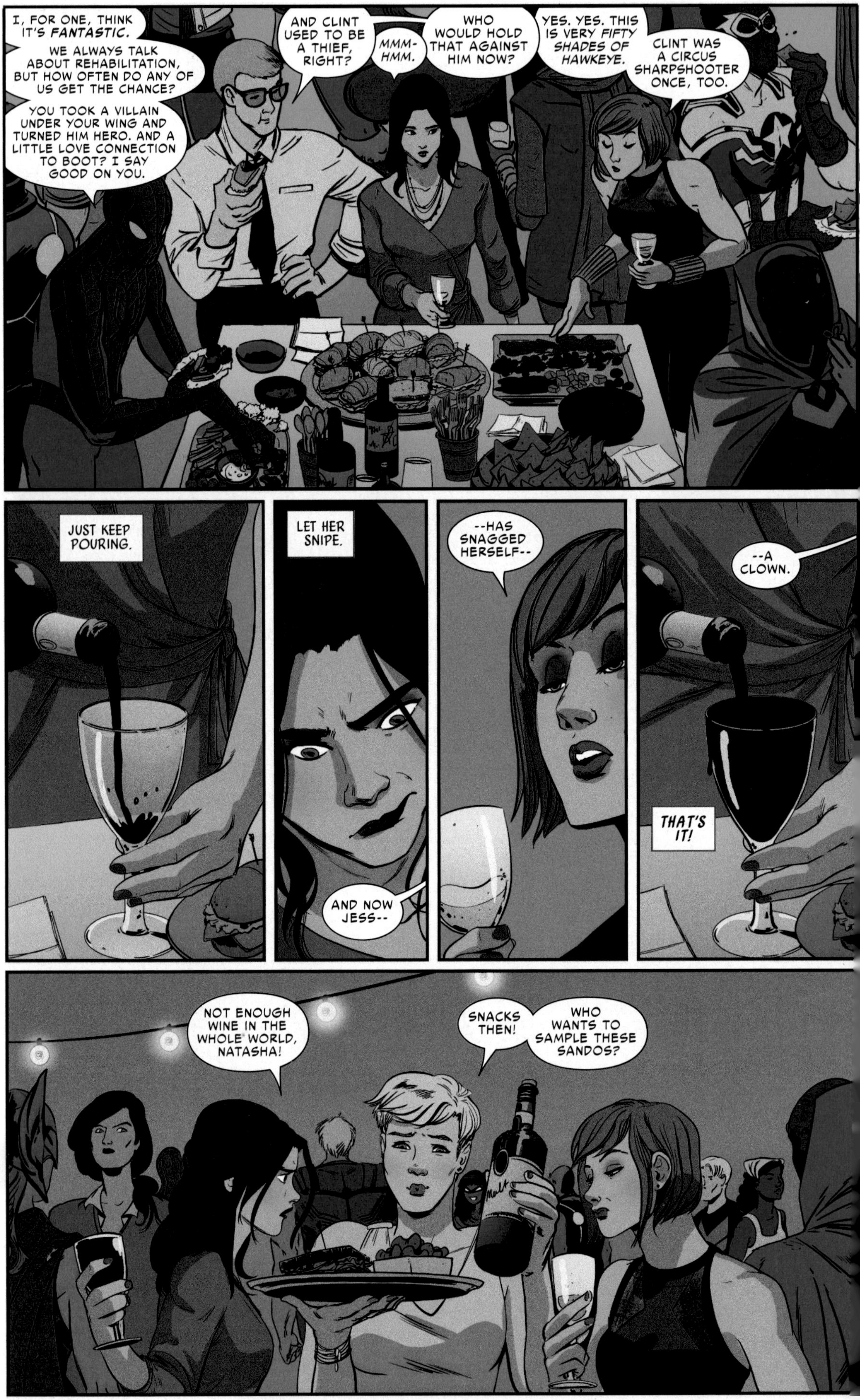
I, FOR ONE, THINK IT'S FANTASTIC.
WE ALWAYS TALK ABOUT REHABILITATION, BUT HOW OFTEN DO ANY OF US GET THE CHANCE?
YOU TOOK A VILLAIN UNDER YOUR WING AND TURNED HIM HERO. AND A LITTLE LOVE CONNECTION TO BOOT? I SAY GOOD ON YOU.
AND CLINT USED TO BE A THIEF, RIGHT?
MMM-HMM.
WHO WOULD HOLD THAT AGAINST HIM NOW?
YES. YES. THIS IS VERY FIFTY SHADES OF HAWKEYE.
CLINT WAS A CIRCUS SHARPSHOOTER ONCE, TOO.
JUST KEEP POURING.
LET HER SNIPE.
AND NOW JESS--
--HAS SNAGGED HERSELF--
--A CLOWN.
THAT'S IT!
NOT ENOUGH WINE IN THE WHOLE WORLD, NATASHA!
SNACKS THEN!
WHO WANTS TO SAMPLE THESE SANDOS?

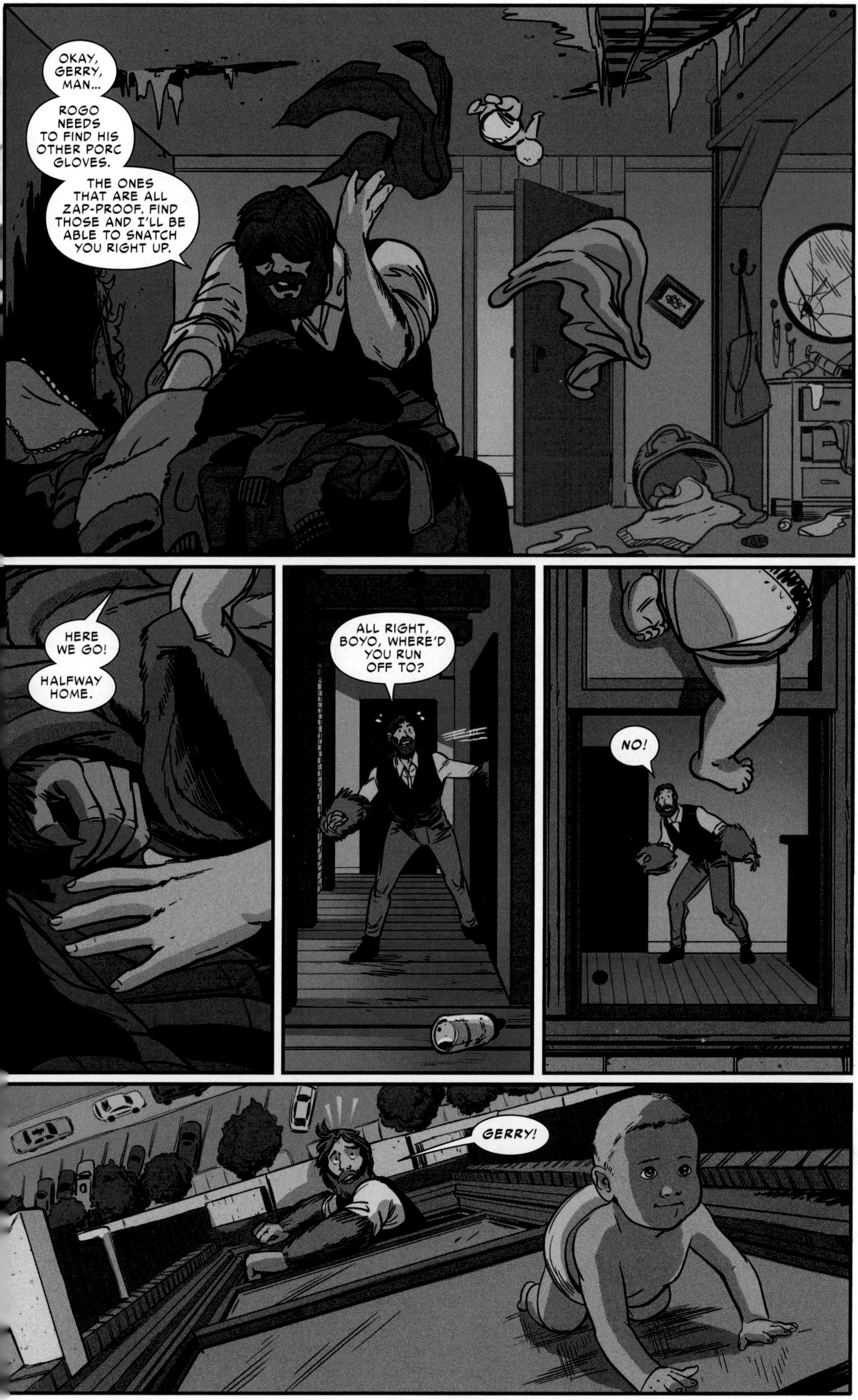
OKAY, GERRY, MAN...
ROGO NEEDS TO FIND HIS OTHER PORC GLOVES.
THE ONES THAT ARE ALL ZAP-PROOF. FIND THOSE AND I'LL BE ABLE TO SNATCH YOU RIGHT UP.
HERE WE GO!
HALFWAY HOME.
ALL RIGHT, BOYO, WHERE'D YOU RUN OFF TO?
NO!
GERRY!

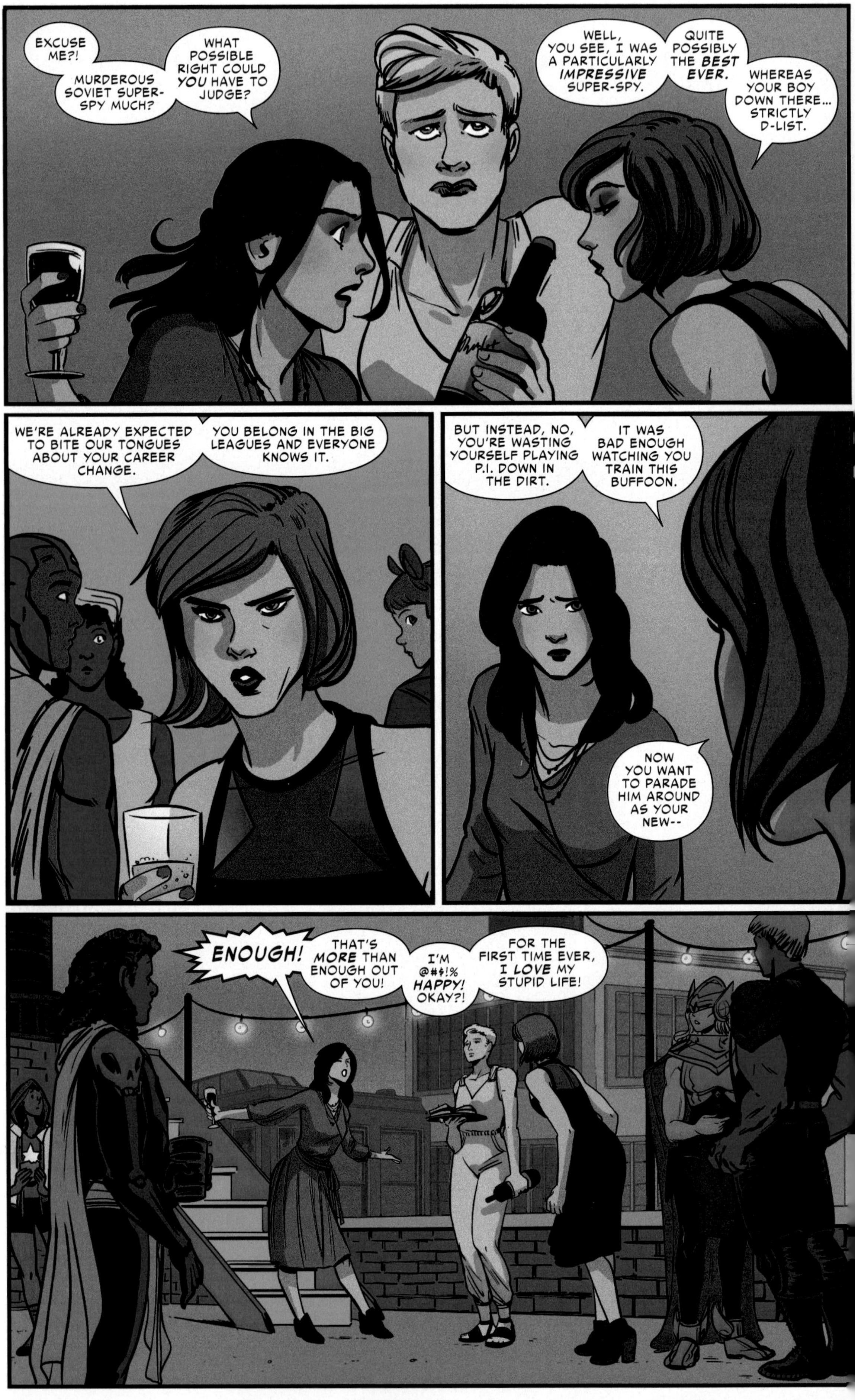

EXCUSE ME?!
MURDEROUS SOVIET SUPER-SPY MUCH?
WHAT POSSIBLE RIGHT COULD YOU HAVE TO JUDGE?
WELL, YOU SEE, I WAS A PARTICULARLY IMPRESSIVE SUPER-SPY.
QUITE POSSIBLY THE BEST EVER.
WHEREAS YOUR BOY DOWN THERE... STRICTLY D-LIST.
WE'RE ALREADY EXPECTED TO BITE OUR TONGUES ABOUT YOUR CAREER CHANGE.
YOU BELONG IN THE BIG LEAGUES AND EVERYONE KNOWS IT.
BUT INSTEAD, NO, YOU'RE WASTING YOURSELF PLAYING P.I. DOWN IN THE DIRT.
IT WAS BAD ENOUGH WATCHING YOU TRAIN THIS BUFFOON.
NOW YOU WANT TO PARADE HIM AROUND AS YOUR NEW--
ENOUGH!
THAT'S MORE THAN ENOUGH OUT OF YOU!
I'M @#$!% HAPPY! OKAY?!
FOR THE FIRST TIME EVER, I LOVE MY STUPID LIFE!

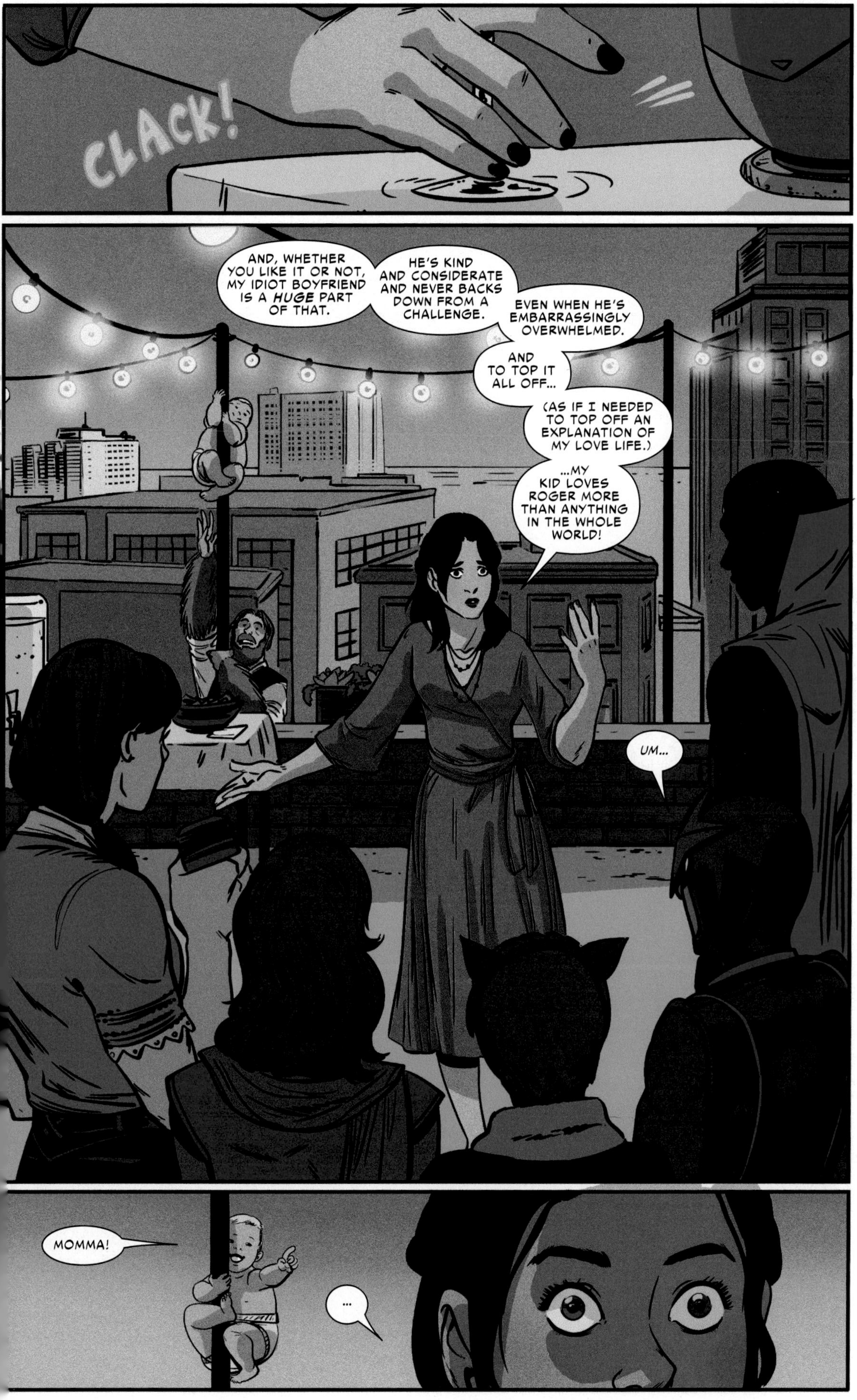
CLACK!
AND, WHETHER YOU LIKE IT OR NOT, MY IDIOT BOYFRIEND IS A *HUGE* PART OF THAT.
HE'S KIND AND CONSIDERATE AND NEVER BACKS DOWN FROM A CHALLENGE.
EVEN WHEN HE'S EMBARRASSINGLY OVERWHELMED.
AND TO TOP IT ALL OFF...
(AS IF I NEEDED TO TOP OFF AN EXPLANATION OF MY LOVE LIFE.)
...MY KID LOVES ROGER MORE THAN ANYTHING IN THE WHOLE WORLD!
UM...
MOMMA!
...

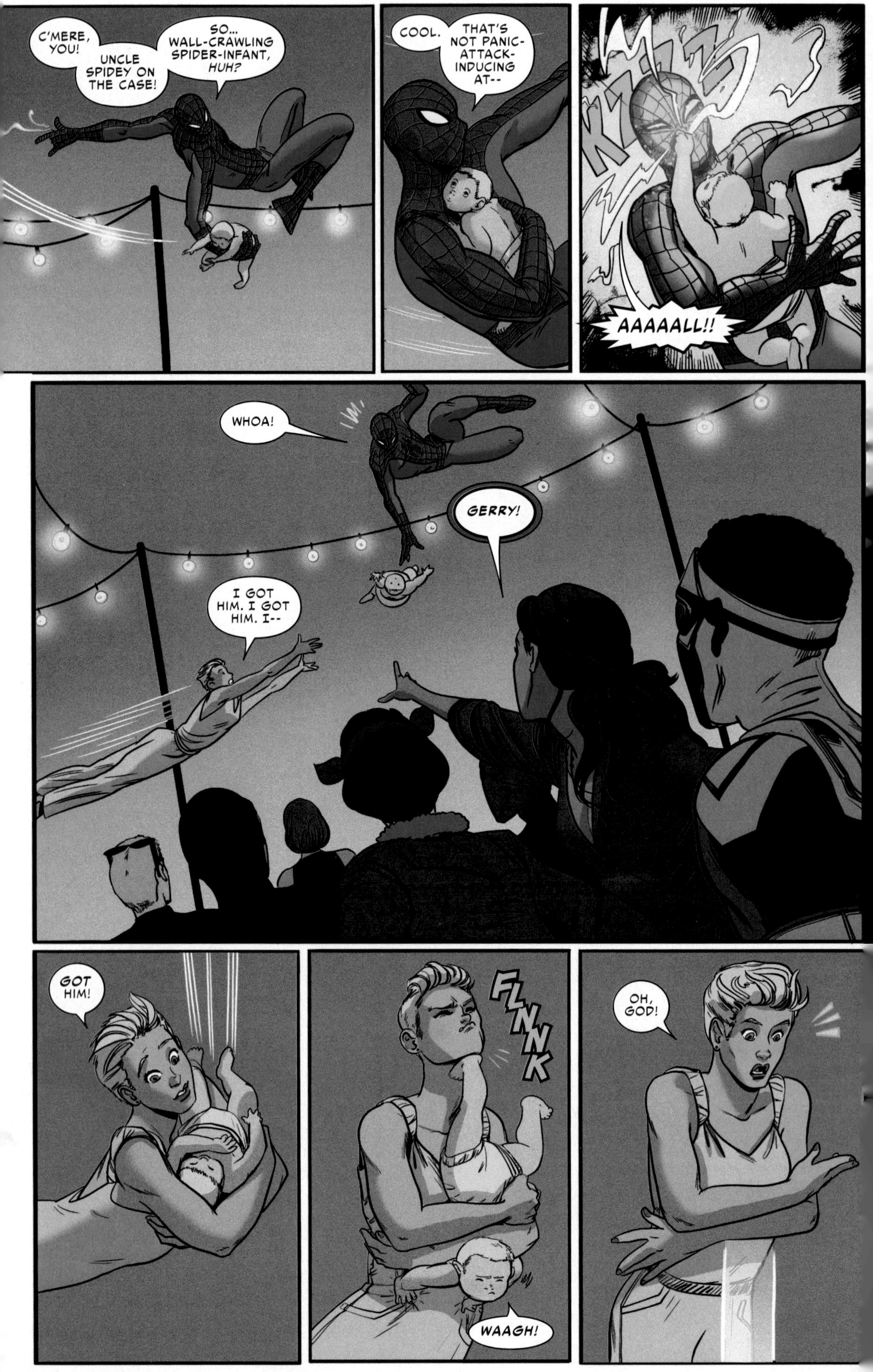
C'MERE, YOU!
UNCLE SPIDEY ON THE CASE!
SO... WALL-CRAWLING SPIDER-INFANT, HUH?
COOL.
THAT'S NOT PANIC-ATTACK-INDUCING AT--
KZZZZZ
AAAAALL!!
WHOA!
GERRY!
I GOT HIM. I GOT HIM. I--
GOT HIM!
FLNNK
WAAGH!
OH, GOD!

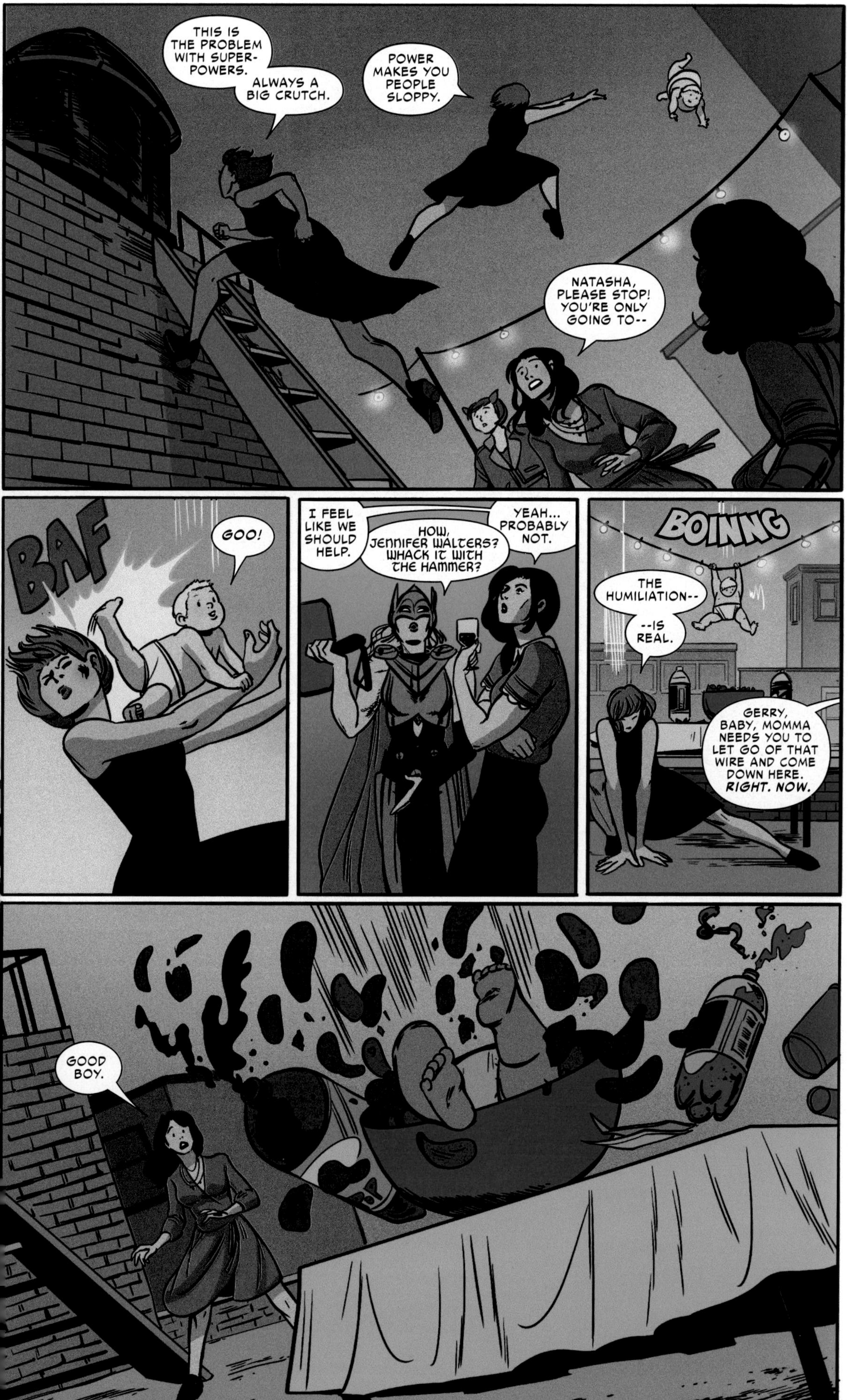
THIS IS THE PROBLEM WITH SUPER-POWERS.
ALWAYS A BIG CRUTCH.
POWER MAKES YOU PEOPLE SLOPPY.
NATASHA, PLEASE STOP! YOU'RE ONLY GOING TO--
BAF
GOO!
I FEEL LIKE WE SHOULD HELP.
HOW, JENNIFER WALTERS? WHACK IT WITH THE HAMMER?
YEAH... PROBABLY NOT.
BOINNG
THE HUMILIATION--
--IS REAL.
GERRY, BABY, MOMMA NEEDS YOU TO LET GO OF THAT WIRE AND COME DOWN HERE. RIGHT. NOW.
GOOD BOY.

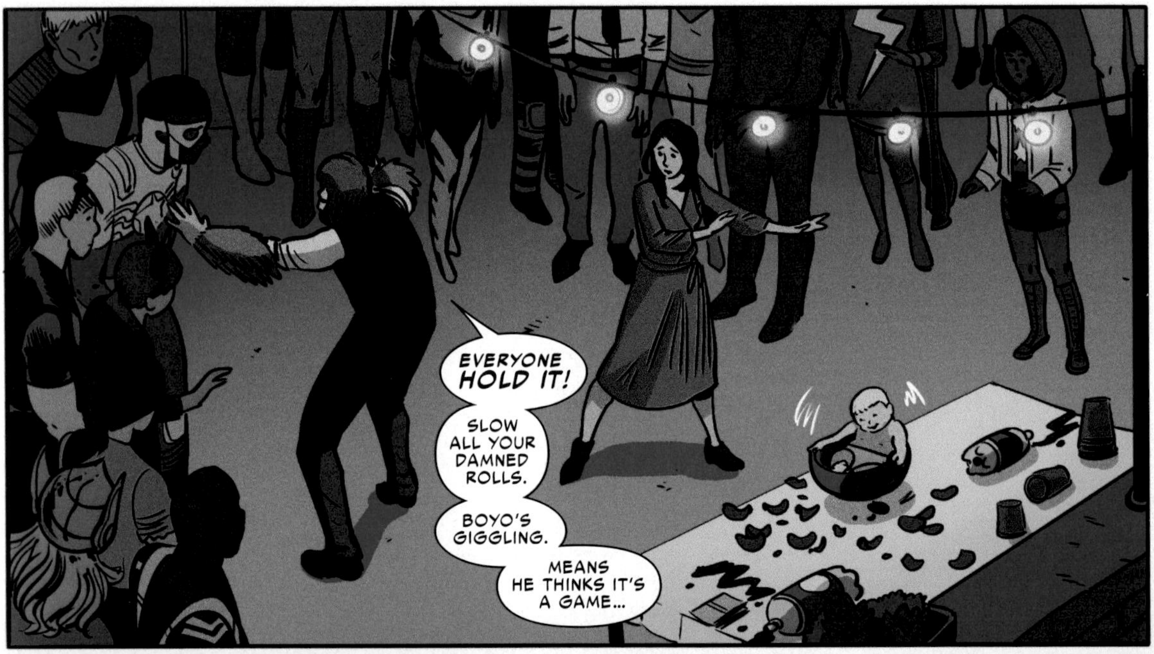
EVERYONE HOLD IT!
SLOW ALL YOUR DAMNED ROLLS.
BOYO'S GIGGLING.
MEANS HE THINKS IT'S A GAME...

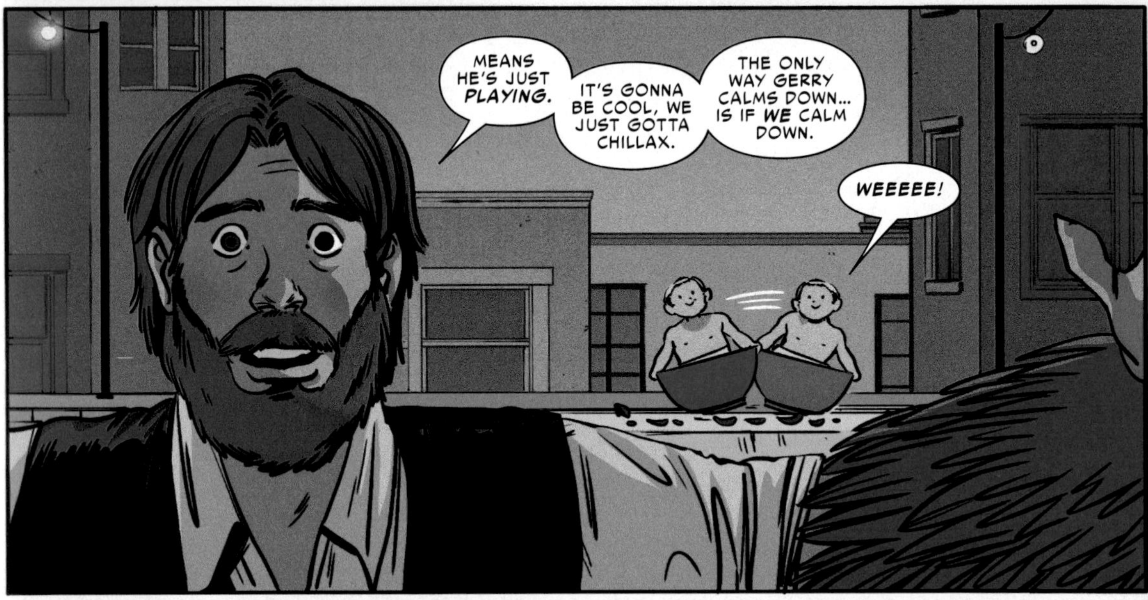
MEANS HE'S JUST PLAYING.
IT'S GONNA BE COOL, WE JUST GOTTA CHILLAX.
THE ONLY WAY GERRY CALMS DOWN... IS IF WE CALM DOWN.
WEEEEE!

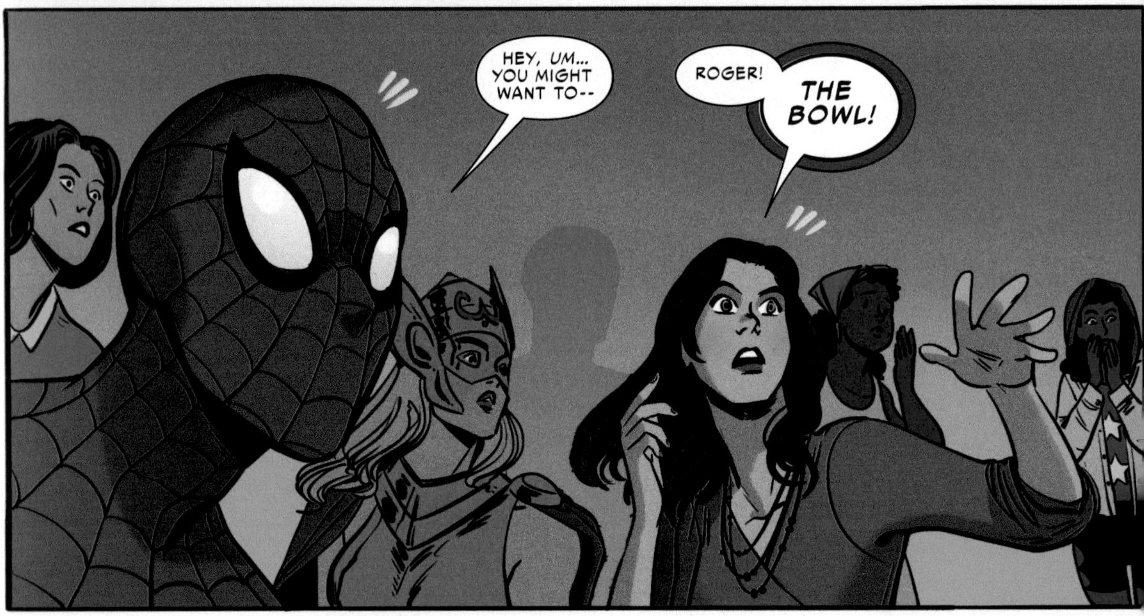
HEY, UM... YOU MIGHT WANT TO--
ROGER!
THE BOWL!

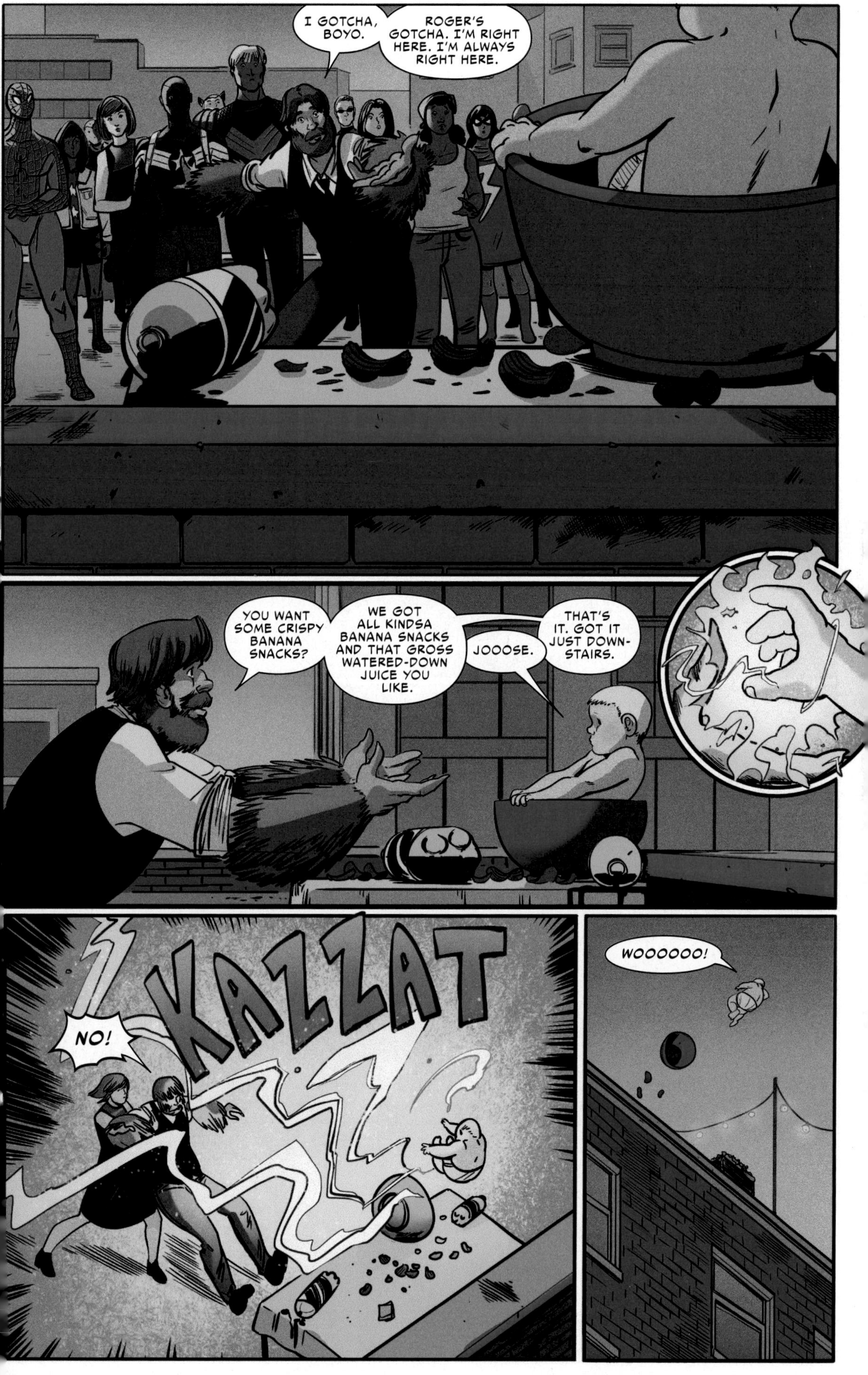
I GOTCHA, BOYO.
ROGER'S GOTCHA. I'M RIGHT HERE. I'M ALWAYS RIGHT HERE.
YOU WANT SOME CRISPY BANANA SNACKS?
WE GOT ALL KINDSA BANANA SNACKS AND THAT GROSS WATERED-DOWN JUICE YOU LIKE.
JOOOSE.
THAT'S IT. GOT IT JUST DOWN-STAIRS.
NO!
KAZZAT
WOOOOOO!

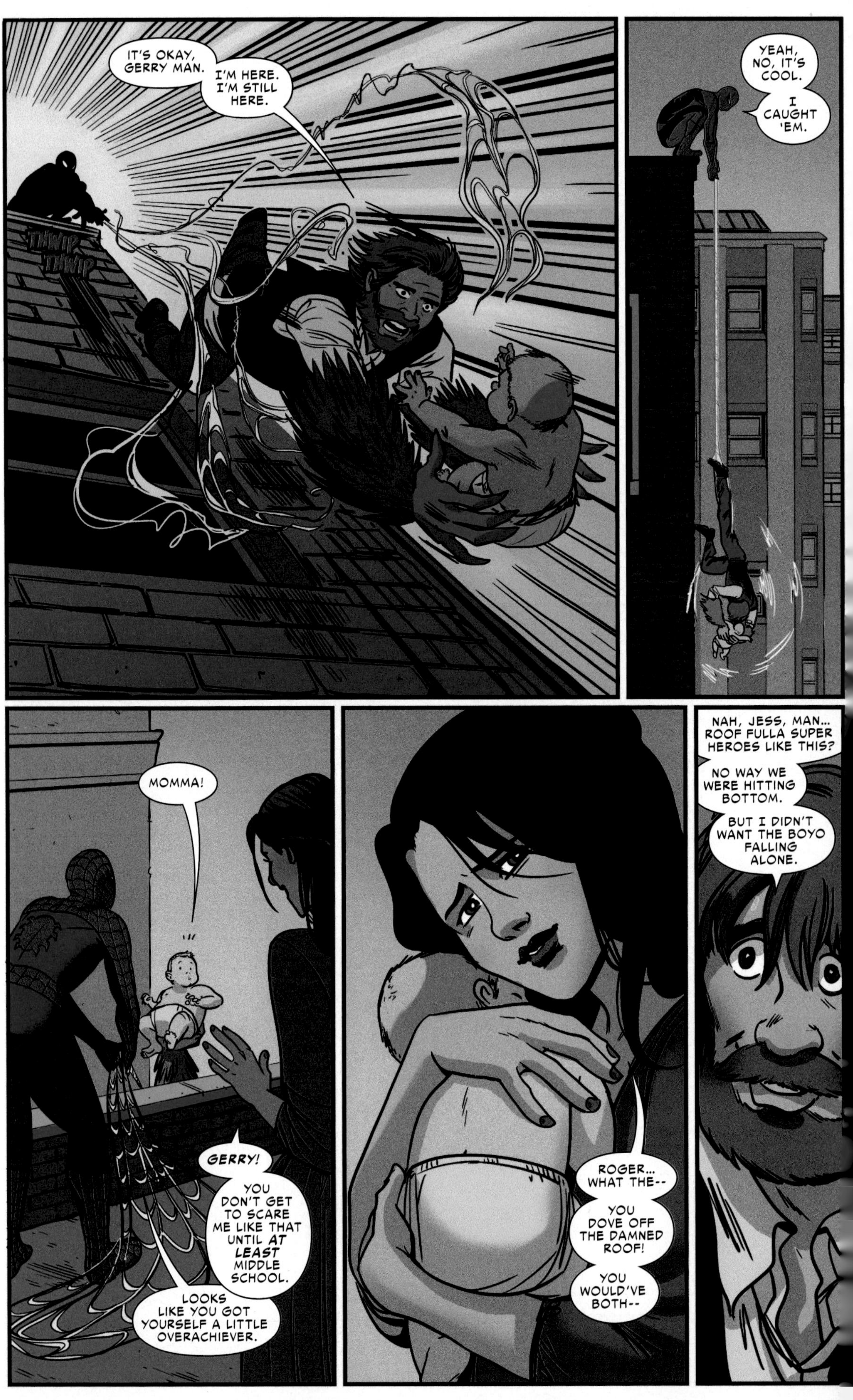
IT'S OKAY, GERRY MAN.
I'M HERE. I'M STILL HERE.
THWIP THWIP
YEAH, NO, IT'S COOL.
I CAUGHT 'EM.
MOMMA!
GERRY!
YOU DON'T GET TO SCARE ME LIKE THAT UNTIL AT LEAST MIDDLE SCHOOL.
LOOKS LIKE YOU GOT YOURSELF A LITTLE OVERACHIEVER.
ROGER... WHAT THE--
YOU DOVE OFF THE DAMNED ROOF!
YOU WOULD'VE BOTH--
NAH, JESS, MAN... ROOF FULLA SUPER HEROES LIKE THIS?
NO WAY WE WERE HITTING BOTTOM.
BUT I DIDN'T WANT THE BOYO FALLING ALONE.

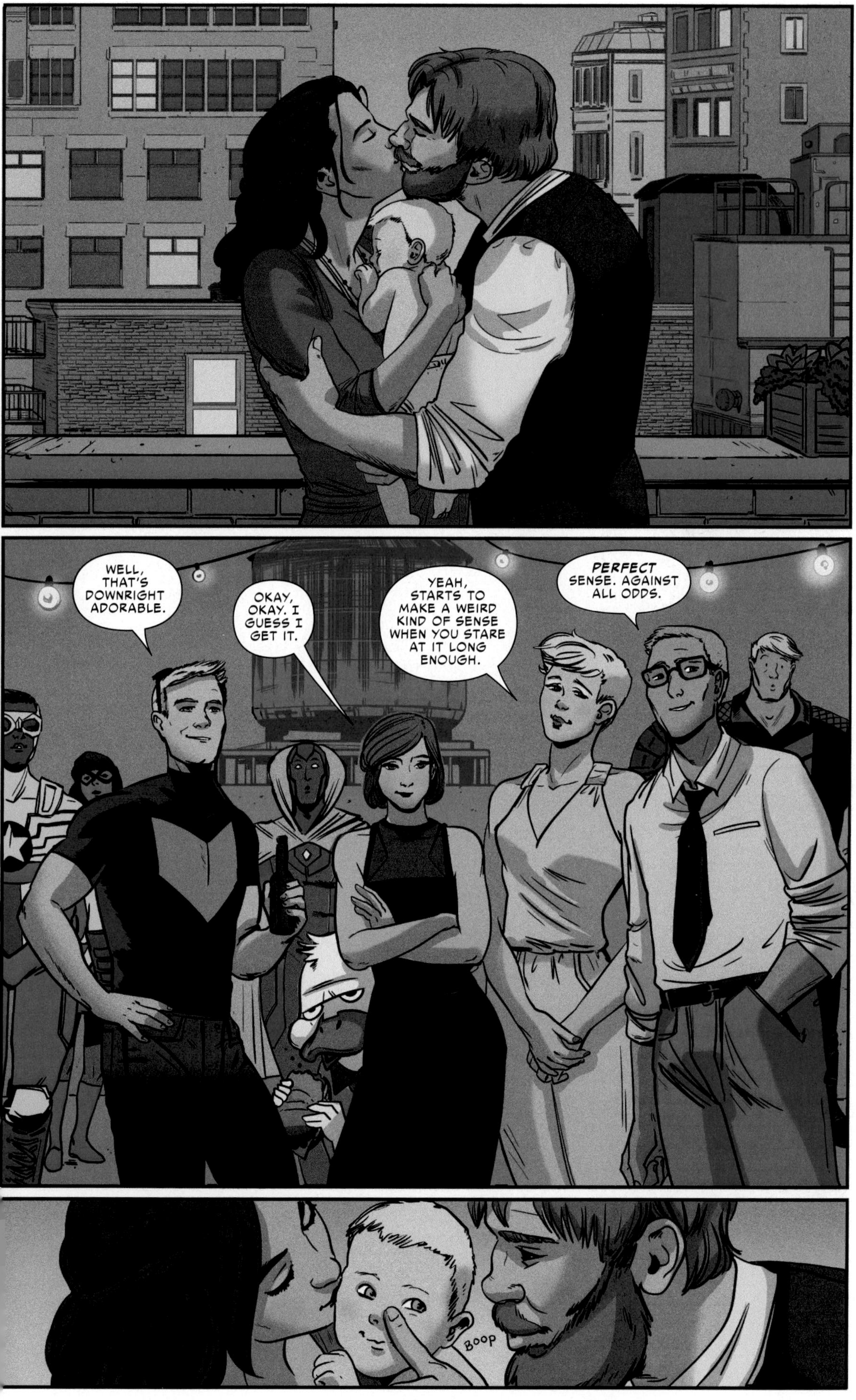
WELL, THAT'S DOWNRIGHT ADORABLE.
OKAY, OKAY. I GUESS I GET IT.
YEAH, STARTS TO MAKE A WEIRD KIND OF SENSE WHEN YOU STARE AT IT LONG ENOUGH.
PERFECT SENSE. AGAINST ALL ODDS.
BOOP

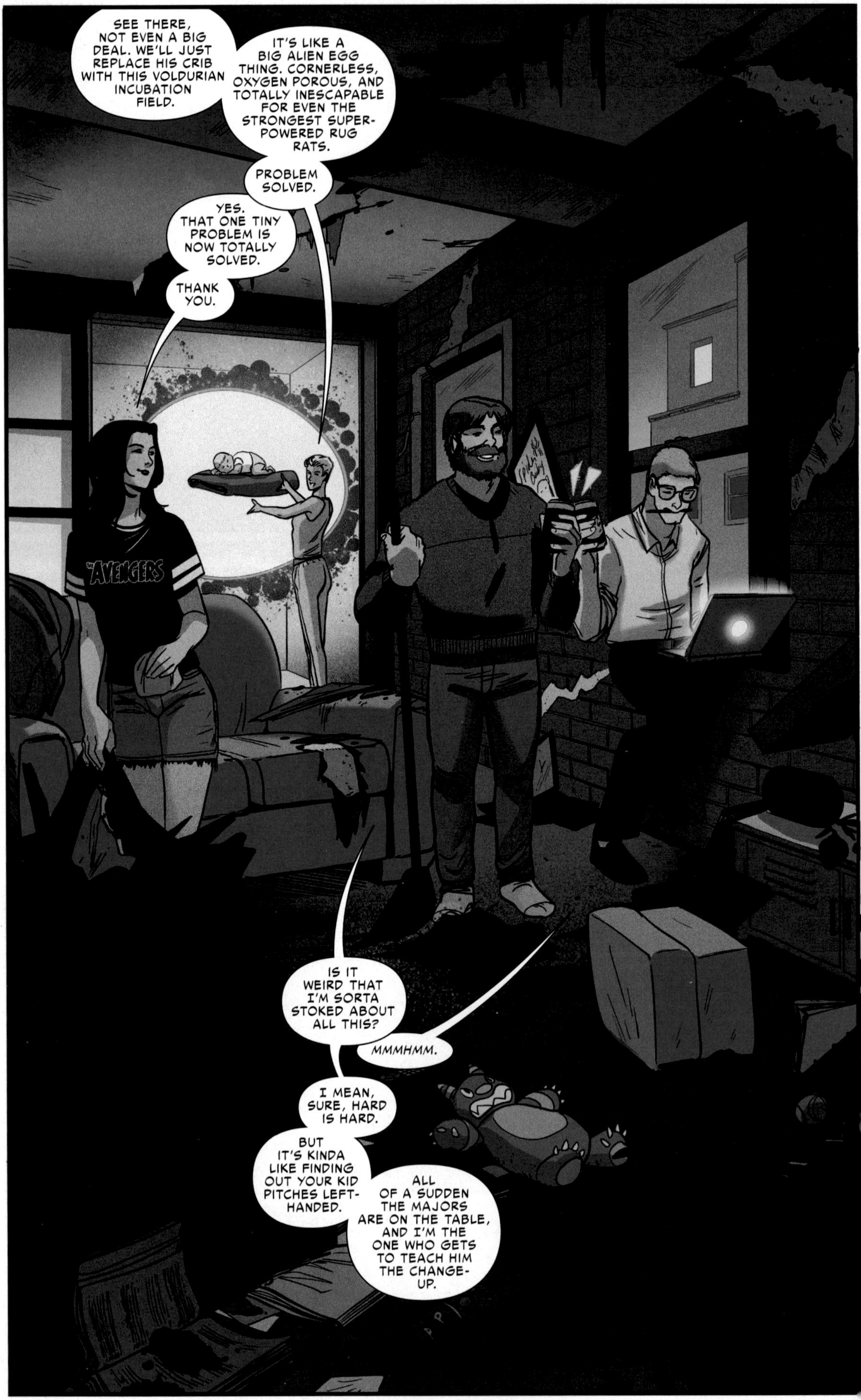
SEE THERE, NOT EVEN A BIG DEAL. WE'LL JUST REPLACE HIS CRIB WITH THIS VOLDURIAN INCUBATION FIELD.
IT'S LIKE A BIG ALIEN EGG THING. CORNERLESS, OXYGEN POROUS, AND TOTALLY INESCAPABLE FOR EVEN THE STRONGEST SUPER-POWERED RUG RATS.
PROBLEM SOLVED.
YES. THAT ONE TINY PROBLEM IS NOW TOTALLY SOLVED.
THANK YOU.
AVENGERS
IS IT WEIRD THAT I'M SORTA STOKED ABOUT ALL THIS?
MMMHMM.
I MEAN, SURE, HARD IS HARD.
BUT IT'S KINDA LIKE FINDING OUT YOUR KID PITCHES LEFT-HANDED.
ALL OF A SUDDEN THE MAJORS ARE ON THE TABLE, AND I'M THE ONE WHO GETS TO TEACH HIM THE CHANGE-UP.

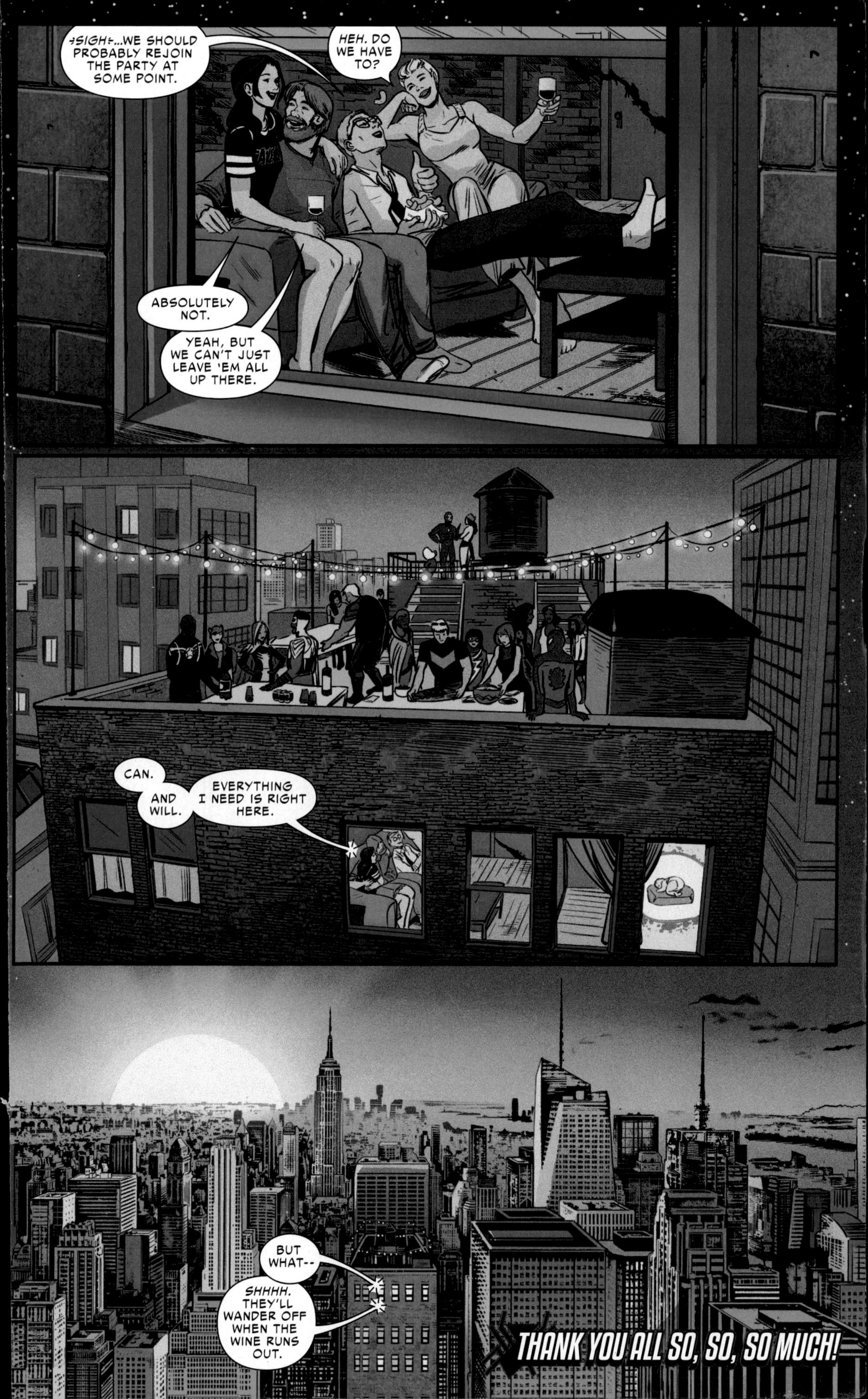

SIGH...WE SHOULD PROBABLY REJOIN THE PARTY AT SOME POINT.
HEH. DO WE HAVE TO?
ABSOLUTELY NOT.
YEAH, BUT WE CAN'T JUST LEAVE 'EM ALL UP THERE.
CAN.
AND WILL.
EVERYTHING I NEED IS RIGHT HERE.
BUT WHAT--
SHHHH. THEY'LL WANDER OFF WHEN THE WINE RUNS OUT.
THANK YOU ALL SO, SO, SO MUCH!

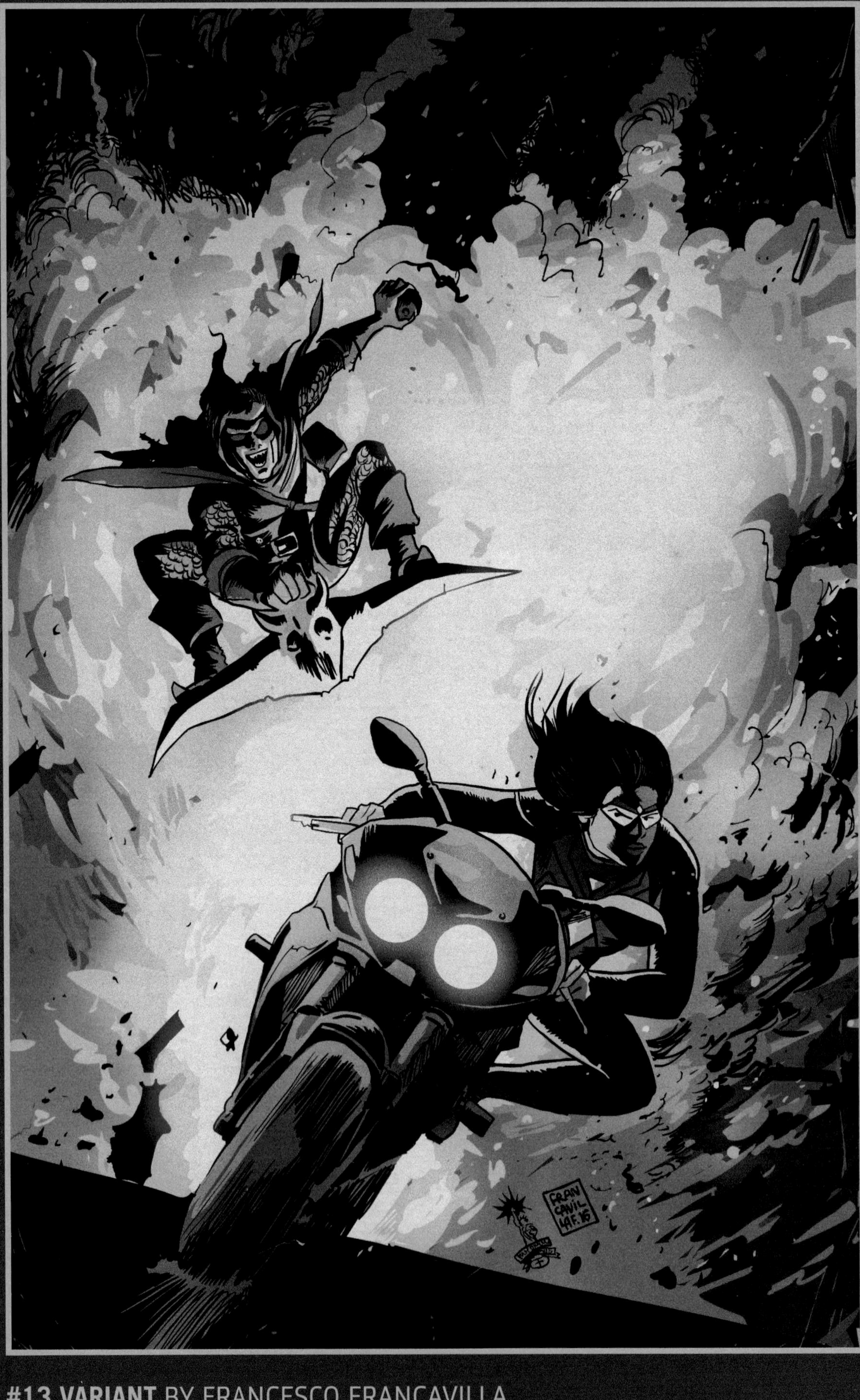

#13 VARIANT BY FRANCESCO FRANCAVILLA

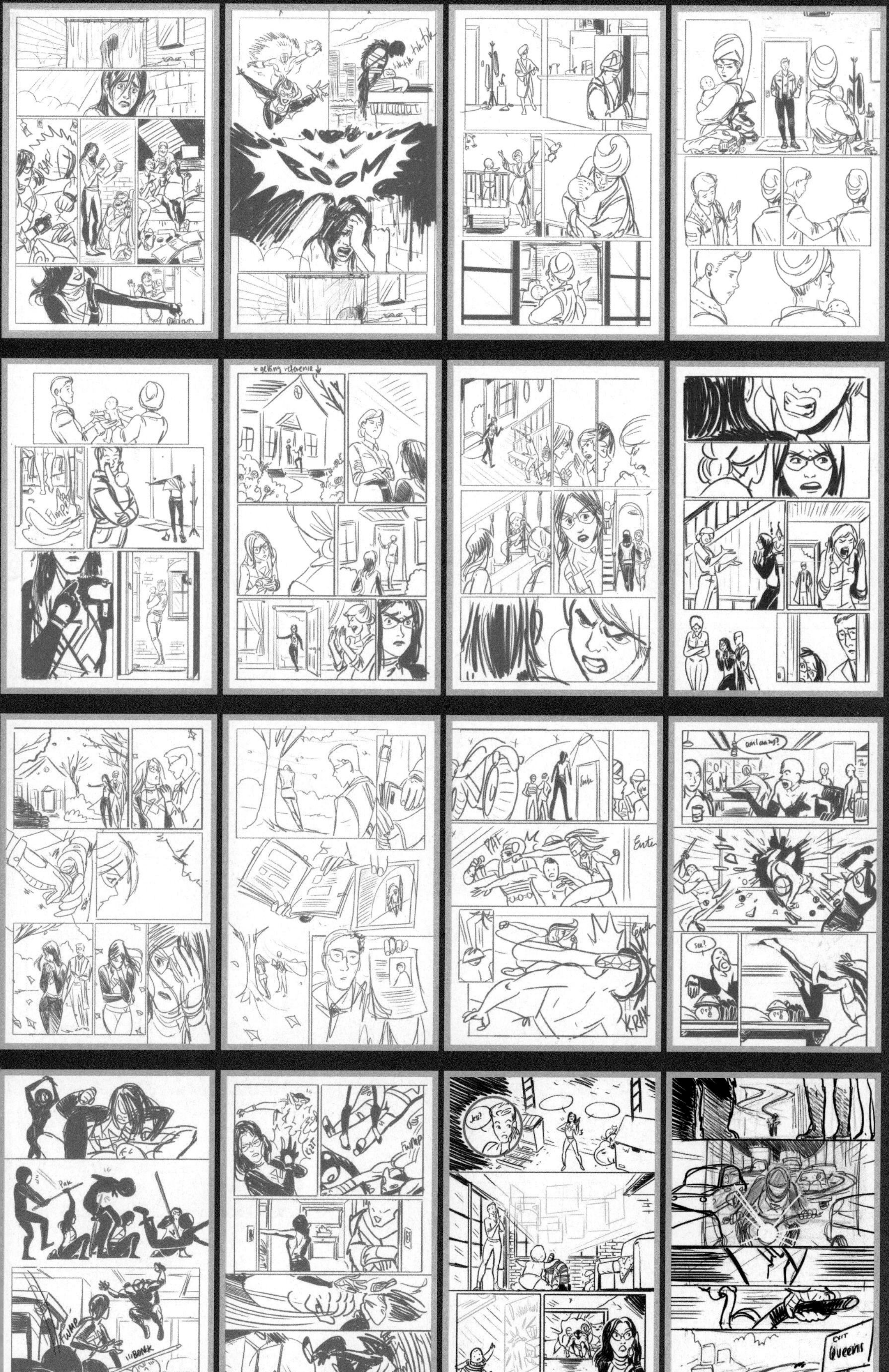
BOOM
KRAK
EXIT
Queens

#14, PP. 1-16 **LAYOUTS** BY VERONICA FISH

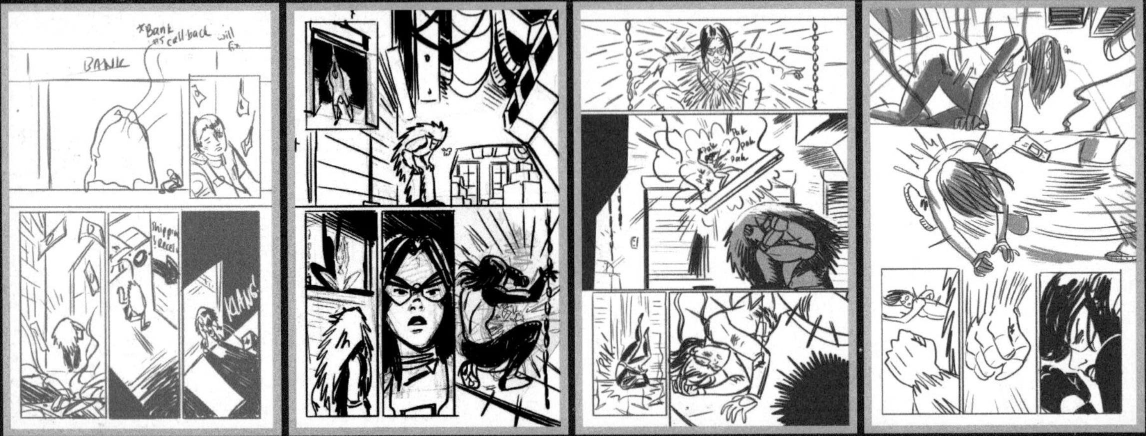
BANK

#14, PP. 17-20 LAYOUTS BY VERONICA FISH

COVER SKETCHES
BY JAVIER RODRIGUEZ

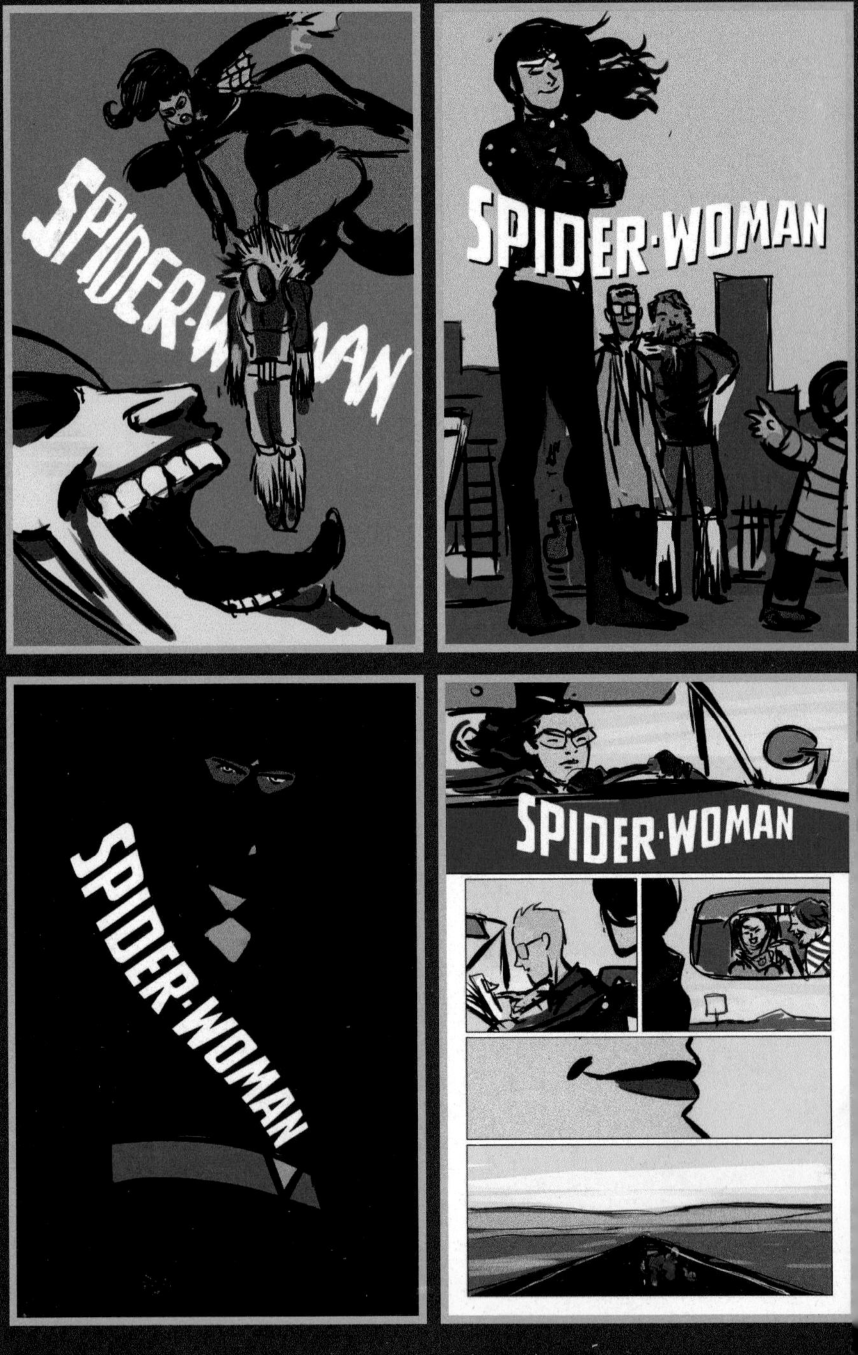
SPIDER-WOMAN
SPIDER-WOMAN
SPIDER-WOMAN
SPIDER-WOMAN